CW00551629

City & Guilds
Level 2 Diploma for IT Users

IT Principles

Level
2

David Broughton

Heinemann Educational Publishers
Halley Court, Jordan Hill, Oxford OX2 8EJ
Part of Harcourt Education

Heinemann is the registered trademark of
Harcourt Education Limited

© David Broughton 2004

First published 2004

09 08 07 06 05 04
10 9 8 7 6 5 4 3 2 1

British Library Cataloguing in Publication Data is available
from the British Library on request.

ISBN 0 435 46284 9

Typeset by Tech-Set Ltd, Gateshead, Tyne and Wear
Printed in the UK by Thomson Litho Ltd

Publisher's note
The materials in this Work have been developed by Harcourt Education and the
content and the accuracy are the sole responsibility of Harcourt Education. The City
and Guilds of London Institute accepts no liability howsoever in respect of any
breach of the intellectual property rights of any third party howsoever occasioned or
damage to the third party's property or person as a result of the use of this Work.

The City & Guilds name and logo are the registered trade marks of The City and
Guilds of London Institute and are used under licence.

Acknowledgements
I would like to thank my wife Lynne and my sons, Tom, Matthew and Joseph for
their support and patience during the writing of this book.

Additionally, I thank Northbrook College, Sussex, Sheila, and Janice Chester in
particular for the assistance they gave me.

The publishers wish to acknowledge that the screenshots in this book have been
reprinted with permission from Microsoft Corporation and to thank the following
for the use of photos: Epson (pages 4, 8, 9); Chris Honeywell (page 3, bottom);
Anthony King, Medimage (page 2).

Tel: 01865 888058 www.heinemann.co.uk

Contents

Introduction

City & Guilds developed in consultation with leading industry experts a new range of IT qualifications called e-Quals. These exciting qualifications have been developed for those wishing to improve their IT skills from the IT user level to the IT professional level.

There are three standard routes to e-Quals: the Computer User, the Software Developer and Systems Support. The Software Developer and Systems Support Practitioner qualifications (Levels 2–3) have been developed for those who wish to improve and extend their technical and professional skills in these fields.

Within the Computer User's qualification, there are three levels, Levels 1–3, and these are particularly suitable for individuals who use IT both at home and in the office. e-Quals enables you to develop and improve your skills and achieve a qualification that is recognised internationally.

e-Quals is supported by web-based support materials and online testing. To obtain the qualification for the Diploma for IT Users, candidates must successfully complete the assessments for the IT Principles core unit, plus two optional units.

The IT Principles (Core) is divided into five outcomes. You will learn to:

- prepare peripheral devices and hardware for use
- use software applications
- manage and maintain directory structures
- use the operating environment
- identify health and safety requirements

This book covers the learning requirements within the five outcomes. These outcomes have been covered within the eight sections of the book. The beginning of each section indicates which objectives are covered, with each section giving specific information and practical tasks to complete.

Throughout the book reference is made to a case study of the company called Boris Badges in giving practical examples of how the applications are used in a modern office.

At the end of the book there is a practice assignment similar to the final City & Guilds assignment for this unit.

This book refers to Microsoft Office 2000 applications throughout but the City & Guilds unit is not specific to a particular suite of applications and operating systems.

Section 1 — Selecting hardware

You will learn to

- Select hardware for use with specified software applications
- Describe the functions of input devices
- Describe how hardware affects the efficiency of the computer
- Describe the functions of output devices
- Identify the features of: VGA, Super VGA and XGA
- Use suitable media/storage devices
- Identify the main types of memory storage devices and give comparisons in terms of speed, cost and capacity
- State the standard capacities for different types of storage media
- Describe precautions when handling and storing floppy disks, CDs, zip drives

Information: The computer

Computers are used in every aspect of our lives, not only to surf the Internet or produce letters at home or in the office but also, for example, in our cars, washing machines, televisions and hi-fis. Computers are used extensively in business, industry and home. They have revolutionised the way we communicate. Using the internet we can send text, images and sound across the world in seconds when in the past it would have taken hours or days. This flexibility has an implication for employment and the way we work and live.

Computers have the same general characteristics in that data is input, processed and output, and there is backing storage for future retrieval of data.

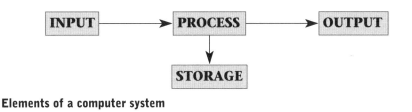

Elements of a computer system

Hardware consists of the physical parts of the computer you can touch, such as the VDU (visual display unit), keyboard and mouse, and printer.

Input devices

An input device is the method by which data is entered into the computer. The most commonly used input devices are the keyboard and the mouse.

Keyboard

The keyboard is used for text and numerical entry of information into the computer. It enables the user to enter text, for example letters, memoranda or reports, and is also used to type commands into the computer.

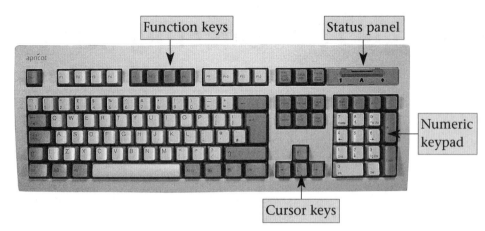

Figure 1.1 A keyboard

The letter keys on the keyboard are arranged in the same pattern as that of a standard typewriter, but have additional function and numeric keys. The keyboard is referred to as a QWERTY layout, after the first six top row alphabetic characters on the keyboard.

The QWERTY keyboard consists of different types of keys. These keys represent letters and numbers, the alphanumeric keys, and there are keys used for punctuation, such as **, ? , . " !**

Cursor keys
Cursor movement keys are used to control the direction of the cursor on the screen.

Function keys
Function keys are located along the top of the keyboard.

Function keys are used to perform specific functions according to the application being used. F1, for example, is commonly used to obtain Help.

Numeric keypad
The computer keyboard has a separate numeric keypad to facilitate faster entry of numerical data. To use the keypad you must have the numeric lock (Num Lock) pressed down.

A light will appear in the status panel to indicate that the Num Lock is selected. If the numeric lock is not selected then some of the keys will function as additional cursor keys.

Status panel
The status panel is lit when the numeric keypad, caps lock or scroll lock is on.

Keyboards are available in a variety of different shapes and designs and can now incorporate wrist rests for the user to relax their wrists in between typing, and may contain additional shortcut keys for surfing the net. Keyboards are available incorporating infrared technology to reduce the amount of cabling required.

Mouse
In a graphical user interface (GUI), such as Windows, a pointing device is used to select icons and commands. The mouse is the most commonly used pointing device.

Figure 1.2 Mouse

Underneath the mouse there is a ball which moves in the same direction in which the mouse is moved. If you remove the plastic ring, which holds the ball in place, and take out the ball, you will see two rollers inside. One roller controls the vertical movement and the other horizontal movement. As the mouse ball travels across the flat surface it touches these rollers underneath and these movements are then translated into electrical signals, which control the mouse pointer on the screen.

On top of the mouse there are two or more buttons. When the user moves the pointer to the icon or option of their choice it is selected by using either a single or double click on the mouse button. In addition to the buttons, a scroll wheel may also be seen which can be turned to make scrolling easier.

Trackball

A trackball is an alternative to a mouse and is used on laptop computers. It looks like an upturned mouse, in that there is a ball which the user moves with their fingers in order to move the pointer around on the screen.

Figure 1.3 A trackball

Touch pad

The touch pad is situated on a laptop computer. It is a touch-sensitive pad on which the user moves their finger, and the motion is detected. These movements are converted into electrical signals which are sent to control the direction of the pointer on the computer screen. By a single or double tap on the pad the user replicates the single or double mouse click.

Joystick

A disadvantage of using a keyboard is that it is not user-friendly for controlling movement on the screen. With games software, such as flight simulation, a joystick is often used as it gives the user more control of movement compared with the keyboard. The joystick also has buttons which can be programmed for different functions according to the game or simulation.

Touch screen

A touch screen is used to make selections by touching areas of the screen. They are used, for example, in supermarkets to display special offers and recipes and in tourist information offices to display information on tourist attractions.

Scanner

A scanner allows the reproduction of documents, graphics and photographs. Documents can be scanned into computer software which you can then edit and print. A scanner works in a similar way to a photocopier by reproducing an exact image. In order to edit text, which has been scanned in, additional software is required, which is normally supplied with your scanner, called optical character recognition (OCR). This software translates the text into a format recognisable by a word processor, and the text can then be edited.

Figure 1.4 A scanner

Light pen

A light pen is used in specialist applications to draw and edit graphics. It works by having at its tip a sensor which detects light in order to select objects on a computer screen.

Plotter

A plotter is used to produce specialist drawings such as engineering designs, architectural drawings and ordinance survey maps. A series of pens are used to plot accurate drawings onto paper.

Microphone

A microphone allows speech and sound to be input into the computer. It can be used, for example, to enable the spoken word to be translated into text via speech recognition software.

Digital cameras

Digital and video cameras allow digital images to be captured, which can then be downloaded to a computer. The user can then view and edit the images via appropriate software.

Processors

Inside the computer there are a number of hardware components which work together to process data.

Motherboard

The motherboard is a printed circuit board which enables the hardware components to connect together.

Central processing unit (CPU)

The central processing unit is the brain of the computer. It fetches, decodes and executes all computer instructions.

Information: Processor speed

How fast a processor works is determined by its clock speed, which is the time it takes to fetch and execute instructions. Clock speed is measured in megahertz (MHz); the higher the megahertz the faster the processor. Processor speed has increased significantly in recent years and there are now processors whose clock speed is measured in gigahertz (GHz) rather than megahertz.

Read Only Memory (ROM)

Read Only Memory is non-volatile, i.e. when the power is switched off the memory remains. ROM is used to store programs required for starting up and enabling the computer to operate.

Random Access Memory (RAM)

Random Access Memory is memory that you can read and write to. It is a temporary storage area for processing, and it is sometimes referred to as primary storage, or main memory, as it stores the program instructions and the data whilst it is being processed. RAM is volatile, which means that all information held temporarily on it is lost when the power is switched off.

Information: Measurement of memory – bits and bytes

Inside the computer electrical current is measured in terms of two states, high and low, and is represented in the binary system with 1 representing high and 0 representing low. These two states are referred to as a bit (binary digit).

A byte is a collection of 8 bits and can store one character or number.

- A kilobyte (KB) can store 1,024 characters.
- A megabyte (MB) can store 1,048,576 characters.
- A gigabyte (GB) can store 1,073,741,824 characters.

The larger the number of bytes, the greater the capacity of memory that can be stored. Software applications require a significant amount of memory to be temporarily stored in RAM. Running more than one application at the same time requires additional memory to work efficiently. It is therefore important to have sufficient RAM in the computer to be able to use these modern applications. A computer with insufficient RAM will either not be able to load the program or will be slow in its operation.

Output devices

An output device is used to portray data after it has been processed. Examples include: visual display unit, printer, plotter, speakers, speech synthesisers and projection devices.

Visual display unit or monitor

A visual display unit or monitor enables the user to view text and graphics on screen. Computer monitors vary in the technology used and their size, typically to a maximum of 21 inches.

Types of monitors

- **Cathode ray tube (CRT)** The cathode ray tube is used in the majority of desktop computers and is the same technology as used in a television set. CRT technology operates by projecting three beams of electrons onto a glass screen, which is covered by triangular patterns of phosphor-coloured dots which are red, green and blue in colour. When the electrons hit the dots they react to them by giving out light. Together the three dots of primary colour make up a single pixel of colour. Different colours are created by varying the power of the electron beams hitting each of the small dots of red, green or blue phosphor.

- **Liquid crystal display (LCD)** Liquid crystal displays are used for laptops and increasingly for flat screens for desktop computers. LCDs work by using the reflective properties of liquid crystals. When electrical current is passed through them they emit light.

  Liquid crystal displays have advantages over cathode ray tubes in that they are lighter and take up less space and therefore can be used in laptops.

- **Thin film transistor (TFT)** technology, which uses LCDs, provides a high resolution flat screen which has the benefits of quality and space saving. The disadvantage is that this technology is still relatively expensive.

Hint:

Before purchasing games software make sure your graphics card has sufficient memory to ensure best performance.

Information: Graphics cards

All visual display units require a video adapter (graphics card) to work. The graphics card creates the image displayed on the computer screen. Instructions are sent from the computer software to the graphics card. The card interprets these signals, and sends a signal to the monitor showing the amount of the three primary colours required for each individual pixel.

The resolution and quality of graphics shown on the screen is determined by the amount of memory on the graphics card. 3D graphics applications required in games software need more memory than 2D text used for a word processor. The minimum standard requirement for graphics cards is 16 MB, however applications such as simulation games require more than this to operate. The minimum standard for simulation games is 32 MB or higher.

Graphics cards require software drivers to function properly. The correct driver should be installed, as an incorrect driver will affect the performance of the graphics card and therefore the quality of the image on the screen. You should invest in a good quality graphics card with sufficient memory as a low quality graphics card will compromise the overall quality on the computer display.

Information: Screen resolution

The screen resolution refers to the number of pixels (**pi**cture **el**ements) displayed on the screen. A pixel is the smallest element that makes up the text and graphics. A character displayed on the monitor, for example, is made up of a series of pixels or 'small dots'. A pixel is made up of three primary colours, red, green and blue. The more pixels displayed the clearer the image will be. Visual displays which have a large number of pixels are referred to as having high resolution, those with fewer pixels and therefore less clearly defined images are referred to as having low resolution. The number of pixels on a screen is measured by the amount displayed in the horizontal position, which is the first number quoted, and the vertical surface of the screen, which is the second number.

There are a number of different video standards which define the resolution of the computer and the number of colours it can display.

The number of bits per pixel determines the number of colours available. For example, 4 bits per pixel produces 16 colours because $4^2 = 16$. If the number of bits double to 8 the number of available colours increases to 256, i.e. $8^2 = 256$. When 16 bits are used, 65,536 colours are produced and this is known as *high* colour. When 24 bits are used, 16.7 million colours for the palette can be used and this is known as *true* colour.

Information

Monitor settings

Resolution measures the number of pixels or picture elements on the screen; the larger the screen the higher the potential for increasing the resolution, providing your graphics card supports it. Changing the monitor settings is covered in Section 4.

Some common standards for video are:

- **Video graphics array (VGA)** This video standard supports 256 colours at a resolution of 320×200 or 16 colours at a resolution of 640×480.
- **Super video graphics array (SVGA)** SVGA supports a higher resolution than VGA and creates up to 16.7 million colours. Resolutions of 1280×1024 in 256 colours are supported, although smaller screen sizes will use the smaller resolution of 800×600.
- **Extended graphics array (XGA)** The XGA standard can support resolutions of up to 1024×768 pixels but can provide a larger number of colours.

Refresh rate

CRT monitors light up as electrons hit the phosphor dots. This effect is only temporary, and without further electrons hitting the phosphor dots the image fades. To maintain a constant image on the screen, the monitor needs to be refreshed continuously. The speed of the refresh rate is measured in Hertz (Hz); one Hz is equal to one cycle per second. A typical refresh rate for the monitor is 60 Hz or higher. With lower refresh rates you may notice the screen flicker whilst it is being refreshed, whereas with higher refresh rates this flicker will not be as noticeable.

Printers

Dot matrix

These were the most popular type of printer used at one time but have now been largely replaced by inkjet or laser printers as the technology has advanced and the cost of these printers has fallen significantly.

Dot matrix printers are impact printers, in that a series of pins within a matrix hits the printer ribbon to form individual characters. The quality is poor by comparison with inkjet and laser printers and they are slower.

Figure 1.5 A dot matrix printer

Inkjet

Inkjet printers are non-impact printers. They use a print cartridge rather than a ribbon. Small jets of ink are electrically charged and sprayed onto the paper to form the individual characters. These printers have fallen in price in recent years and are now used as the entry-level printer in the home and in the office.

Figure 1.6 An inkjet printer

Laser

Laser printers produce fast, high-quality print copies, but are more expensive than inkjet printers because replacement toners cost more. A laser beam is directed onto the surface of a drum and is switched on and off to create a series of dots which are used to form the printed characters. Where the laser hits the drum it changes the charge at that position. The surface is then coated by toner, which sticks to the surface made by the electrical charge. The ink is then heated to stick it to the paper.

A standard laser can be used for black and white printing; colour laser printers are required for colour printing. These printers require four separate toners to produce the range of colours. They are more expensive to buy and maintain.

Figure 1.7 A laser printer

Speakers

Speakers are used in multimedia to output sound such as music from an audio CD, musical instruments and for speech recognition. For the sound from the speakers to be heard a sound card or built-in sound capabilities on the motherboard is required. Speakers can be separate or built in.

Speech synthesisers

A speech synthesiser is software that converts text into voice output; the synthesiser 'reads' the text.

Storage devices

RAM is primary storage or main memory. RAM is a temporary storage and is lost when the power is switched off. To keep data so it can be retrieved for future use, a secondary form of storage is required. There are different types of secondary storage, i.e. backing storage:

Hard disk

Inside the computer there is a hard disk which stores the operating system, application programs and files for your computer. The computer hard drive is supplied with an internal disk drive, although you can purchase external hard drives.

Hard disks can store large amounts of data, and the amount they can hold is increasing significantly as technology develops. It is usual to find entry-level computers with hard drives with 60 or 80 GB capacity and higher. The price of these drives is also decreasing; making larger capacity drives a common feature.

Inside a sealed casing, which protects the inside from dust, there is a series of disks (platters) which are rotated via a spindle attached to a motor. Magnetic material covers the surface of these platters. Read/write heads, controlled by an actuator, hover above the surface of the platters and are controlled by an actuator, which moves over the disk

As the disk spins an electromagnetic charge is switched on and off. Binary data is recorded on to the disk by changing the composition of the magnetic surface in a similar way that iron filings change when a magnet is placed over them. This is achieved by switching an electrical current on and off over the disk surface, representing the 0s and 1s in binary, and allows for data to be both read and written to.

Precautions in handling and storing hard disks

There are a number of precautions you should take to protect the hard disk, some of which relate to the installation of the disk drive:

- Avoid extremes in temperature and humidity. Do not place the disk in direct sunlight.
- Avoid moving the computer when it is turned on as this could misalign the read/write heads and damage the drive.
- Avoid electrostatic discharges when installing the disk drive.
- Don't make connections to the hard drive with the power on when installing the disk drive.

Floppy disks

Floppy disks allow data, typically up to 1.44 MB, to be transferred from one computer to another. They are so called because in the past the outer case was made of cardboard and the diskette would 'flop'! They now have a hard plastic outer case to protect the data inside.

The case contains a thin disc made of magnetic film coated on both sides. The disk surface is made up of a series of tracks subdivided into sectors. The principle for storing data on a floppy disk is the same as a hard drive.

Precautions in handling and storing floppy disks

Floppy disks are cheap to purchase and will last a long time provided the following precautions are taken in handling and storing:

- Floppy disks store information by changing the properties of magnetic film. Keep the diskette away from other magnetic sources as this could affect the data stored on it!
- Floppy disks do not like extremes in temperature. Do not place the disk in direct sunlight.
- Although it is called a floppy disk, do not bend it.
- Do not touch the disk surface, as this will damage it.

Optical storage devices

There are different types of optical devices and their advantage is that they can store large amounts of data, which is portable for use in compatible computers.

CD-ROM (Compact Disc-Read Only Memory)

CD-ROMs can store text, images, sound and video, and up to a maximum of 650 MB of data. Compact disks are made from plastic with an outer aluminium coating called a land. A laser beam 'burns' into the surface of the land creating small 'pits' on the surface. A laser scans the disk surface and detects the differences in the light reflected from the land and pits. These differences are used to represent binary data.

The speed of a CD-ROM is compared to the speed of an audio CD player which has a transfer rate of 150 kilobytes (Kbps) per second. A 2X CD-ROM, for example, rotates at twice the speed of an audio player (2X) and allows twice the amount of information to be read at 300 Kbps. CD-ROM speeds have increased significantly in recent years; speeds of 52X are now common.

CD-R (Compact Disc-Recordable)

CD-R disks have the same capacity as normal CD-ROMs, on which data can be recorded. They are sometimes referred to as WORM (Write-Once, Read-Many) and they can store large amounts of data. They are often used in preference to floppy disks when transferring data from one standalone computer to another. CD-Rs are often used for making backups.

CD-RW (Compact Disc-Re-Writable)

These have a storage capacity of 650 MB and are used for general storage and backups. They can be recorded on more than once and therefore have the advantage over CD-R disks. To use CD-RW disks you need a CD-RW drive and associated software. CD-RW drives are more expensive than ordinary CD-ROM drives but the cost has fallen dramatically and CD-RW drives are now installed as a standard item.

DVD (Digital Versatile Disks)

DVDs can store significantly larger amounts of data than an ordinary CD-ROM. The capacity of the disk varies from 4.7 GB to 17 GB. The difference in capacity is due to some DVDs having two storage layers on each surface and being able to store data on both sides of the disk.

To use a DVD you need a DVD player; these also read other types of compact discs. The cost has fallen significantly and DVDs are now standard on most new computers.

Precautions in handling and storing optical disks

The precautions for handling and storing are the same for all optical disks:

- Avoid touching the disk surface as the grease or dirt can transfer onto it; use a CD-ROM disk cleaning kit to clean the disks.
- Keep away from extreme heat; do not leave in direct sunlight.
- To avoid accidental scratches on the disk surface put the disk away immediately when you have finished with it.

Zip drives

Zip drives are similar to floppy disks in appearance but can store larger amounts of data – 100 MB to 250 MB. They are used to store large files and are useful for transferring files between computers or as backing storage. Zip drives are internal or external to the computer.

Magnetic tape (data cartridges)

Magnetic tape is similar in appearance to audiotapes and is usually stored in data cartridges. Data cartridges are used for backing up large amounts of data, typically to backup data from a network server. Unlike magnetic disks, which are direct access media, magnetic tape is serial access, i.e. the tape has to be read through from the beginning until the data is located. It is therefore slower than magnetic disk, which is direct access media.

Precautions when handling and storing zip drives and magnetic tape

You should follow the same precautions for handling and storing zip drives and magnetic tapes as for floppy disks.

→ Check your knowledge 1

1 What are the four elements of a computer system?
2 ROM is a temporary store of data. True or False?
3 A megabyte is larger than a gigabyte. True or False?
4 A dot matrix printer is an impact printer. True or False?
5 DVD is an abbreviation for Digital Video Disks. True or False?

→ Check your knowledge 2

1 Identify the features of VGA, Super VGA and XGA, including monitor settings, resolution, refresh rate.
2 Identify the main types of memory storage devices and give comparisons in terms of speed, cost and capacity, e.g. floppy disk, internal/external drives, CD-ROM/CD writers.
3 State the standard capacities for different types of storage media.
4 What are the precautions to take when handling and storing hard disks?
5 What precautions do you need to take when handling and storing floppy disks, zip drives and magnetic tape?
6 What are the precautions you need to take when handling and storing optical disks?

Section 2 | Using software

You will learn to

- Describe, select and use software applications for word processing
- Use settings for margins, page size and orientation and text enhancement
- Use spell and grammar checker and help facilities in application software packages
- Describe, select and use software applications for databases
- Identify the field names and field types in a database structure
- Identify the eight principles of the Data Protection Act
- Describe, select and use software applications for spreadsheets
- State the meaning of the terms: cell address, row, columns, formulae
- State the advantages of using integrated software
- Use integrated software to merge documents from different applications
- Describe the advantages of mail merge
- Describe the main uses of commonly used packages: financial applications, presentation graphics
- Describe the function of projection devices
- Describe the main uses of commonly used packages: computer-aided design (CAD)/ vector-based graphics

Software refers to the programs used in a computer system. A typical computer system needs systems software for the machine to operate and applications software to perform the required tasks.

The Windows operating system is an example of systems software. It is the instructions which control the computer's hardware and is essential to enable the computer to operate. The operating system controls file management and the ability to run applications software.

Applications software is a set of instructions normally dedicated to a set of tasks, such as word processing, creating spreadsheets, or creating databases. Microsoft Word is an example of applications software. Microsoft Office comprises a suite of applications software.

In order to run applications software you require hardware, such as the main system unit, the keyboard, mouse and visual display unit, and systems software such as Microsoft Windows.

Information: Case study

You will find various tasks throughout this section that use the Boris Badges company as a case study.

Boris Badges Limited is a family owned business which specialises in the design and production of promotional marketing products for business, clubs and societies. They manufacture small items including corporate badges, pens and key rings. The company currently employs 75 people and is seeking to further expand its operations. It has a hierarchical organisational structure consisting of a Board of Directors with separate departments for Sales and Marketing, Accounts, Purchasing, Production and Human Resources.

The Board of Directors recognise that the IT systems in the company are not as sufficiently integrated or as effective as they would like them to be. Some computers in the company can communicate and share information with each other as they are linked together in a computer network whereas others, such as the General Office and the Production department, use standalone computers. Standalone computers are computers which are not physically connected to one another.

Information: Word processing – creating various documents

Word processing is a software application which is used to produce, edit and print text. The tasks that follow will involve using word processing software to solve the problems faced by the Boris Badges company.

In the General Office at Boris Badges a word processor is used to create a variety of documents. In the following tasks you will select and use software applications for word processing the following documents:

- **Newsletters** – used to inform individuals about what is happening in the organisation.
- **Letters**
- **Reports**
- **Memorandum** – an internal document to inform or invite comment.
- **Agenda** – this outlines the subjects to be covered in the meeting.
- **Minutes of meetings** – this records the discussion and the outcomes of a meeting.

Personnel Meeting of Boris Badges to be held on 7th December 2003 at 2 pm in Meeting Room 3

AGENDA
1 Minutes of last meeting
2 Apologies for absence
3 Matters arising
4 Extra leave entitlement
5 Travel claims
6 Changes in pension arrangements
7 Health cover insurance
8 Any other business
9 Date of next meeting

MEMORANDUM

TO: All staff
FROM: Susan Oakley, Personnel Officer

DATE: 20th December 2003

SUBJECT: Annual Leave

I am pleased to inform you that one extra day of leave has been awarded to all staff in recognition of the hard work they have done for the company. This extra day can be taken any time from the above date.

The holiday year-end on the 31st March 2004 remains the same.

Minutes of the Personnel Meeting held on 7th December 2003 at 2 pm at Boris Badges in Meeting Room 3.

Present:

1 Minutes of last meeting
   The Minutes of the last meeting were taken as read and agreed as a true record and signed by the Chairman.
2 Apologies for absence
   Apologies for absence were received from Simon Yemon.
3 Matters arising
   There are no matters arising from the previous Minutes.
4 Extra leave entitlement
   A discussion took place on awarding staff extra days' leave as a reward for increased productivity. All members agreed this was a good idea.
5 Travel claims
   Simon Ward presented a revised copy of the Travel Claim form. It was emphasised that this form should be used with immediate effect. This was unanimously agreed.
6 Changes in pension arrangements
   There will be a meeting on 10th January, to discuss proposed changes in pension arrangements. All senior staff are required to attend.
7 Health cover insurance
   At the same meeting on 10th January, health cover insurance will also be discussed.
8 Any other business
   Sheila Smith raised the question of refurbishment of the Staff Canteen. It was agreed that this would be an Agenda item at the next meeting.
9 Date of next meeting
   January 23rd 2004.

Task 2.1	Opening a software application

To open the Microsoft Word application either double-click on the Microsoft Word icon or carry out the following steps.

Method

1   Go to the **Start** button and click.
2   Open **Programs** and select the program you want – in this case Microsoft Word – and click to enter.
3   The Microsoft Word window will appear.

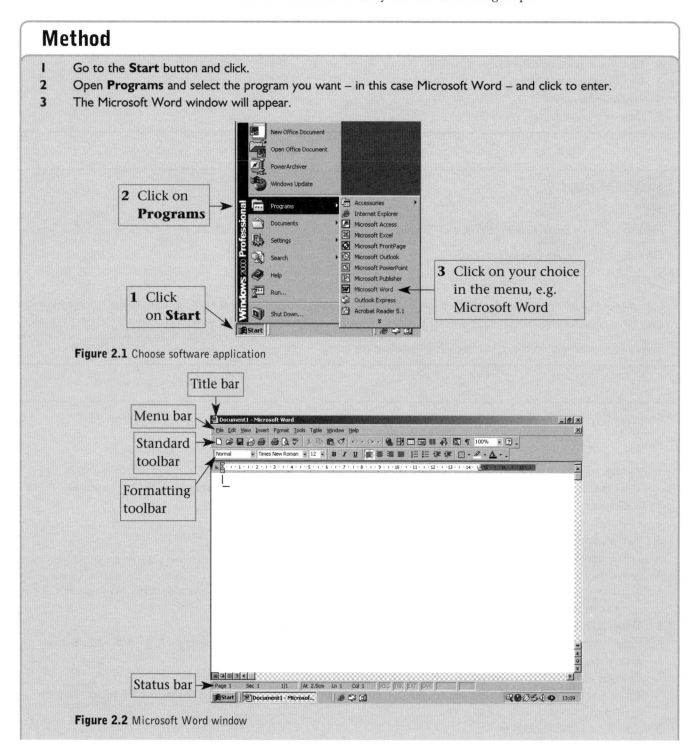

Figure 2.1 Choose software application

Figure 2.2 Microsoft Word window

Task 2.2 — To change margins, page size, page orientation and layout, and printer paper source

Here you will learn to change margins, page size, page orientation and layout, and printer and paper source for any of the documents on page 15.

Method

To change the margins:

1   Select **File** from the bar menu.
2   Select **Page Setup** and click the tab.

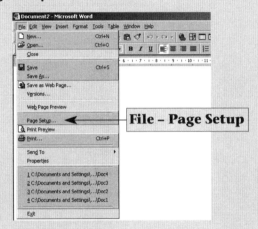

Figure 2.3 Choose document page setup

3   The **Page Setup** dialogue box will be displayed.

At the top of this dialogue box there are four tabs: Margins, Paper Size, Paper Source and Layout.

4   Select the Margins tab to change the current margin settings for the Top, Bottom, Left, Right and the Header and Footer margins.

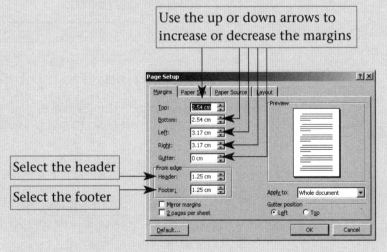

Figure 2.4 Changing margins

●   To change the paper size, select the Paper Size tab to change the paper size, for example from A4 (210 × 297 mm) to A5 (148.5 × 210mm).

- To change the page orientation, select the Paper Size tab to change the page orientation from portrait to landscape.
- To change the layout of the document, use the Layout tab to:
  - Specify where you want the current section to start.
  - Specify different headers/footers for the first page of a section or document.
  - Add or remove line numbering and borders from text.
- To change the printer paper source, select the Paper Source tab to specify which tray of your printer you wish to print from.

Information

Key in the following letter and carry out the tasks that follow.

Boris Badges Limited
Dimension Street
This Town
AAA 123

Mr Prior
Glebe House
Rectory Lane
Puddletown
BBB 345

18th October 2003

Dear Mr Prior

Many thanks for your letter dated 23rd September 2003. The pin type for your Kent badge is no longer in production but there is an alternative fastening in our catalogue reference 298B, on page 13.

I trust this will meet your requirements and look forward to hearing from you.

Yours sincerely
BORIS BADGES LIMITED

Information: Text enhancement

You can change the format of your text to enhance its appearance. Some examples are outlined below:

Normal text
Bold text
Italic text
Underscore (underlined) text
$100°$ – the degree sign is in superscript
10_2 – the 2 is in subscript
Shadow text
Outline text

Method

1   Highlight the text you want to enhance – in this case embolden.

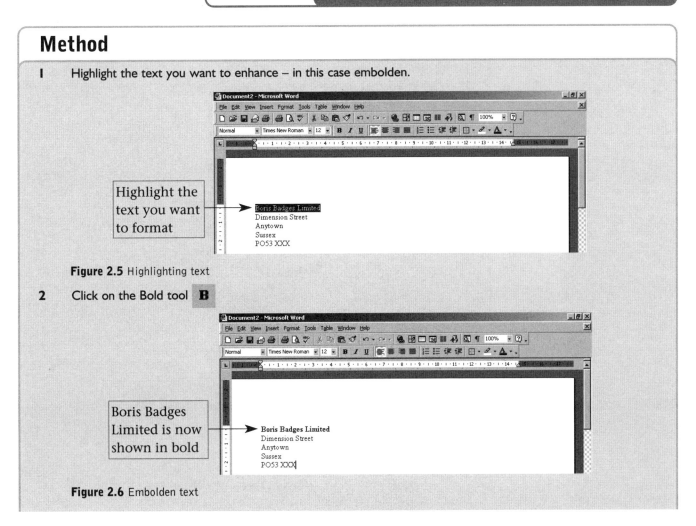

Highlight the
text you want
to format

Figure 2.5 Highlighting text

2   Click on the Bold tool **B**

Boris Badges
Limited is now
shown in bold

Figure 2.6 Embolden text

Task 2.4   To underline text

Method

1   Highlight the text you want to underline.
2   Click on the Underline tool **U**

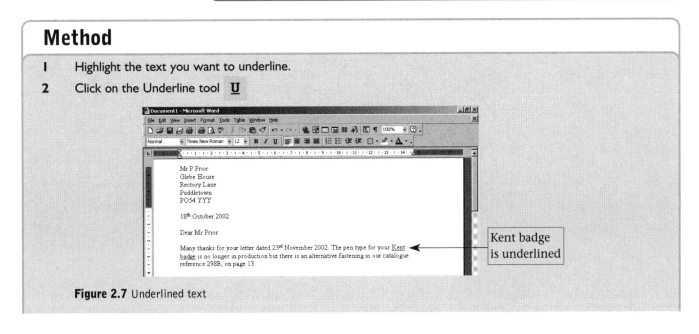

Kent badge
is underlined

Figure 2.7 Underlined text

Task 2.5   Selecting a font

Method

1   Highlight the text you want to change.
2   Select **Format** from the bar menu.
3   Select **Font**.
4   Choose the font you want.
5   Click **OK**.

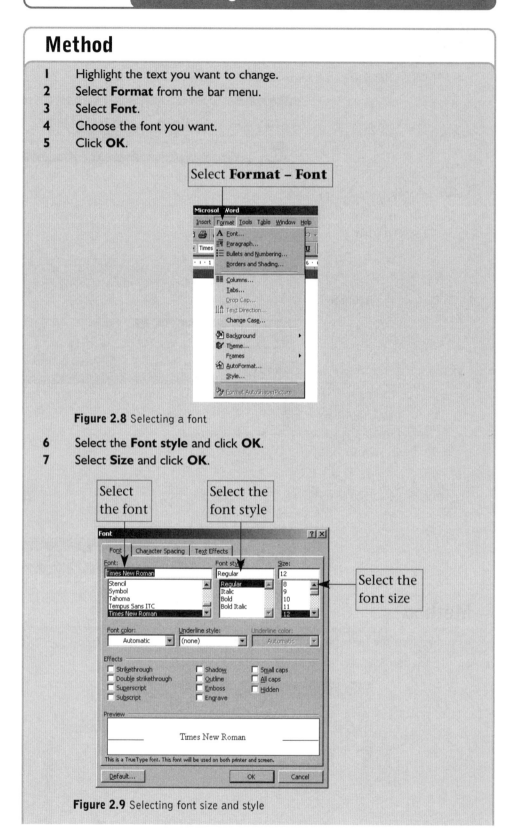

Figure 2.8 Selecting a font

6   Select the **Font style** and click **OK**.
7   Select **Size** and click **OK**.

Figure 2.9 Selecting font size and style

Information: Text alignment

Left alignment   The text is lined up along the length of the left-hand margin and has a ragged right-hand margin.

Centre   The text is centred on the page with an equal distance from both the left- and right-hand margins. The left- and right-hand margins are ragged in appearance.

Right alignment   The text is lined up along the length of the right-hand margin and has a ragged left-hand margin.

Justified   The text has a blocked appearance, as the text lines up along the length of both the left- and right-hand margins.

Task 2.6 To align text

Here is an example of how to centre text. You can apply the same steps as in the other forms of alignment by highlighting the text to be aligned and clicking the appropriate tool button on the Formatting toolbar.

Method

I   Highlight the text to be centred.

2   Go to the **Formatting** toolbar and click on the **Centre** tool button.

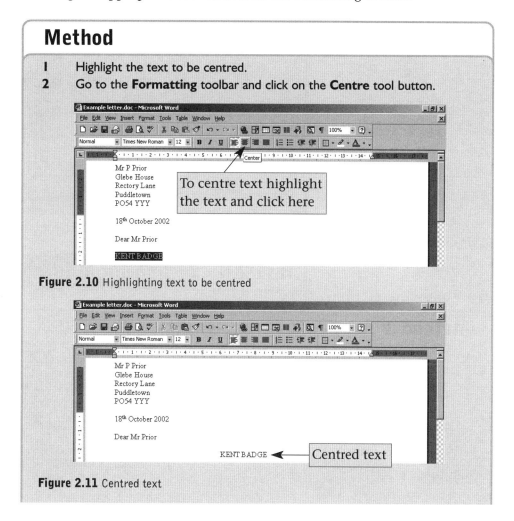

Figure 2.10 Highlighting text to be centred

Figure 2.11 Centred text

Task 2.7 — To save a file

You will now save the current document.

Method 1

1 Open the document.
2 Go to **File** in the bar menu and open.
3 Select the **Save** option and click on it.

Method 2

To save the document with a different name to the current document.

1 Go to **File**.
2 Select **Save As** and click on it.
3 Key in the filename for the document.

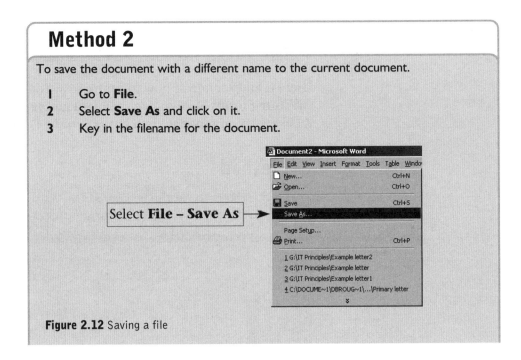

Select **File – Save As**

Figure 2.12 Saving a file

Task 2.8 — To print a file

Method 1

1 Select and open the file to be printed.
2 Select **File** from the menu bar.
3 Select **Print** and click on. The Print dialogue box with print options will appear.

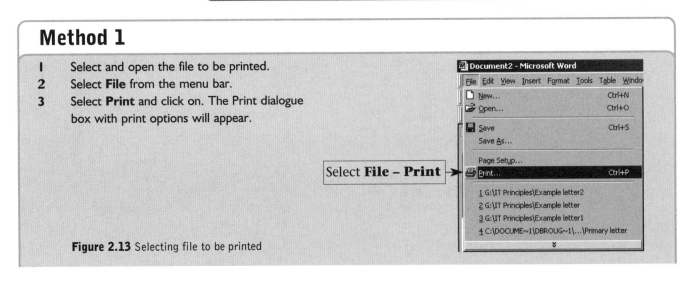

Select **File – Print**

Figure 2.13 Selecting file to be printed

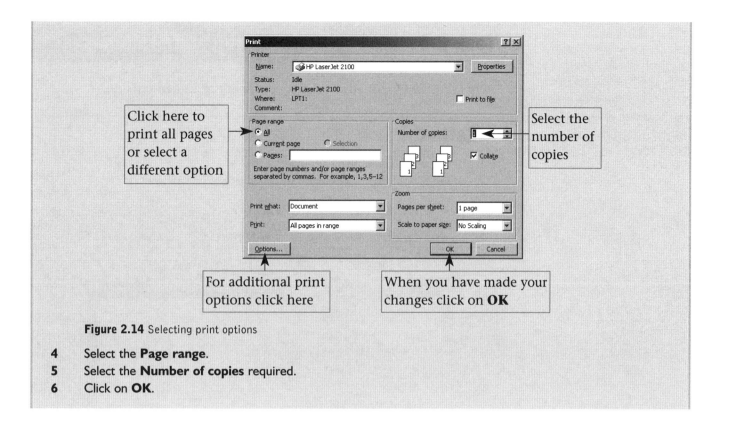

Click here to print all pages or select a different option

Select the number of copies

For additional print options click here

When you have made your changes click on **OK**

Figure 2.14 Selecting print options

4   Select the **Page range**.
5   Select the **Number of copies** required.
6   Click on **OK**.

> # Information: Using spell and grammar checker and help facilities
>
> The Spelling and Grammar facility enables you to check whether you have made spelling or grammatical errors in the text you have created for a document.
>
> A red jagged line under some of the words in your text indicates you may either have an incorrect word spelling or you have repeated the word.
>
> The red line is a guide to highlight potential problems, however you should always check the words which have the red line under them before altering them. This is because the word highlighted may not be a misspelling, but is highlighted because it is either not recognised in the current dictionary or it indicates that you have repeated a word. Words can be added to the dictionary, however be careful when adding them to make sure you spell them correctly. If a misspelling is added to the dictionary, Word will not recognise it as being incorrect in your text. There is no substitute for carefully proofreading your work.
>
> A jagged green line under any of the words in your text indicates that there are grammatical errors in your text.

Task 2.9 — Checking spelling and grammar

There are several methods to check your spelling and grammar.

Method 1

1 Go to the **Tools** menu and open.
2 Select **Spelling and Grammar**. The dialogue box appears.

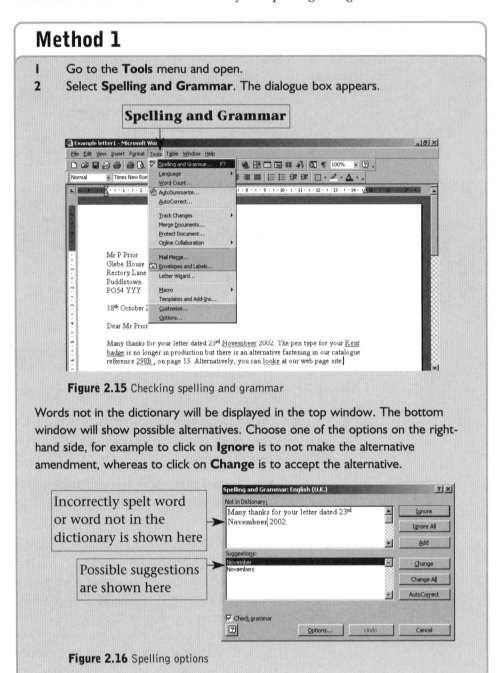

Figure 2.15 Checking spelling and grammar

Words not in the dictionary will be displayed in the top window. The bottom window will show possible alternatives. Choose one of the options on the right-hand side, for example to click on **Ignore** is to not make the alternative amendment, whereas to click on **Change** is to accept the alternative.

Incorrectly spelt word or word not in the dictionary is shown here

Possible suggestions are shown here

Figure 2.16 Spelling options

Method 2

Spelling can also be checked in the following way.

1 Right-click on the red ragged line in the document. You will see a list of possible spellings.

2 Either left-click on the correct spelling or click Add to add to the dictionary.

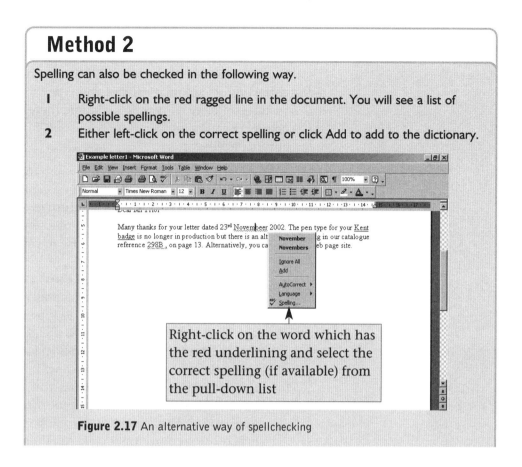

Right-click on the word which has the red underlining and select the correct spelling (if available) from the pull-down list

Figure 2.17 An alternative way of spellchecking

Method 3

Grammar is checked in the following way.

1 Right-click on the green ragged line.

2 Either click on the suggested change of grammar or select **Ignore**.

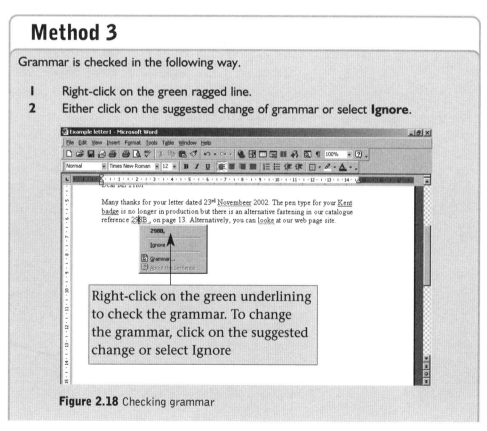

Right-click on the green underlining to check the grammar. To change the grammar, click on the suggested change or select Ignore

Figure 2.18 Checking grammar

Information: Using AutoCorrect

Word has an AutoCorrect feature in Microsoft which can be used to correct errors automatically as you type. You can specify which errors to automatically correct, for example there are several options for changing capitalisation. Here is a list of things you can set to automatically correct:

- **Correct two initial capitals** – use to correct where a second capital letter has been typed after a capital letter.
- **Capitalise first letter of sentences** – use to automatically put a capital letter at the beginning of a sentence.
- **Capitalise names of days** – use to capitalise the first character of the days of the week.
- **Correct accidental usage of Caps Lock key** – if you type the capital letter by mistake by accidentally touching the Caps Lock key, for example if you wanted to type the word **book** but hit the Caps Lock key and typed **bOOK**, the mistake would be corrected.
- **Replace text as you type** – the default can be set to automatically correct and replace text as you type if there is a tick in the checkbox **Replace text as you type**. For example, if you accidentally typed in **across**, AutoCorrect will, when you type a space, automatically correct the spelling to **across**. Click on the checkbox to remove the tick if you do not want Word to automatically correct your text as you type.

Task 2.10   Using AutoCorrect

Method 1

I   Go to **Tools** in the menu.
2   Select **AutoCorrect**.
3   Select the option you require by ticking the appropriate checkbox.

Select this tab to select your preferred options for AutoCorrect text

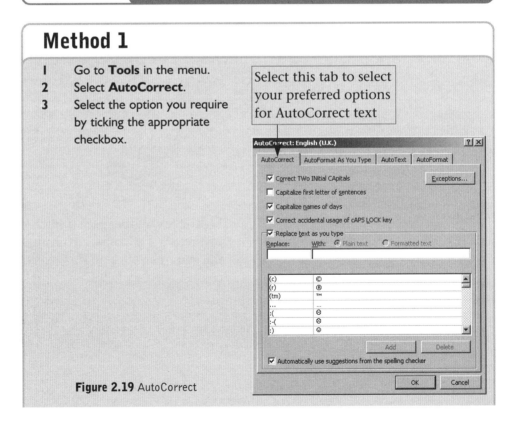

Figure 2.19 AutoCorrect

Task 2.11 | Getting help

Here you will learn how to get help on to how to print.

Method 1

1   Select **Help** (first row of the pop-up menu).
2   Click on **Microsoft Word Help** and then key in the topic you want help with in the search window. Alternatively, to obtain Help press the F1 key or single-click on the Microsoft Office Assistant, which is in the form of an animated graphic on your screen.

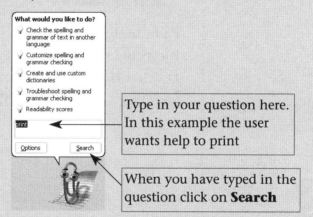

Type in your question here. In this example the user wants help to print

When you have typed in the question click on **Search**

Figure 2.20 Getting help

3   In our example type in Print to obtain help and then click on **Search**.
4   Click on the radial button which matches your question, or refine your search by typing in the search window.

Figure 2.21 Refining the search

Information: The Office Assistant

The Office Assistant is a facility from which you can obtain help and it provides tips on producing your documents.

There are a variety of animated characters available, for example

a paper clip cat  dog and the Genius

To display the Assistant

If the Assistant is not displayed on your screen:

1 Click on **Help**.
2 Click on **Show the Office Assistant**. The Assistant will appear on the screen.

To obtain help from the Office Assistant

1 Single-click on the **Office Assistant**. Either select a topic from the list shown or type in your question in the dialogue box and click on **Search**.

To hide the Assistant

The Assistant can be annoying to view but can be hidden from view.

1 Select **Help** from the menu.
2 Hide the **Office Assistant**.

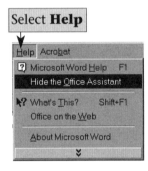

Figure 2.22 Hiding the Office Assistant

To change the Office Assistant

1 Right-click on the **Office Assistant**.
2 Select **Choose Assistant**.
3 Follow the onscreen instructions.

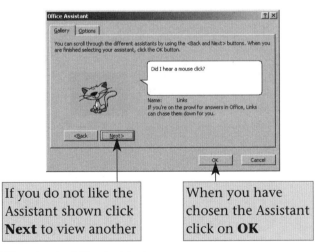

If you do not like the Assistant shown click **Next** to view another

When you have chosen the Assistant click on **OK**

Figure 2.23 Changing the Office Assistant

→ Practise your skills 1

1   Type in the following text:

Boris Badges Limited
Dimension Street
This Town
AAA 123

Mrs S Norris
15A Firetree Avenue
Priory Lane
Pianotown
ABV 34X

18th September 2002

Dear Mrs Norris

Thank you for your letter dated 16th April 2002. I apologise for the delay
in sending you the new Sussex Badge catalogue. Your new catalogue
should arrive in the next few days.

Thank you for your interest in our products.

Yours sincerely

David Smith
BORIS BADGES LIMITED

---

2   Change the margins to 1.5 cm for the right and left margins.
3   Embolden the text BORIS BADGES LIMITED.
4   Change the font to Arial and the size to 12.
5   Save the file.
6   Print a copy of the letter.

Information: Databases

A database is an electronic method of organising data. Storing data electronically, rather than using a manual paper-based filing system, has distinct advantages. Searching for data and producing reports using a computer database is relatively straightforward. A database held on computer in comparison to a manual system can be shared and accessed by authorised users from different locations, which is more efficient, cost effective and avoids the duplication of data. Different types of businesses and organisations use electronic databases including government departments such as customs and excise, the health service, education, as well as commercial organisations such as travel agents, retail stores and financial institutions.

Information: Case study – creating a database

Claire Downs, Sales Manager of Boris Badges, wishes to store customer details on an electronic database. At present the customer files are held on a paper-based system stored in a filing cabinet. Claire is unfamiliar with creating a database. The following section describes how to set up the database. You start by opening Microsoft Access.

Task 2.12 Opening Microsoft Access

Method 1

I   Double-click on the **Access** icon on the desktop.

Method 2

1   Select **Start**.
2   Select **Programs** and click on.
3   A list of programs will appear. Select **Microsoft Access** and click to open.

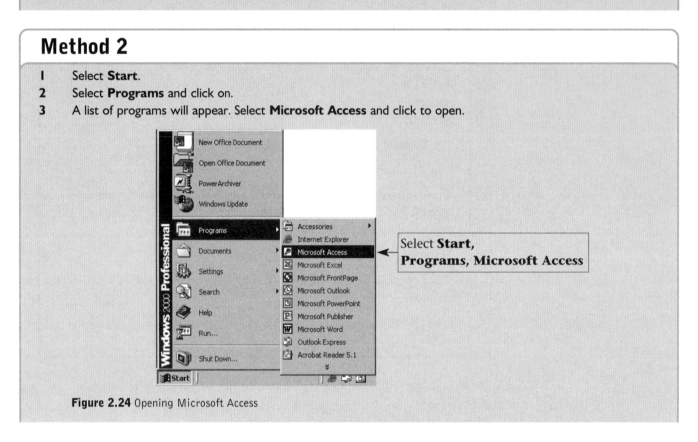

Figure 2.24 Opening Microsoft Access

Task 2.13 To create a new database

Method

I   With Microsoft Access open, select **Blank Access database**.

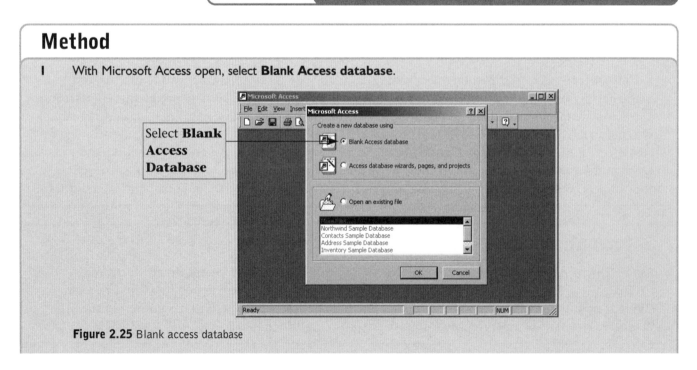

Figure 2.25 Blank access database

2 In the **Save in** dialogue box select the location where to save the database.

3 Key in the name of the database file in the **File name** dialogue box.

4 Click on **Create** when you have keyed in your filename.

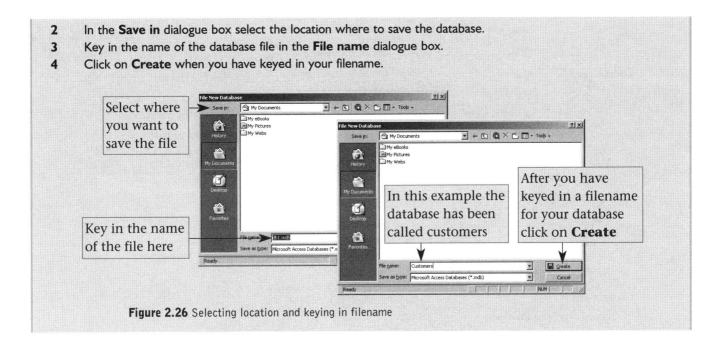

Select where you want to save the file

Key in the name of the file here

In this example the database has been called customers

After you have keyed in a filename for your database click on **Create**

Figure 2.26 Selecting location and keying in filename

Task 2.14 — To create a table

A table stores the data for your database. Before you can enter the data you must first create a structure for the table, which defines what type of data is stored in it.

Method

I   Select **Tables** on left-hand side of window.

2   Click on **Create table in Design view**.

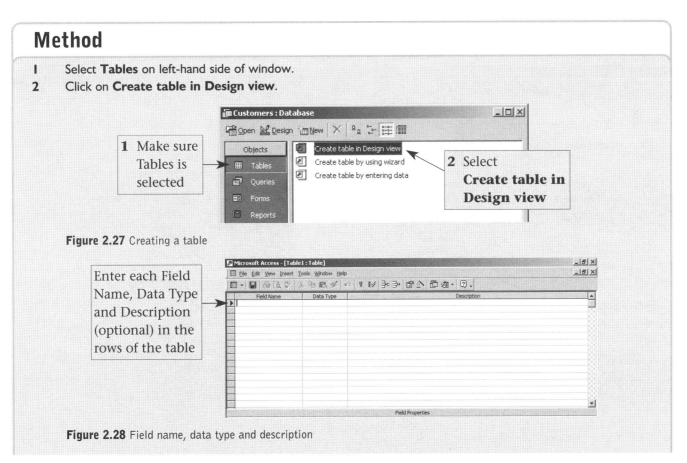

1 Make sure Tables is selected

2 Select **Create table in Design view**

Figure 2.27 Creating a table

Enter each Field Name, Data Type and Description (optional) in the rows of the table

Figure 2.28 Field name, data type and description

3   Key in the name for the field in Field Name row, for example Surname.

This is optional. It is used to descirbe the field. This is, in many cases, obvious and is therefore optional

Data Type for this field is Text

The first field name to add is, in our example, Surname

This is the field size. You want to make this large enough to contain the data in the field but not too large that it takes up disk space

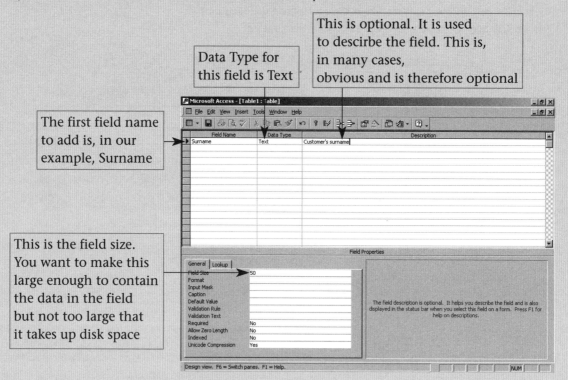

Figure 2.29 Entering field names, data types and description

4   Key in the data type, for example Text for a text field such as Surname, or Date for a date field. In Figure 2.30 the Date/Time data type has been selected.

Select **Date/Time**

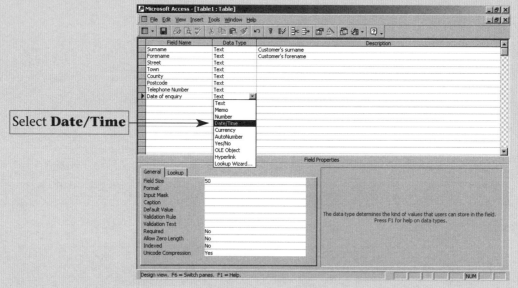

Figure 2.30 Selecting the date/time

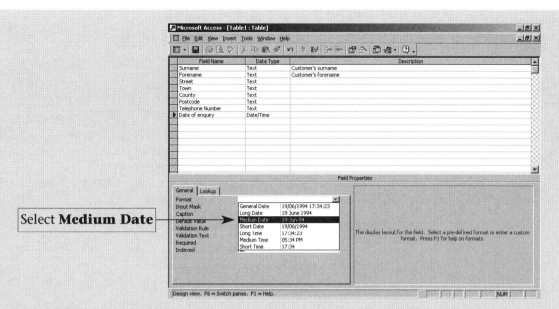

Select **Medium Date**

Figure 2.31 Selecting medium date

Select the format for the date. In our example the medium date has been selected from the Format properties box.

In Figure 2.32 the format for the field **Product interested in** is Number and the chosen format for that number is Long Integer.

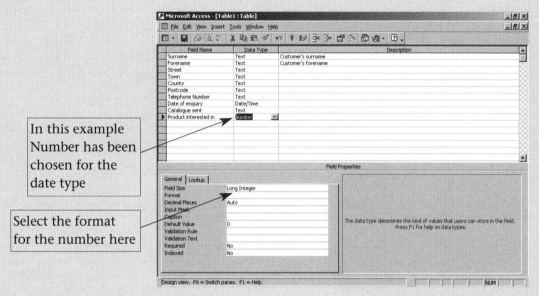

In this example Number has been chosen for the date type

Select the format for the number here

Figure 2.32 Selecting number

5   You can add a description to give more details about the field, but this facility is optional.
       When you have finished entering the structure, save the table.
6   Select **File** from the menu.

7 Click on **Save As**.

8 Key in the name for the table.

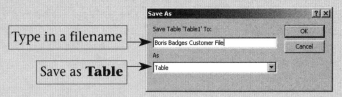

Type in a filename

Save as **Table**

Figure 2.33 Keying in filename

9 The prompt states that 'There is no primary key defined'. A primary key is used to link more than one table in a relationship. In our example, select **No** as we are working from a single table.

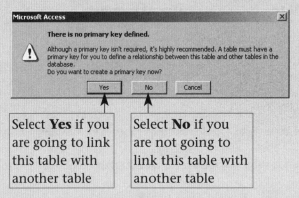

Select **Yes** if you are going to link this table with another table

Select **No** if you are not going to link this table with another table

Figure 2.34 Choosing primary key

10 The table name will be shown in the window.

11 Double-click on the filename.

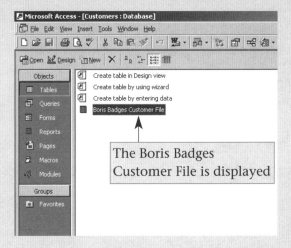

The Boris Badges Customer File is displayed

Figure 2.35 Table name

12 Enter in the data.

13 Save the data by clicking on **File – Save**.

Surname	Forename	Street	Town	County	Postcode	Telephone Nu	Date of enquir	Cata	Product Interes
Jones	Simon	88 The Street	Portsmouth	Hants	PO21 BBB	01853 234562	16-Aug-02	Yes	8926
Frost	George	67 Grange Road	Portsmouth	Hants	PO18 FFF	04869 394817	05-Mar-02	Yes	4380
Monet	Claude	189 Linden Avenue	Portsmouth	Hants	PO22 HHH	01546 098769	25-Aug-02	Yes	956
Lane	Penny	82 Gordon Terrace	Portsmouth	Hants	PO22 JJJ	01674 492769	06-Jul-02	Yes	3471
Practice	Alice	83 Corrance Road	Portsmouth	Hants	PO23 EEE	01543 765439	05-Mar-02	Yes	8962
Patel	Ali	1a Mistle Close	Southampton	Hants	SO16 DDD	01943 643210	22-Sep-02	Yes	1789
Molley	Mildred	1C Oak Avenue	Southampton	Hants	SO19 GGG	03581 059879	19-Sep-02	Yes	8792
Gordon	Keith	21 The Highlands	Southampton	Hants	SO20 AAA	01293 123453	20-May-02	Yes	1234
Smith	Alias	15 Rainbows End	Southampton	Hants	SO20 CCC	01345 345671	18-Apr-02	No	543
Hardwick	Charles	123 King Street	Southampton	Hants	SO99 ZZZ	01327 960488	01-Feb-02	Yes	4534
									0

Table showing data entered

Figure 2.36 Tables showing data entered

Task 2.15	To create a query

A query is a search on your data. To search for data you need to define the fields you wish to search on and what criteria you want to use for your search.

Method

1   Select **Queries**, which is in the box on the left-hand side of the window.
2   Select **Create query in Design view**.

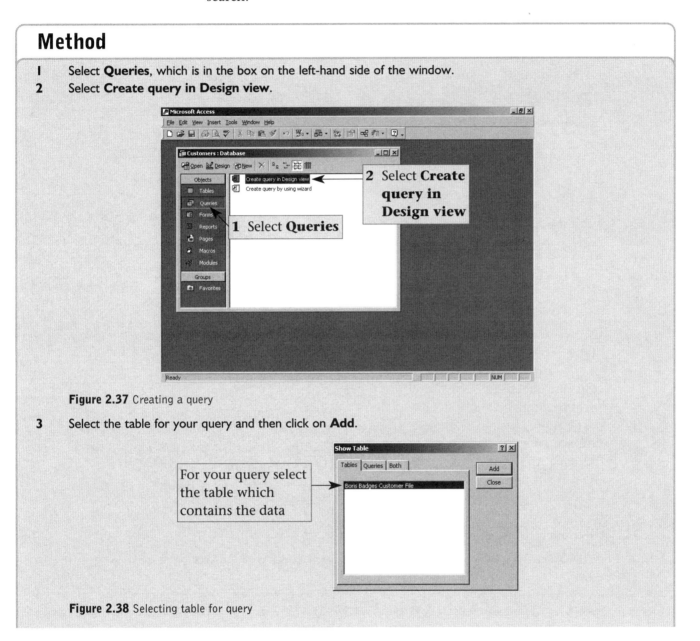

Figure 2.37 Creating a query

3   Select the table for your query and then click on **Add**.

Figure 2.38 Selecting table for query

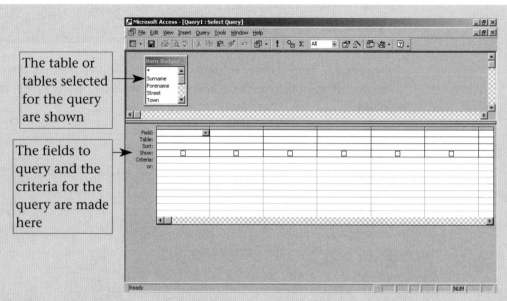

The table or tables selected for the query are shown

The fields to query and the criteria for the query are made here

Figure 2.39 Fields and criteria for query

4   The table selected for the query will be displayed.

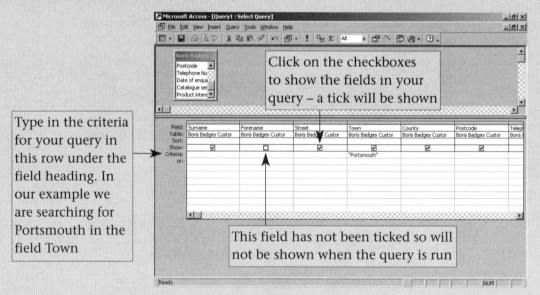

Click on the checkboxes to show the fields in your query – a tick will be shown

Type in the criteria for your query in this row under the field heading. In our example we are searching for Portsmouth in the field Town

This field has not been ticked so will not be shown when the query is run

Figure 2.40 The table for the query

5   Either double-click the fields in the table which you require in your query or click on the field and drag into the Field row.

To display a field in your query ensure there is a tick in the field column you want, displayed in the Show row. In the example there is no tick in the Forename field so this will not be displayed in the answer. You can search for a field but not have the field displayed as part of your answer.

In the Criteria row underneath the field you wish to search, you need to enter the search criteria. In Figure 2.40 the query will search for town, which is Portsmouth, and will display the Surname, Street, Town, County and Postcode.

6   To complete the query, either click on the **Run** tool button to display the results or click on the **Close Query** button (make sure you do not select the top Close button or you will close the database!)

Query showing the
results for the search
on Portsmouth for the
Town. Notice that the
Forename field is not
shown, as it was not
selected in the Show
checkbox when the
query was created

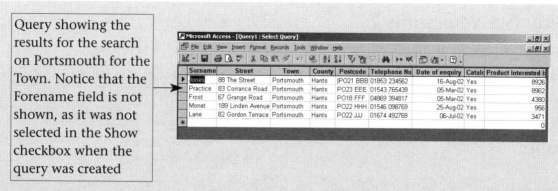

Figure 2.41 Results of the query

7   Key in a name for the query. Make sure the **Save As** dialogue box displays Query.

Type in the name of the query

Save the table as a Query

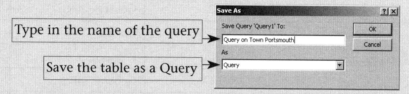

Figure 2.42 Keying in query name and saving table

In Figure 2.42 a new query has been set up. The query searches between two dates using the AND function to search between dates. The criterion >#01/05/2002# and <#01/09/2002# will search for all the dates greater than 1/5/2002 and less than 01/09/2002.

Note: You do not put in the # sign in the query; this will be typed in automatically. You must also ensure there is a space between the beginning and the end of the AND function.

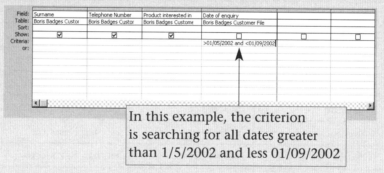

In this example, the criterion
is searching for all dates greater
than 1/5/2002 and less 01/09/2002

Figure 2.43 A date query

The results of the query are shown.
Note the Date of Enquiry field is not
shown as the Show checkbox in this
field was not selected in the query
design. This demonstrates that you
can query a field but not necessarily
show that field in the query results

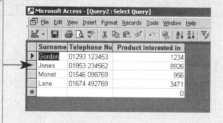

Figure 2.44 Results of the date query

→ Practise your skills 2

Boris Badges require an inventory of all computer equipment used in the company.

1   Create a database with the following fields and enter in the extract of data below:

Reference number
Description
Serial number
Location
Date purchased

Reference number	Description	Serial number	Location	Date purchased
Autonumber	Keyboard	KB675432	General Office	22/8/2002
	Keyboard	KB32142	General Office	22/8/2002
	Mouse	MO29870	Production	13/2/2003
	Monitor	MON777	General Office	19/5/2001
	System unit	SY56741	Production	1/1/2002
	System unit	SY85321	General Office	12/5/2002
	Mouse	MO7654	General Office	18/9/2002
	Monitor	MON123	Production	3/5/2002
	System unit	SYT3421	General Office	19/3/2002
	Mouse	MO98765	General Office	11/7/2003
	Monitor	MON2312	General Office	13/7/2003
	System unit	SY5678	Human Resources	21/5/2003
	System unit	SY6543	Human Resources	11/9/2002
	Monitor	MON4321	Human Resources	16/9/2001
	Monitor	MON6431	Human Resources	22/7/2002
	Mouse	MON1234	Human Resources	14/5/2003
	Mouse	MO8765	Human Resources	19/7/2003
	Keyboard	KB78654	Human Resources	13/6/2003

2   Print all the data.
3   Search for all equipment in the General Office. Print the query.
4   Search for all equipment older than May 2001 and print the query.
5   Change the location for serial number MON2312 to Sales and Marketing.
6   Add the record: System unit;SY76321;Sales and Marketing;24/9/2002.
7   Edit the serial number SYT3421 to read ST3421.
8   Find all records between 31/812002 and 31/7/2003 and display and print out the description and location fields only.

Information: Data Protection Act

The rise in the use of computers and the amount of personal information stored on them raise issues regarding the potential for this information to be inappropriately disclosed or misused. There was concern that personal information was being held which was not relevant for the original purpose and that unscrupulous individuals could gain access to personal data.

In 1984 the UK government passed the Data Protection Act to protect the security of personal data. This Act was further strengthened in 1998.

The Data Protection Act sets out eight principles for data. Data must be:

- fairly and lawfully processed
- processed for limited purposes
- adequate, relevant and not excessive
- accurate
- not kept for longer than necessary
- processed in line with your rights
- secure
- not transferred to other countries without adequate protection.

Information: Spreadsheets

A spreadsheet is used for recording and making numerical calculations. Numerical data is input into a grid made up of rows and columns and calculations are made automatically on this data. Spreadsheets are commonly used for tasks such as sales forecasting, budgeting and payroll. In the following tasks you will learn how to create a spreadsheet, using Microsoft Excel, and learn how to use the SUM, AVERAGE, MIN and MAX formulae to calculate numeric data. You will learn how to replicate formulas, calculate percentages and to format the spreadsheet for currency, alignment and decimal places. Sorting data, inserting columns, changing the print orientation and printing the spreadsheet will also be examined.

Task 2.16   To open Microsoft Excel

The software you will use to create a spreadsheet is Microsoft Excel.

Method

1   Click on the **Start** button.
2   Go to **Programs**.
3   Select **Microsoft Excel**.

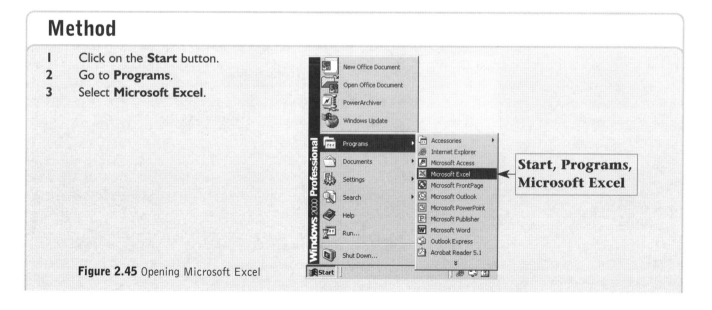

Figure 2.45 Opening Microsoft Excel

Information: Cell addresses, rows, columns, formulae

- **Row**   This is a horizontal line from left to right on the spreadsheet.
- **Column**   This is a vertical line from top to bottom on the spreadsheet.
- **Cell**   A cell is a box which you enter data into.
- **Cell addresses**   Each individual cell has a unique address, which is called an absolute address. The address is made up of the column and row position, e.g. A1.
- **Formulae**   The advantage of the spreadsheet is that you can enter a mathematical formula into a cell to calculate the value from other cells. If, for example, you wanted to add the contents of cell A1 to cell A2 and place the answer in A3 you would place the cursor in A3 and type =A1+A2.

Figure 2.46 shows a spreadsheet made up of rows and columns. Where the rows and columns intersect a cell is formed. Each cell on the spreadsheet has a unique absolute reference identified by the column and row reference, for example A1, B1, B2.

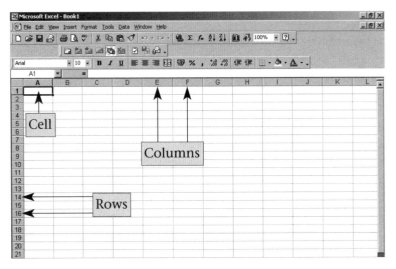

Figure 2.46 Rows, columns and cells

Figures 2.47 and 2.48 show some of the features of the spreadsheet window.

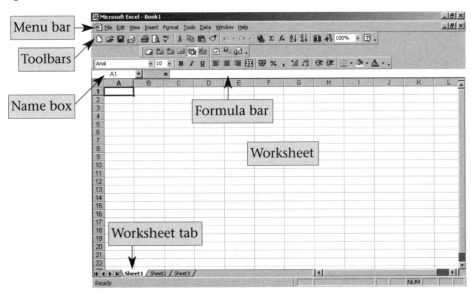

Figure 2.47 Features of the spreadsheet window

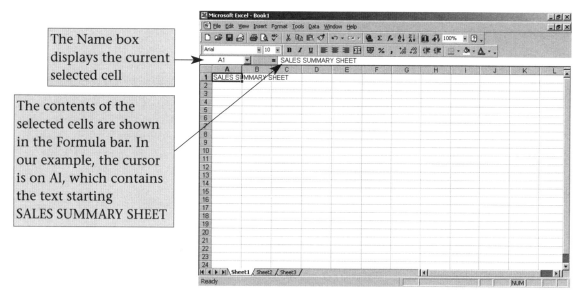

The Name box displays the current selected cell

The contents of the selected cells are shown in the Formula bar. In our example, the cursor is on Al, which contains the text starting SALES SUMMARY SHEET

Figure 2.48 More features of a spreadsheet window

A spreadsheet has been created for the Sales Department of Boris Badges for the first quarter of the year. The sales figure for each of the sales staff is entered on the spreadsheet and a formula is required for the totals. In the following tasks you will learn how to enter formulae and do calculations on a spreadsheet.

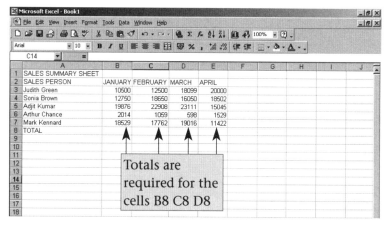

Totals are required for the cells B8 C8 D8

Figure 2.49 Boris Badges spreadsheet

Task 2.17   To enter a formula

Here you will learn how to enter a formula for making spreadsheet calculations.

Method

I	Place the cursor where you want the answer.
2	Key in =
3	Key in **SUM**.
4	Key in an open bracket (
5	Click on the first cell to add :
6	Hold the mouse down and drag down to the last cell to add. You will see dotted lines around your selection.

7 Release the mouse button.

8 Key in a closing bracket **)**

9 Select **Enter** or move to a new cell by moving one of the cursor keys.

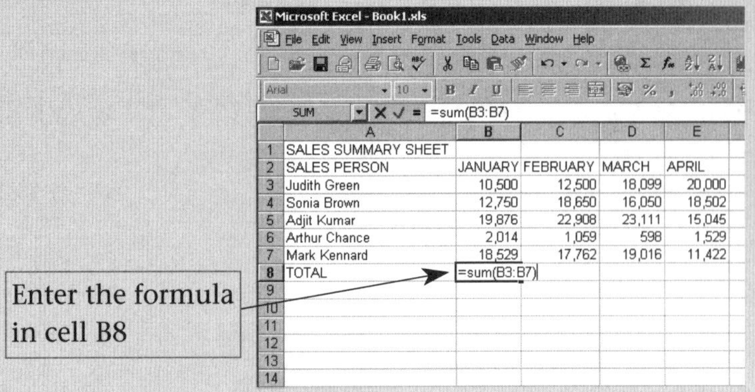

Enter the formula in cell B8

Figure 2.50 Entering a formula

Task 2.18 To replicate a formula

A formula can be replicated in order to make calculations.

Method

1 When you have entered the formula you will see the figure displayed in the cell. Ensure your cursor is on the cell and move the cursor onto the bottom right-hand square of the cell. The large cross displayed will change to a thin cross.

2 Keep the mouse button held down and drag across to the last cell location you want to replicate the cells to.

3 Release the mouse button.

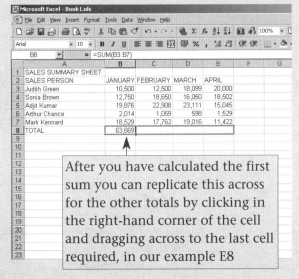

After you have calculated the first sum you can replicate this across for the other totals by clicking in the right-hand corner of the cell and dragging across to the last cell required, in our example E8

Figure 2.51 Replicating a formula

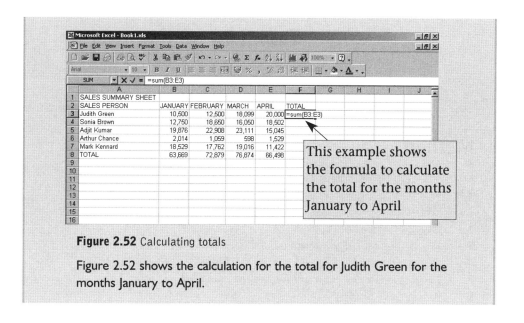

Figure 2.52 Calculating totals

Figure 2.52 shows the calculation for the total for Judith Green for the months January to April.

Task 2.19 To calculate an average using the AVERAGE function

Use the AVERAGE function to calculate an average value within a range.

Method

1 Place the cursor in the position you wish the answer to appear.
2 Key in =
3 Key in **average**.
4 Key in open bracket (
5 Key in the first cell you want for the average, **b3**.
6 Key in a colon :
7 Key in the last cell you want for the average, **e3**.
8 Close the bracket)
9 Press **Enter** or use the down cursor arrow.

Figure 2.53 Calculating an average value

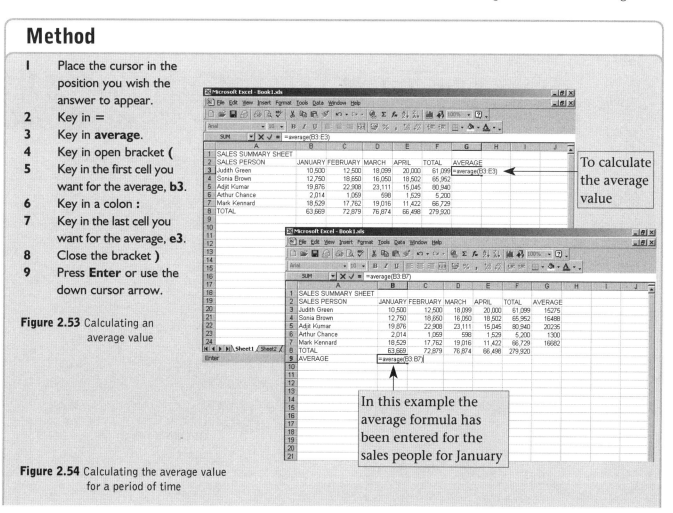

Figure 2.54 Calculating the average value for a period of time

| Task 2.20 | To calculate the minimum value using the MIN function |

You use the MIN function to calculate the minimum value in a list.

Method

1 Place the cursor where you want the answer.
2 Key in =
3 Key in **min**.
4 Key in open bracket (
5 Key in the first cell you want for the minimum, **b3**.
6 Key in a colon :
7 Key in the last cell you want for the minimum, **e3**.
8 Key in close bracket)

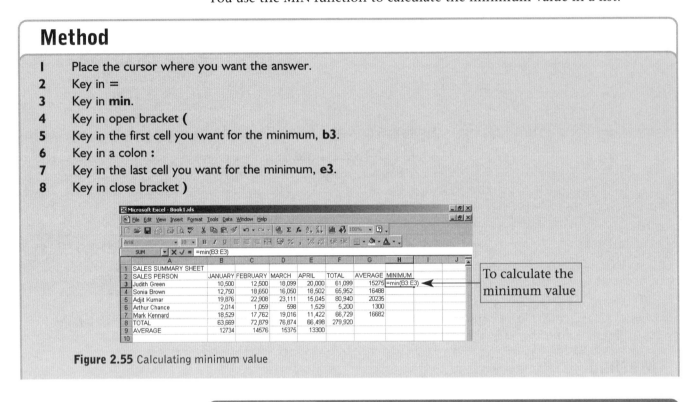

Figure 2.55 Calculating minimum value

| Task 2.21 | To calculate the maximum value using the MAX function |

The MAX function is used to calculate the maximum value of a list.

Method

1 Place the cursor where you want the answer.
2 Key in =
3 Key in **max**.
4 Key in open bracket (
5 Key in first cell you want for the maximum, **b3**.
6 Key in the last cell you want for the maximum, **e3**.
7 Key in close bracket)

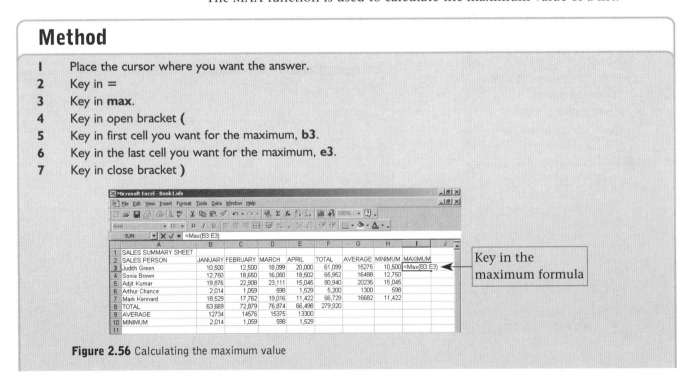

Figure 2.56 Calculating the maximum value

Now your spreadsheet should look the same as in Figure 2.57.

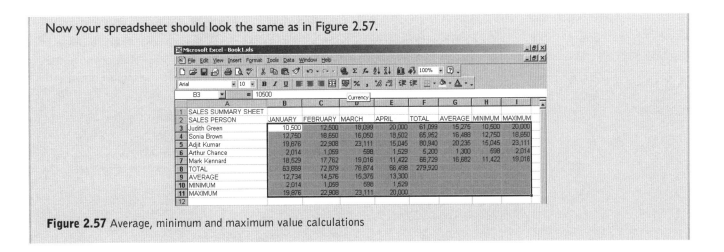

Figure 2.57 Average, minimum and maximum value calculations

Information

If you have used the formulae to calculate the maximum and minimum values, you can then use another formula to calculate the range. The range shows the spread of data and is calculated by subtracting the lowest value from the highest.

In this example, the formula to calculate the range of Judith Green's sales would be = I3 – H3.

Task 2.22 | To format currency

To insert currency in a spreadsheet involves formatting the appropriate cells.

Method

1   Highlight the cells to be formatted.
2   Click on the **Currency** button. The currency selected will be inserted automatically into all the columns highlighted.

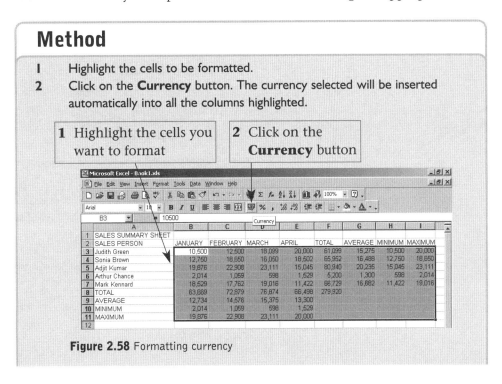

Figure 2.58 Formatting currency

Note: If you see a series of hashes displayed in the cell it indicates that the cell width needs to be widened to accommodate the increase in characters. If this is the case, go to **Format**, then **Column**, then **Width**. Key in a larger size, or move the cursor between the columns on the column names and hold the mouse down and drag to a larger width.

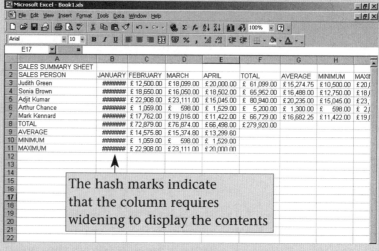

The hash marks indicate that the column requires widening to display the contents

Figure 2.59 Currency inserted

Task 2.23 | To display formulas

The formulas required for making calculations to a spreadsheet are displayed in the following way.

Method

1   Go to **Tools** in the menu.
2   Select **Options**.
3   Click on **Formulas** checkbox in the Options box.
4   The formulas will now be displayed on the screen.

Select **Tools, Options**

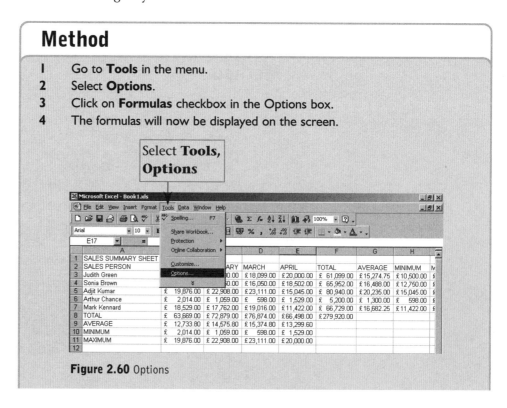

Figure 2.60 Options

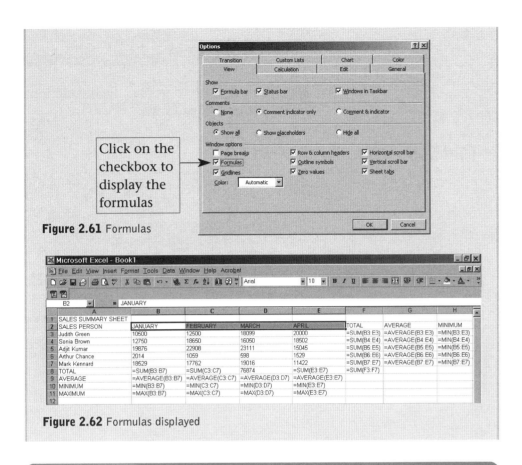

Figure 2.61 Formulas

Figure 2.62 Formulas displayed

Task 2.24 | To align cells

The cells in a spreadsheet need to be aligned to make the data easier to read, and to improve the appearance of the spreadsheet.

Method

1 Highlight the cell to be formatted.
2 Go to **Format** in the menu bar.
3 Click in **Cells**.
4 Choose the alignment from the **Format Cells** dialogue box.

To align the text
1 Highlight the text to be formatted
2 Format
3 Cells

Click on the arrow to select your choice of alignment

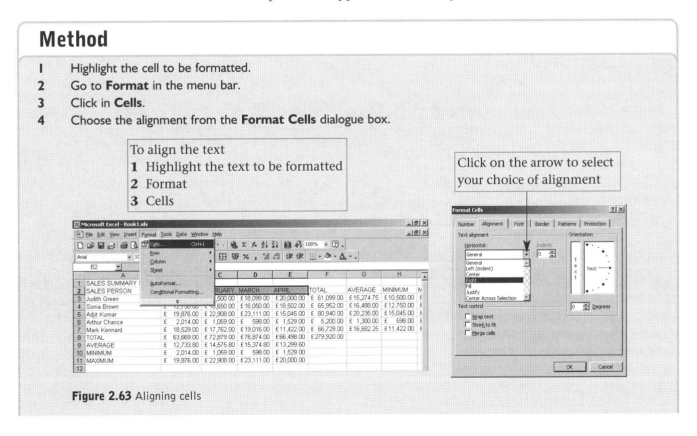

Figure 2.63 Aligning cells

To change the orientation of text

Here you will learn to change the orientation of the text in a spreadsheet to either portrait or landscape.

Method

1 Click on the coloured pointer and move to the position where you want the text to be displayed.
2 Release the mouse button.

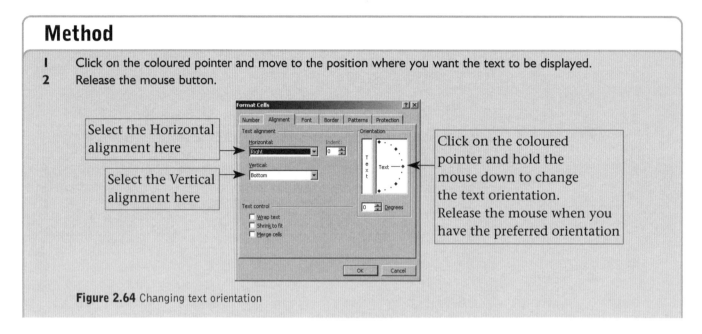

Figure 2.64 Changing text orientation

To change the page orientation

Method

1 Select **File** from the menu.
2 Go to **Page Setup**.
3 Click on **Landscape**.
4 Click **OK**.

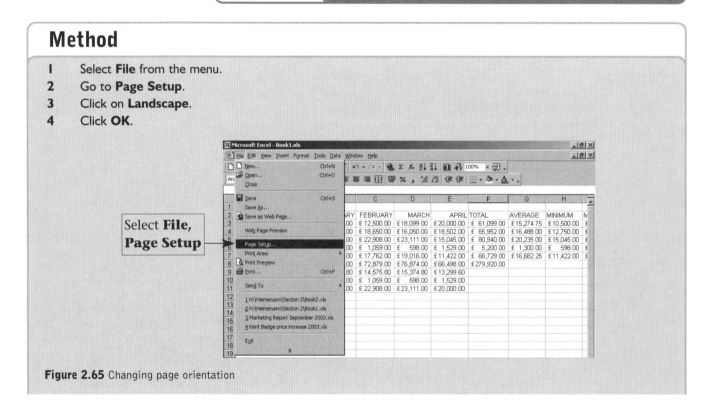

Figure 2.65 Changing page orientation

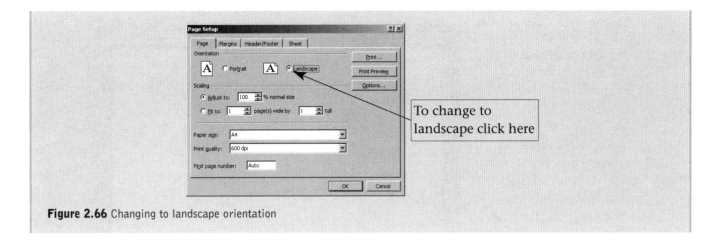

Figure 2.66 Changing to landscape orientation

| Task 2.27 | **To print preview the spreadsheet** |

You may need to print preview the spreadsheet to make sure that it looks satisfactory. By previewing your work prior to printing you can proofread the spreadsheet and make amendments. This will save wasting paper.

Method

1   Go to **File** in the menu bar.
2   Select **Print Preview**.
3   Preview your work on the screen. If the text is too small click on the **Zoom** button.
    Set the margins by clicking on **Margins** and you can print directly from here by clicking on **Print**.
4   Click on **Close** when you have finished previewing your work.

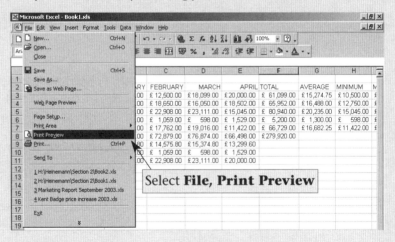

Figure 2.67 To print preview a document

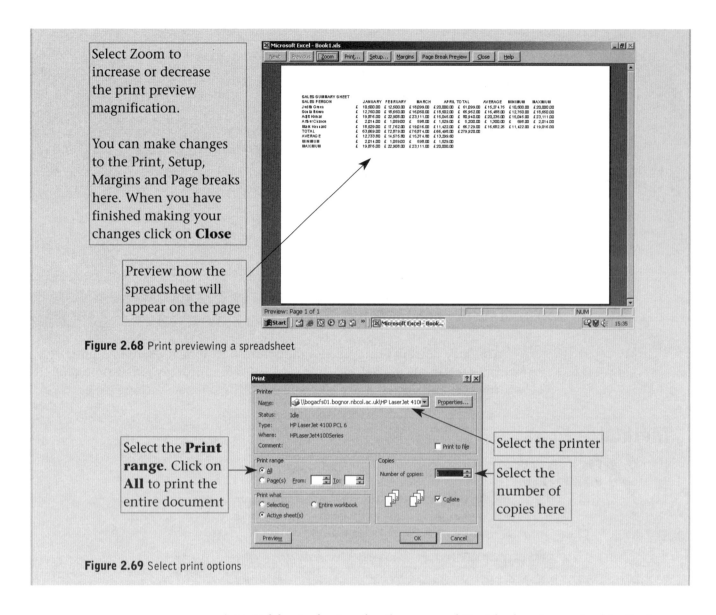

Select Zoom to increase or decrease the print preview magnification.

You can make changes to the Print, Setup, Margins and Page breaks here. When you have finished making your changes click on **Close**

Preview how the spreadsheet will appear on the page

Figure 2.68 Print previewing a spreadsheet

Select the **Print range**. Click on **All** to print the entire document

Select the printer

Select the number of copies here

Figure 2.69 Select print options

A spreadsheet of prices for the range of Kent badges is required by Boris Badges. You will create a spreadsheet, list the prices of the badges and format the spreadsheet. Key in the following data.

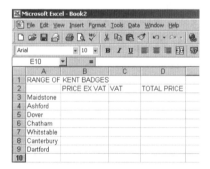

Figure 2.70 Range of Kent badges

Key in the following prices.

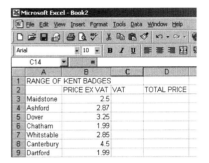

Figure 2.71 Kent badges prices

You will notice that some of the prices are not formatted to 2 decimal places. You will do this in the following task.

Task 2.28   Format to 2 decimal places

Method

1   Highlight the cells to format.
2   Click on the **Increase Decimal** icon as shown in Figure 2.72. Additional mouse clicks on the icon will increase the number of decimal places. If you have selected too many decimal places either select the **Undo** button or select the **Decrease Decimal** button to the right of the Increase Decimal button.

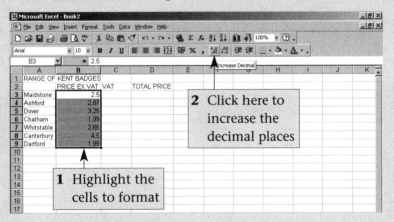

Figure 2.72 Formatting to 2 decimal places

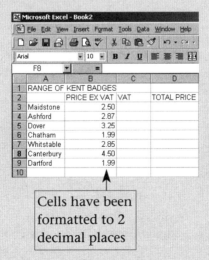

Figure 2.73 Cells formatted to 2 decimal places

Task 2.29	To insert a column

These are the steps to follow if you need to add more columns to your spreadsheet.

Method

1 Place your cursor where you want the new column.
2 Select **Insert**.
3 Select **Columns**. If you want more than one column to be inserted highlight the number of columns required, starting at the first position to be inserted and repeat steps 1 and 2.

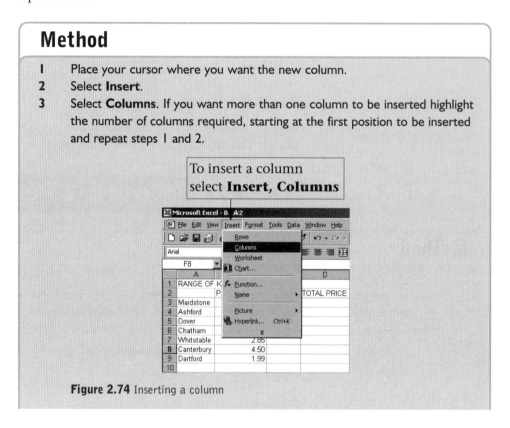

Figure 2.74 Inserting a column

Task 2.30	To calculate percentage increases in price

You have to calculate a 10% increase in the price of each type of badge in Boris Badges' Kent range.

Method

1 Enter the formula =B3*10% in cell C3 to calculate the 10% increase.
2 To replicate the percentage for each type of badge, select the cell and drag down from the right-hand corner.
3 To calculate the new price, excluding VAT, enter the formula =B3+C3.
4 To calculate the VAT, enter the formula =D3*17.5%.
5 To calculate the new total price, add the new price, excluding VAT, with the VAT.

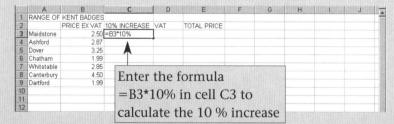

Figure 2.75 Calculating price increase

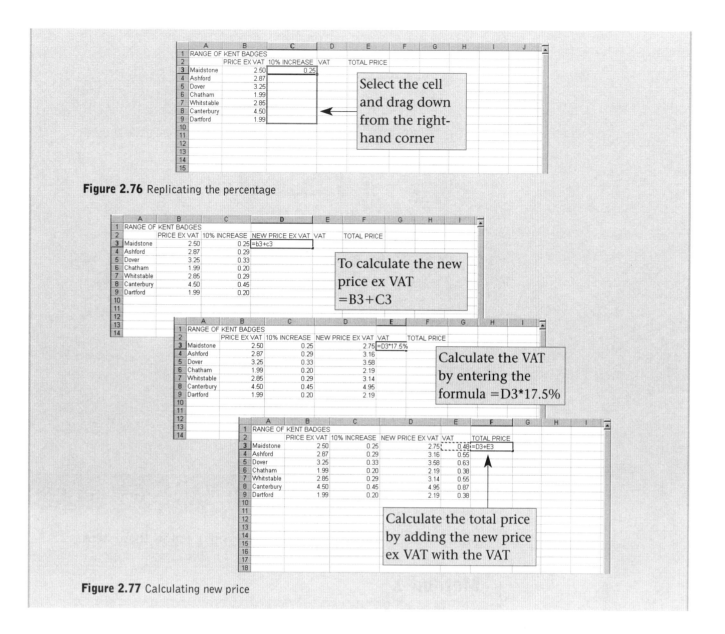

Figure 2.76 Replicating the percentage

Figure 2.77 Calculating new price

Task 2.31 | To sort data

You can sort data into alphabetical order. Here you will sort the towns on the Kent badges spreadsheet into alphabetical order.

Method

1	Select **Data** from the menu bar.
2	Select **Sort**.
3	Select the cells you wish to sort on.
4	Select which column you want to sort by. In the example shown the Sort column is the towns in column A.
5	Click **OK**.

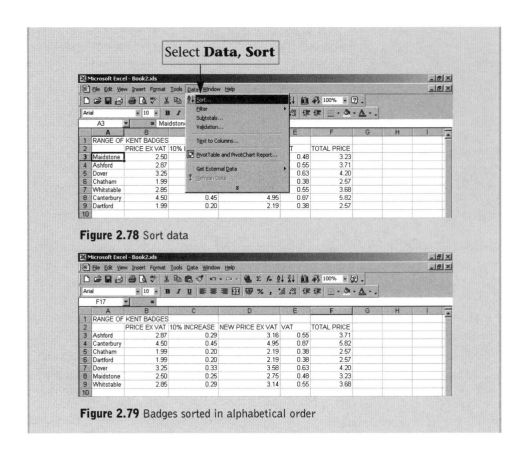

Figure 2.78 Sort data

Figure 2.79 Badges sorted in alphabetical order

Task 2.32 | To print the spreadsheet

To print out a spreadsheet (produce a hard copy), follow these steps.

Method 1

1	Select **File** from the menu.
2	Select **Page Setup**.
3	Select the orientation – either portrait or landscape.
4	From **File** select **Print**.
5	Select the printer.
6	Select **Print range**.
7	Select number of copies required.
8	Click **OK**.

Method 2

1	Select **File**.
2	Go to **Print**.
3	Click **OK**.

→ Practise your skills 3

1 Load Excel.

2 In cell A1 type in Sussex Badge Sales 2003

3 In the row below enter the headings:

Salesperson	September	October	November	December	Total

4 Enter the following salespeople in column A: Dave Pickles, Sandra Johns, Paula Chan, Arthur Chance.

5 Enter the following data:

Salesperson	September	October	November	December	Total
Dave Pickles	303	466	828	911	
Sandra Johns	388	931	564	499	
Paula Chan	225	809	246	812	
Arthur Chance	246	802	308	280	

6 In the Total column enter a formula to calculate the total sales for Dave Pickles.

7 Replicate this formula for the other salespersons.

8 Format the numerical data to currency.

9 Insert a new column after Total labelled Commission.

10 Calculate a 5.5 % commission on each salesperson's total sales.

11 Sort the data alphabetically by Salesperson.

12 Change the print orientation to landscape.

13 Display the formulas.

14 Print a copy of the formulas.

15 Print a copy of the spreadsheet.

16 Save the spreadsheet as **Sales1**.

Information: Mail merge

You can use mail merge to send a standard letter to numerous people. You can use it to create form letters, mailing labels, envelopes or catalogues. To create a mail merge you create a main document (e.g. standard letter) containing information which remains the same for each document of the mail merge, and you create a data source for information which alters for each of the individual documents. In a letter, for example, the individual name and address of the recipient will be held on the data source and the content of the letter will be stored in the main document. The data source can be contained in a variety of applications, for example it might be from a Word table, a spreadsheet, or a database. When creating your mail merge, you may have an existing data source, which you want to use for the mail merge, or you can create an entirely new data source. Similarly, you may have an existing data source that you want to use but the contents need to be edited.

The Marketing Department of Boris Badges has designed and produced promotional literature detailing a new range of badges. It wants to send this literature out to existing and new customers. The easiest way to send the literature is to create a mail-merged document. It needs a standard letter to be sent to its customers promoting the range of badges, and each letter needs to be personalised to include the name of each customer and their address.

Here you will set up a mail merge for sending Boris Badge's promotional literature to existing and new customers.

Method 1

I   Select **Tools** from the menu.

2   Select **Mail Merge** from the drop-down list.

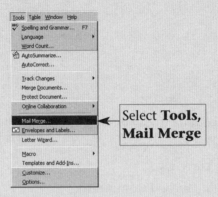

Figure 2.80 Starting a mail merge

The next step is to create the main document containing the main body of text, which is the same for all recipients of the document.

3   Either open an existing document, which you want to use for your main document, or create a new document containing the information you want in your form letter.

4   Select **Tools**, then **Mail Merge**. The Mail Merge Helper will appear on the screen.

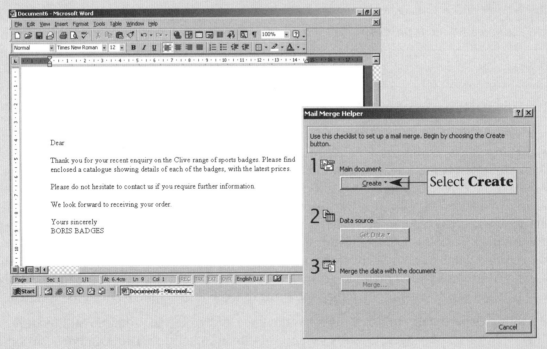

Figure 2.81 Creating mail merge

5   Click on **Create** under the Main document.

6   Select from the list. In our example we are creating a form letter, so click on **Form Letters**.

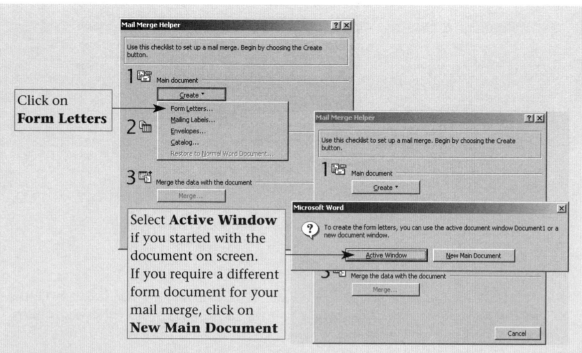

Figure 2.82 Creating a form letter

7 Select **Active Window**.
8 Click on **Get Data**, in the Mail Merge Helper window.
9 Click on **Create Data Source**.

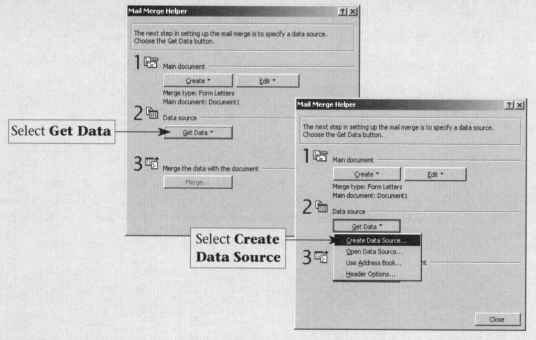

Figure 2.83 Getting data and creating a data source

10 In our example we are going to use the field names which are shown in the right windowpane of the Create Data Source window. We will remove the field names which are not required.

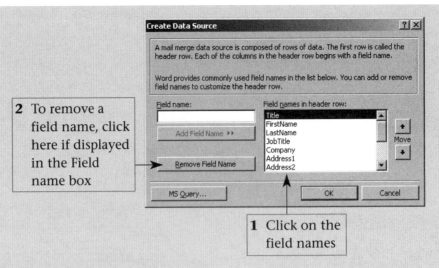

2 To remove a field name, click here if displayed in the Field name box

1 Click on the field names

Figure 2.84 Removing field names

11 Select Title in the **Field names in header row** box and click on **Remove Field Name**. Click on Company and Remove Field Name. Repeat this process until you have only the remaining: Title, FirstName, LastName, Address1, Address2, City and PostalCode.

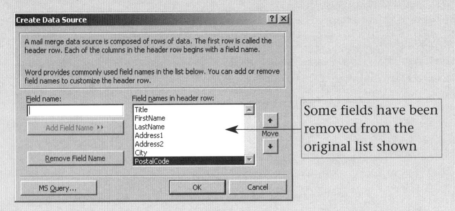

Some fields have been removed from the original list shown

Figure 2.85 Data field names

12 Click on **OK**. The Save As menu appears. Save the document with an appropriate name, e.g. Catalogue Request Data.

13 At this point you will be given the option to edit either the data source or the main document. In our example you do not need to edit the main document because we created it at the start of this exercise. However you will need to edit the data source as the data does not currently exist, so click on the Edit Data Source option.

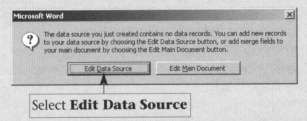

Select **Edit Data Source**

Figure 2.86 Edit the data source

14 In our example we will enter the data of the following four customers:
Mr Simon Smith, The Ravens, 345 The Street, Sunnytown, KL14 7TY
Mrs Cherie Patel, The Croft, 98 High Road, Seatown, BL20 8FG
Mr Stuart Peters, Sunnyside, 123 Low Road, Seatown, BL21 7PG
Mrs Bianca Jade, The Cottage, 2 Eagles Close, New Harriet, NH15 2YJ
As you enter this data on the data form, in order to move from one field to another either press the Tab key or the Enter key on the keyboard.

To move from one record to another, either click on **Add New** or press the Enter key on the keyboard.

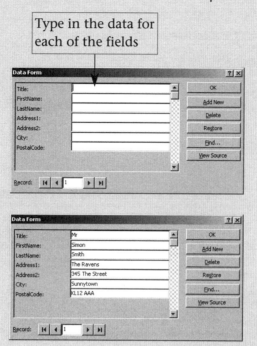

Figure 2.87 Data entered in the data form

15 When you have finished entering the data click on **OK**. A new toolbar will appear, showing **Insert Merge Field** and **Insert Word Field**.

Insert Merge Field and **Insert Word Field** are shown on the toolbar

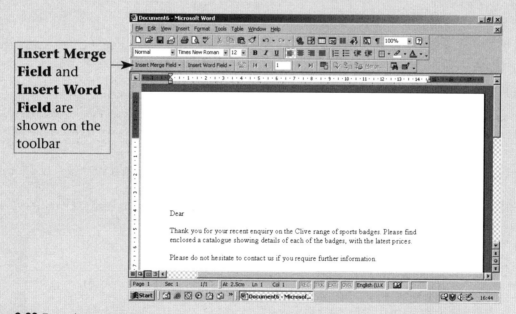

Figure 2.88 Form document

16 Place your cursor where you wish the first field to appear (i.e. Mr).

17 Click on **Insert Merge Field** and choose **Title**. You will see the field name appear. Press the space bar to add a space and click on Insert Merge Field and choose **FirstName**.

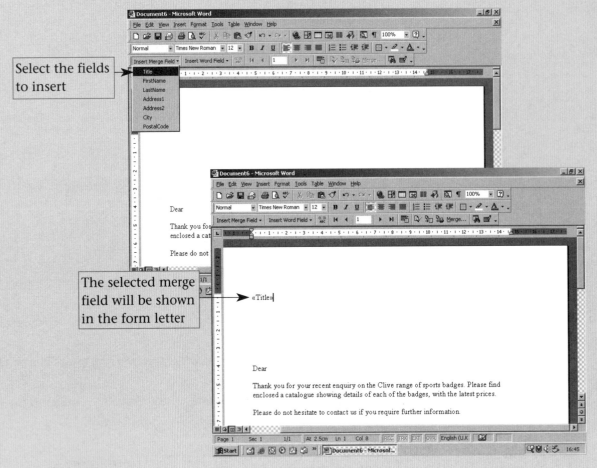

Select the fields to insert

The selected merge field will be shown in the form letter

Figure 2.89 Selecting field to insert

18 Continue until you have selected all the fields as shown in the example, remembering to add the spaces and line returns as required. Note also the use of the fields Title and LastName after the word Dear at the start of the letter.

Merge fields are shown inserted in the form document

Figure 2.90 Merge fields inserted

19 When you have entered all the fields, you have a number of options on your Mail Merge toolbar to use:

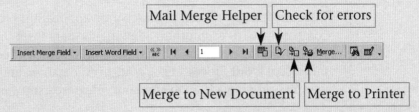

Figure 2.91 Mail Merge toolbar

In our example, we are going to use the Merge to New Document option. When you have clicked on this, you will see that the form letter and the data have been merged and a new document has been created. This option prior to printing has been chosen because it gives you the opportunity to proofread your document and make any amendments which may be required.

Information: External data source

Files may have been created in a number of different applications programs, for example a letter in a word processor, sales figures in a spreadsheet and customer details in a database. When working in one application you may wish to import the data from another application. The data from another application which is imported is an external source.

Task 2.34	**Creating a mail merge using an external data source**

In this task you will create a mail-merged letter using data from a database as the external source.

Method

I To create a mail merge document using an existing data source, follow steps 1–6 as shown in Task 2.33.

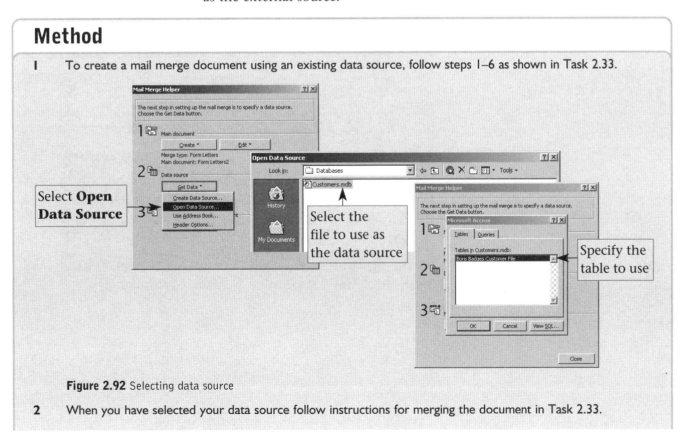

Figure 2.92 Selecting data source

2 When you have selected your data source follow instructions for merging the document in Task 2.33.

Information: Integrated software

Integrated software comprises separate application programs compatible with each other, allowing for data from one application program to be easily used by another. Microsoft Office with its individual word processing, spreadsheet, database and presentation graphics programs is an example of integrated software.

In Task 2.35 you will use integrated software to merge documents from different applications.

Task 2.35 | To integrate data from a spreadsheet into a database

Here you will integrate software to merge documents from different applications. The following are the documents you will work with.

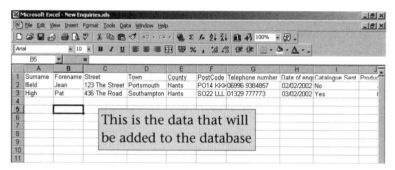

Figure 2.93 Spreadsheet data

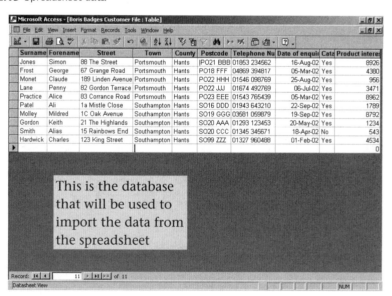

Figure 2.94 Database file

Method

1 Go to the Access database file.
2 Select **File**.
3 Select **Get External Data**.
4 Select **Import**.
5 Select the file to import.
6 Select the sheet which contains the data.

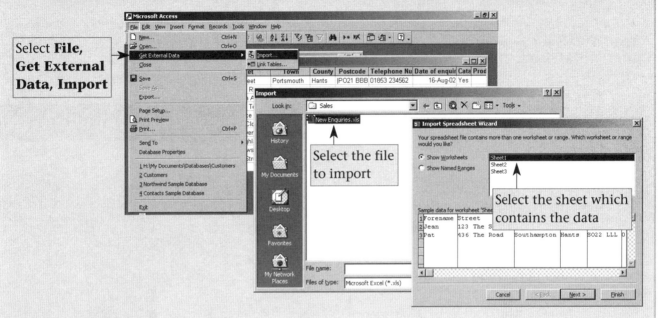

> Select **File**, **Get External Data**, **Import**

> Select the file to import

> Select the sheet which contains the data

Figure 2.95 Selecting file to import

7 If the spreadsheet contains column headings click in **First Row Contains Column Headings** checkbox.
8 Select where you want to store your data, either **In a New Table** or **In an Existing Table**.
9 Click on **Finish**.
10 Click on **OK**.

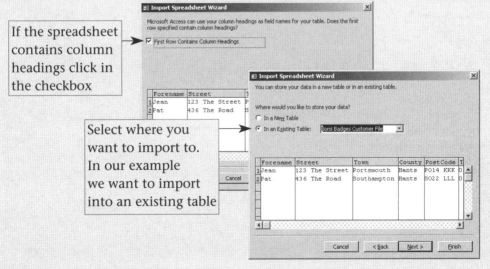

> If the spreadsheet contains column headings click in the checkbox

> Select where you want to import to. In our example we want to import into an existing table

Figure 2.96 Importing data into existing table

The spreadsheet data will be integrated into the database.

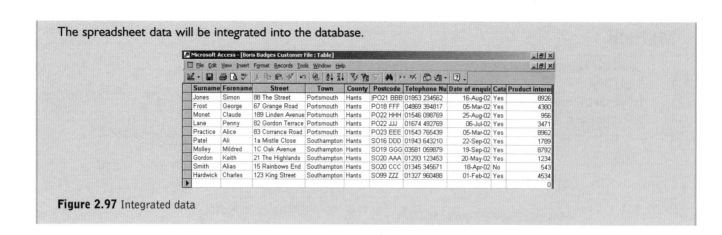

Figure 2.97 Integrated data

Task 2.36 — To integrate a spreadsheet into Word

Method

1   Open Word and key in the text below.

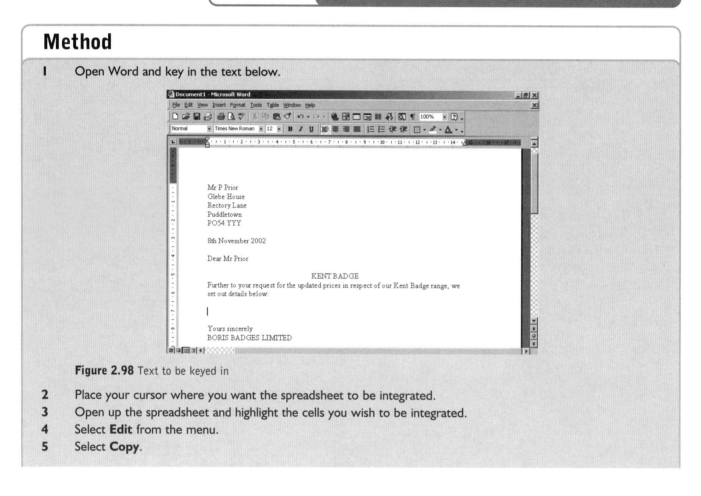

Figure 2.98 Text to be keyed in

2   Place your cursor where you want the spreadsheet to be integrated.
3   Open up the spreadsheet and highlight the cells you wish to be integrated.
4   Select **Edit** from the menu.
5   Select **Copy**.

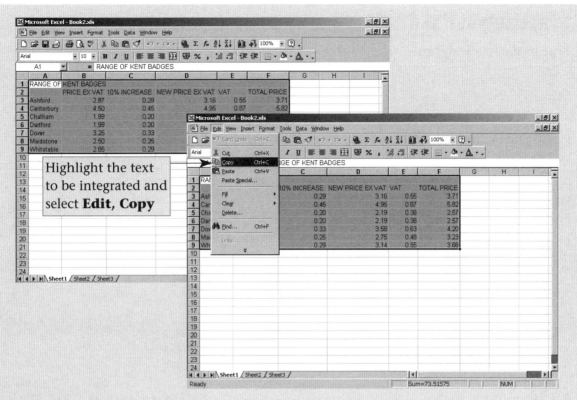

Figure 2.99 Copying text

6   Go back to **Edit**.
7   Select **Paste**.

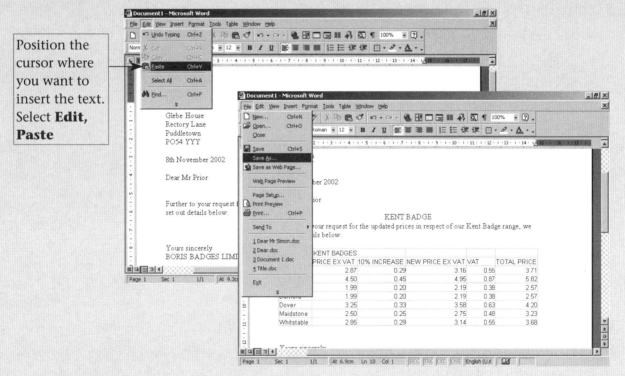

Figure 2.100 Pasting in text

8   The selected spreadsheet cells will be integrated into the Word document.
9   To save the document, select **File** and **Save As**.
10   Select the destination where the document is to be saved.

→ Practise your skills 4

1 Type in the following letter:

Dear

Please find below the prices requested for the Sussex range of badges. On receipt of your order badges will be delivered within 28 days.

Please make cheques payable to Boris Badges Limited.

I look forward to receiving your order.

Yours sincerely

Bob Jackson

Sales and Marketing

2 Save the file as **Sussex Letter**.
3 Create the following spreadsheet.

Sussex and Kent Badge Prices 2003

Catalogue number	Range	Product name	Price excluding vat	17.5% VAT	Total
1234	Kent	Canterbury	1.45		
1356	Kent	Ashford	2.15		
2456	Kent	Dover	2.87		
7653	Kent	Sandwich	2.54		
8765	Kent	Folkestone	1.76		
5643	Sussex	Chichester	2.66		
8999	Sussex	Westbourne	1.11		
78654	Sussex	Brighton	2.63		
44448	Sussex	Worthing	1.45		
9099	Sussex	Lewes	1.77		

4 Calculate the VAT.
5 Calculate the total price including VAT.
6 Print out the spreadsheet.
7 Print out the formulae.
8 Save the file as **Sussex and Kent badges**.

→

9   Create a database containing the following data:

Title	Surname	Street	Town	County	Postcode
Mr	Clue	56 The Avenue	Westbourne	Sussex	BA87 3SS
Mrs	Knight	45 Fine Street	Chichester	Sussex	PO98 5TT
Mrs	Jamm	22 Plum Street	Worthing	Sussex	BY65 7HH
Mr	Apple	56 Larynx Road	Brighton	Sussex	PO99 3ED
Miss	Belinda	66 New Street	Lewes	Sussex	BN99 M09

10 Save the database file as **Sussex Customers**.

11 Print the database.

12 Integrate the Sussex and Kent badges into the Sussex Letter.

13 Create a mail merge letter using the Sussex Letter as the main document and the Sussex Customers database as the data source.

14 Merge the document.

15 Print the mail-merged letters.

Information: Financial applications software

The Finance Department of Boris Badges uses accountancy software for financial accounting. Using computer software has significant advantages over manual bookkeeping.

Prior to using computerised accounts the accounts were held in ledgers and the calculations and entries were entered manually. It was easy to make mistakes, so great care and time was used to check the accounts were accurate. The task was time-consuming, labour intensive and required skilled personnel. The introduction of financial software packages enable the same work to be undertaken in much less time, as the calculations and the transfer from one ledger to another are automated, as is the transfer from one ledger to another. In addition to the time saved, accountancy packages can also produce reports which may help in the financial forecasting and planning of the business.

In the Accounts Department the accounts software is used to record the following.

Invoicing
When a customer orders goods from Boris Badges an invoice (bill) is raised. Invoices contain the terms and conditions of the sale of goods and will include the following: description of the goods, including details of the name and address of the company; the date of issue; a reference number and price details including unit price; discounts; charges; VAT; and a total price payable. The benefit of using a computer to produce an invoice is that the invoice can be set up as a standard form and calculations generated and printed on it.

Purchase ordering
Boris Badges sell a wide range of badges and office stationery. To manufacture their products they require raw materials and buy in some pre-manufactured parts. →

Purchase ordering is used to check the original ordering of goods against the supplier invoices, and if there are any discrepancies such as return of goods due to damage of the goods or non-delivery of items, to record this and amend payments.

Information on payments to suppliers and outstanding debts is recorded in the purchase ledger.

Sales ledger
This contains details of company sales. Records are kept of all sales orders and payments in the sales ledger. Storing sales and payments on the computer makes it easier and quicker to track payments and to identify non-payments or late payments. It is very important for the company to maintain cash flow to ensure profitability.

Nominal ledger
Information from the other accounts ledgers is combined into a single ledger, the nominal ledger, which shows the overall expenditure of different accounts and displays the company income.

Stock control
Boris Badges uses a stock control application to control the stock. It is important for the company to ensure that there are sufficient raw materials or components to manufacture the different products which it supplies. If one component is out of stock it affects the overall production. The stock control system ensures that supplies do not fall below a minimum level, and there is sufficient time to reorder the supplies before they run out. Maximum stock levels must not be exceeded, as stock in storage costs the company money as unsold stock.

A computerised stock control system records the input and output of stock and automatically triggers the reordering of stock if the minimum level is reached or notifies when the maximum stock level has been reached. The company does not therefore have stock tied up which is not selling and does have stock which it requires to manufacture products which are selling.

Payroll
The payroll of Boris Badges is calculated using a payroll system. The application calculates the amount of pay, tax, national insurance, holiday entitlement, pension, sick pay, and other benefits or deductions, and automates the printing of payslips and, if required, payment of cheques.

Financial projections
The company uses financial software to enable it to forecast the costs of producing each of its products by entering in prices for each stage of the process. By evaluating the costs the company can make a decision as to whether it is profitable to produce a new product before it commits to manufacturing it.

Information: Presentation graphics software

Paula Radcliffe is the western Sales Manager for Boris Badges. She has been asked to give a presentation on a new range of pens the company produces. She designs slides and handouts using presentation software to produce a professional presentation to her audience.

In the following tasks you will learn how to use software for creating a presentation using graphics.

Task 2.37 | To create a new presentation

Method

1   Click on **Start**.
2   Select **Programs**.
3   Open **Microsoft PowerPoint**.
4   Select **Blank presentation** and click to open.

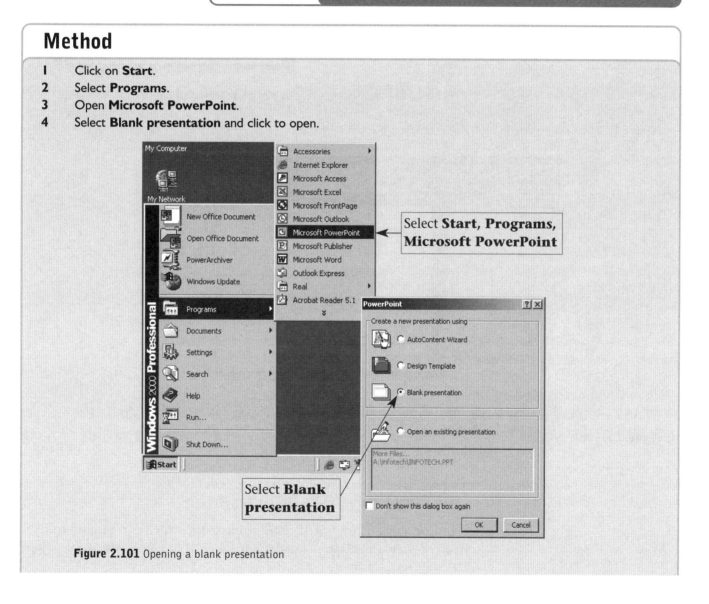

Figure 2.101 Opening a blank presentation

5 Create a title slide. When you open a Microsoft PowerPoint blank presentation there are a number of autolayouts you can use. For your first slide select the title slide.

6 Click on **OK**.

7 Click in the text box and add your titles.

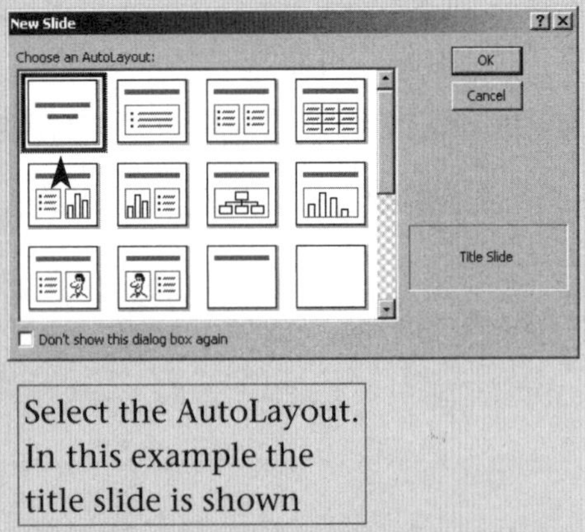

Select the AutoLayout. In this example the title slide is shown

Figure 2.102 Creating a title slide

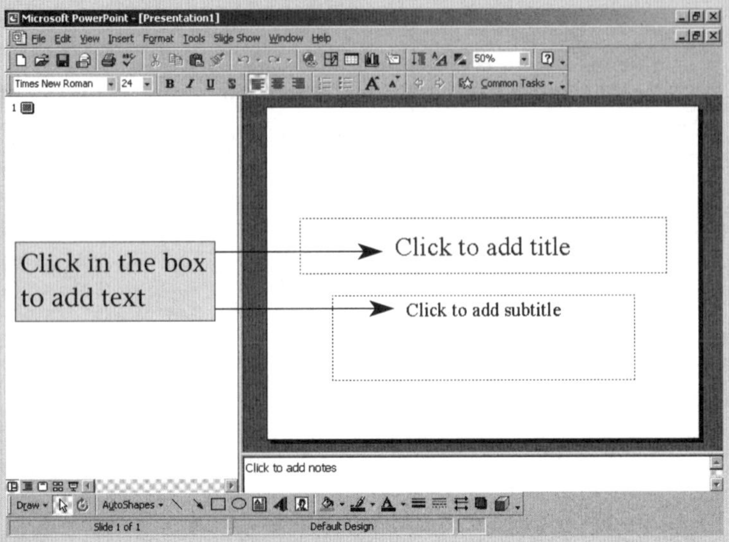

Click in the box to add text

Figure 2.103 Adding text

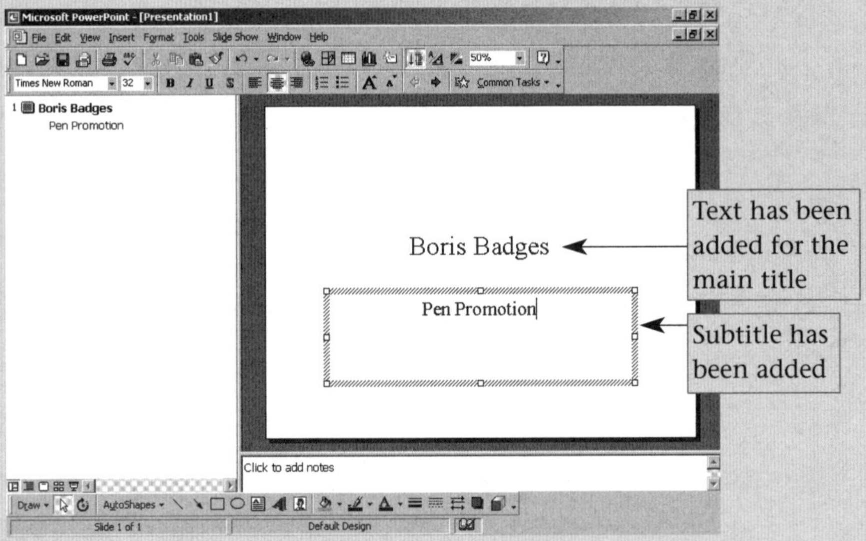

Text has been added for the main title

Subtitle has been added

Figure 2.104 Titles added

Information: Autolayout slides

Microsoft PowerPoint has 12 autolayout slides, which can be used to create specific slide layouts, making it easier to produce your slides. The slide layouts are:

- Title slide
- Column text
- Text and chart
- Organisation chart
- Text and clip art
- Title only

- Bulleted list
- Table
- Chart and text
- Chart
- Clip art and text
- Blank

Method

1   Select **Insert** from the menu.
2   Select **New Slide**.

To create a new slide select **Insert, New Slide**

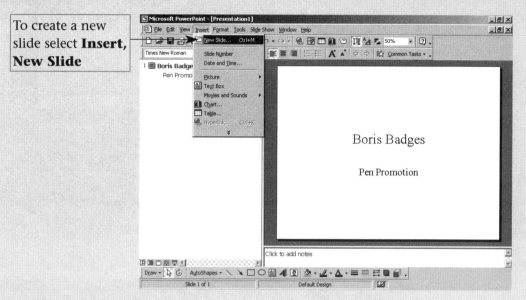

Figure 2.105 Selecting new slide

3   Select the slide AutoLayout. In the example, Figure 2.105, this is a title slide.
4   Click on **OK**.

Bulleted list

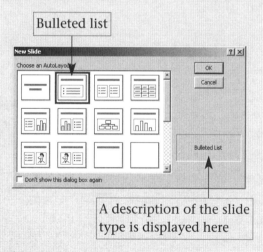

A description of the slide type is displayed here

Figure 2.106 Choosing the AutoLayout

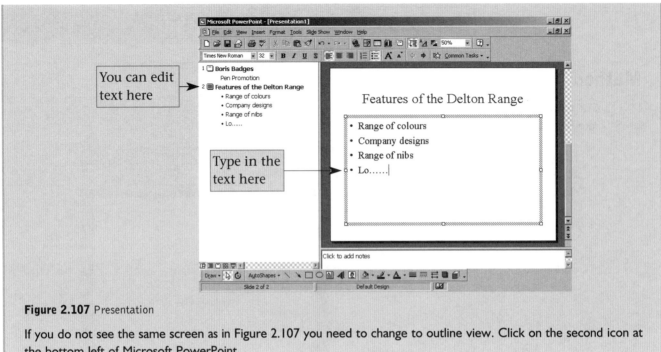

Figure 2.107 Presentation

If you do not see the same screen as in Figure 2.107 you need to change to outline view. Click on the second icon at the bottom left of Microsoft PowerPoint.

Task 2.39 — To add clip art to your presentation

You can add clip art to your slides by using either AutoLayout or by using blank slides.

Method 1

Here you can build a presentation using AutoLayout.

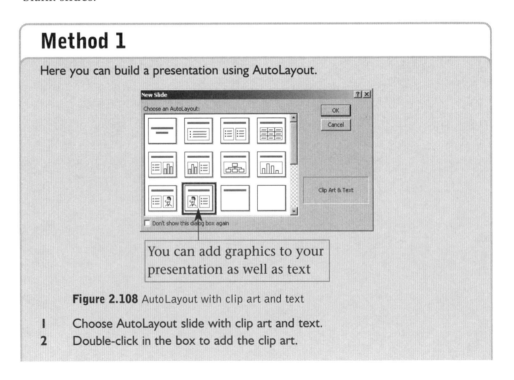

Figure 2.108 AutoLayout with clip art and text

1 Choose AutoLayout slide with clip art and text.
2 Double-click in the box to add the clip art.

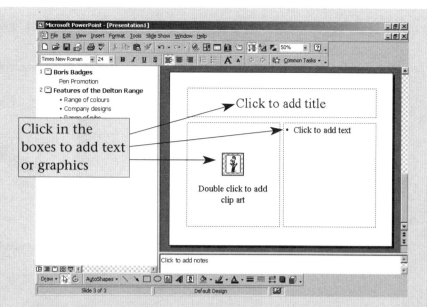

Figure 2.109 Adding clip art

3   Open clip art gallery and select a clip art category by double-clicking on the category.

Figure 2.110 Clip art gallery

4   Find a suitable picture. Click on the thumbnail. Four pop-up buttons will appear.

5   Click on the first of the pop-up buttons to insert the picture.

6   Close the clip art window by selecting the **Close** button. Make sure you close the clip art window and not the presentation window!

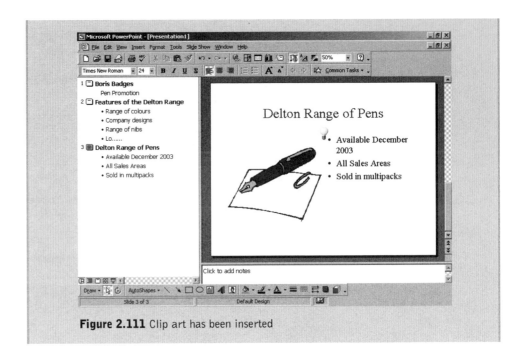

Figure 2.111 Clip art has been inserted

Method 2

Here you can build a presentation by using an AutoLayout slide which has preset formats to make building a slide easier. Alternatively, you can choose the blank AutoLayout slide where you add text boxes and clip art if required, to build the slide.

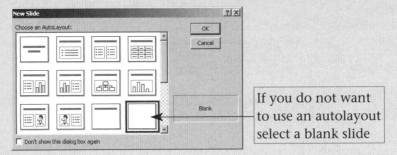

If you do not want to use an autolayout select a blank slide

Figure 2.112 Choosing a blank slide

1   Create a new slide by selecting **Insert.**
2   Select **New Slide.**
3   Choose **Blank** from the **AutoLayout** slides.
4   To insert a picture select **Insert**, **Picture**, **Clip Art** or select **Insert**, **Picture**, **From File.**

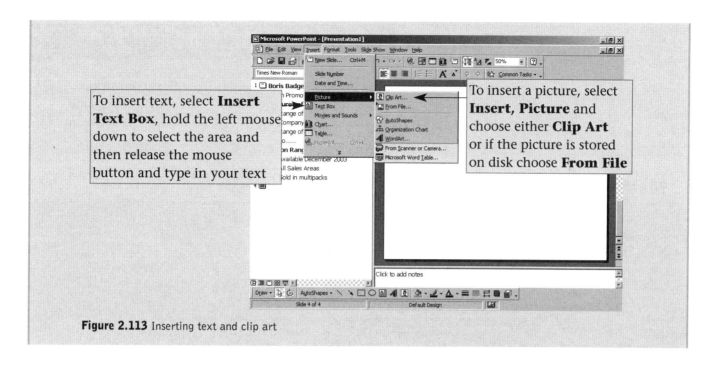

Figure 2.113 Inserting text and clip art

Task 2.40 To view a presentation

Method

1 Select **Slide Show** from the menu bar.
2 Select **View Show** from the drop-down list.

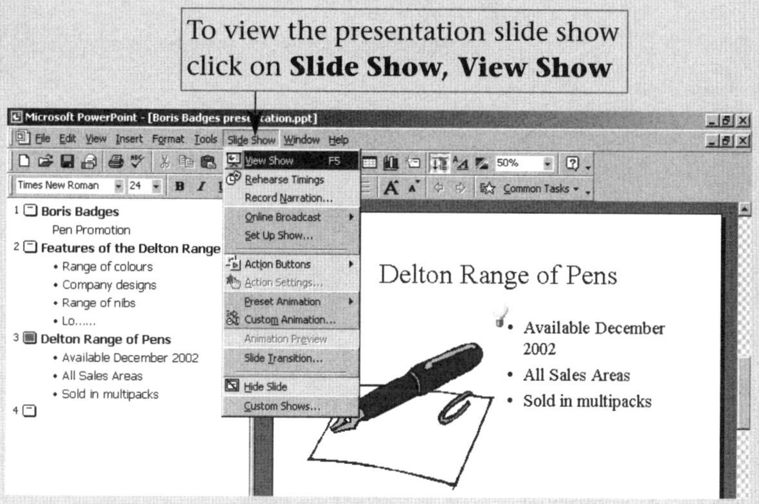

To view the presentation slide show
click on **Slide Show, View Show**

Figure 2.114 Viewing a presentation

3 The first slide will be displayed on the screen.
4 To view the next slide click the mouse button or click on button at the bottom left of the screen and click **Next** to view the next slide.
5 Continue to click through the slides until the end of the presentation.
6 Press the **Esc** key to exit the slide view.

In a presentation showing one slide after another with no transition between can make the presentation appear disjointed. By using a slide transition you can avoid this. Here you will create transitions between slides.

Method 1

1. Click on the slide you want to apply the transition to.
2. Select **Slide Show** from the menu bar.
3. Select **Slide Transition**.

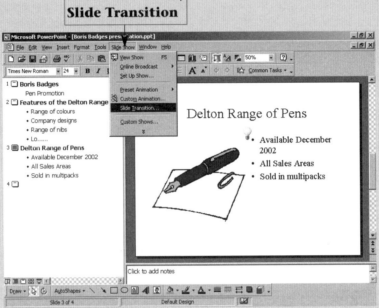

Figure 2.115 Choosing slide for transition

4. Click on the pull-down arrow and choose a transition.

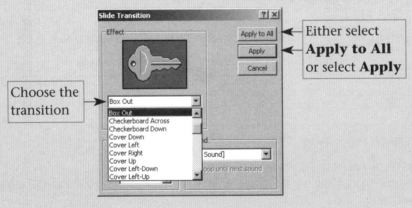

Figure 2.116 Choosing a transition

The preview of this is shown in the graphic above the pull-down menu.

5   Select the speed for the transition: **Slow**, **Medium** or **Fast**.

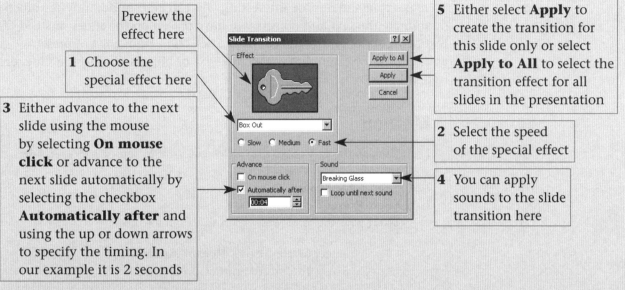

Preview the effect here

1 Choose the special effect here

3 Either advance to the next slide using the mouse by selecting **On mouse click** or advance to the next slide automatically by selecting the checkbox **Automatically after** and using the up or down arrows to specify the timing. In our example it is 2 seconds

5 Either select **Apply** to create the transition for this slide only or select **Apply to All** to select the transition effect for all slides in the presentation

2 Select the speed of the special effect

4 You can apply sounds to the slide transition here

Figure 2.117 Select transition speed

6   To apply this transition in your slide show, select either **On mouse click** or **Automatically after** and then use the arrows to specify the number of seconds for the transition.

7   You can use this transition for all your slides by selecting **Apply to All**, or just for this slide by selecting **Apply**.

Method 2

I   In slide view, click on the slide.

2   Change the **Transition** and **Effect** by selecting your choice using the pull-down arrows and clicking once on your choice.

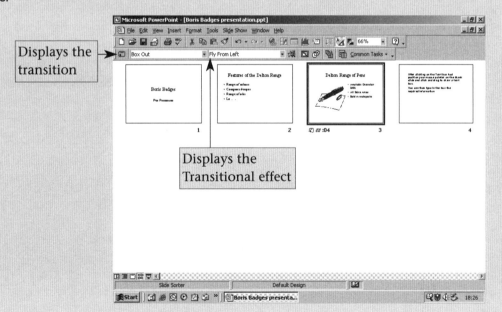

Displays the transition

Displays the Transitional effect

Figure 2.118 Changing the transition and effect

Task 2.42 Using preset animation

To make your slides more interesting you can add sound, movies and charts or animate the text and objects you have placed on the slides. Instead of the text being static on the screen make a selection from a list of preset animations, for example to make the text or objects fly into the slide, drop in text letter by letter.

Method

I	Click on the part of the slide which you want to apply the **Preset Animation** to.
2	Select **Slide Show**.
3	Select **Preset Animation**.
4	Select your choice of preset animation from the menu.

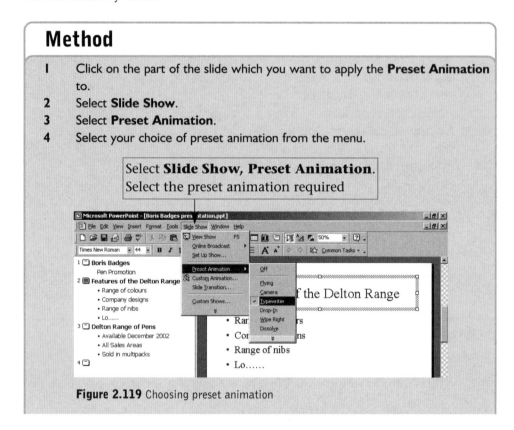

Figure 2.119 Choosing preset animation

Task 2.43 To print a presentation

You can now print out your presentation.

Method

I	Select **File**.
2	Go to **Print**.
3	Select the **Print range**.
4	Select in the **Print what** box what you want to print.
5	Click on **OK**.

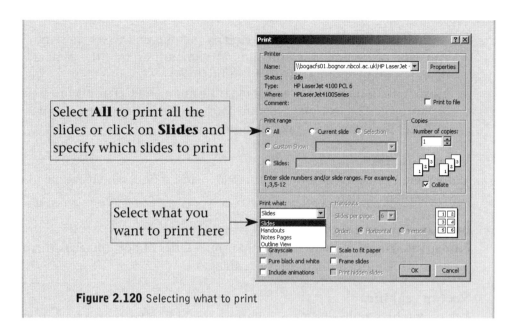

Select **All** to print all the slides or click on **Slides** and specify which slides to print

Select what you want to print here

Figure 2.120 Selecting what to print

Information: Projection devices

Projection devices magnify the display from the computer and project it on a large screen. Projection devices are used within the classroom, for teaching purposes, for running PowerPoint presentations at conferences, presentations and exhibitions.

Information: Computer-aided design (CAD)/Vector-based graphics

Computer-aided design

Computer-aided design (CAD) is specialist software enabling a user to draw designs using a computer, to accurately plot coordinates and draw lines and shapes. With CAD software images can be changed easily, for example the colour can be altered, images can be rotated, enlarged, reduced and stretched, all of which would take considerable time to draw by hand.

Graphics tablet

Designers use a graphics tablet to draw designs. The tablet consists of a flat surface (tablet) which has a stylus (pen) attached to it. This stylus is moved across the surface, and as it touches the tablet it makes an electrical connection so that its position on the tablet is translated to a corresponding position on the screen.

Saved designs can be linked to CAM software (computer-aided manufacture) which controls automated equipment, such as lathes, to produce, for example, the badges manufactured by Boris Badges.

Information: Photographic image/bitmap graphics

Digital photography

A digital camera works by capturing images not on a film but on an image sensor.

When purchasing a digital camera there are a number of factors to consider:

- There are many affordable digital cameras on the market, however if you compromise on cost you also compromise on quality.
- Digital images are made up of pixels and the more pixels there are the better the quality of the image. Digital images do not enlarge well as they are made up of individual pixels which distort when enlarged, therefore an image with more pixels will appear less distorted. Purchase a camera with the highest resolution you can afford.

→

- With digital cameras you can take many pictures and reject those not required, saving the time and expense of developing the film. The amount of RAM the camera contains determines the potential number of images that can be stored.
- Most digital cameras have as a standard feature an LCD display to frame the image prior to capturing it. These displays require considerable battery power, so it is useful to carry additional batteries with you when taking photos.

Video cameras
Many digital cameras can now capture video and sound, which can be manipulated using software on the computer.

Bitmap (Raster graphics)
Bitmaps are graphical images made up from a series of dots (pixels). Microsoft Paint is an example of a program which uses bitmaps to create images.

Vector graphics
Vector graphics, unlike bitmaps, comprise solid lines based on x y coordinates. The advantage of using vector graphics is that they do not become distorted when enlarged.

→ Check your knowledge 1

1 In word processing, what does a jagged green underline represent?
2 How do you ensure a capital letter is automatically placed at the beginning of a sentence?
3 In a database, what is a field and what is a record?
4 What is a cell in a spreadsheet?
5 How do you display a formula?
6 In mail merge, what is a form letter?
7 What is a slide transition?

→ Check your knowledge 2

1 What are the eight principles of the Data Protection Act?
2 What do the following terms mean: cell address, row, column, formula?
3 What are the advantages of using integrated software?
4 What are projection devices used for?
5 What are the functions of computer-aided design and vector-based graphics?
6 What are the main uses for photographic images?

Consolidations 1–3

Consolidation 1

Boris Badges requires a spreadsheet to record the value of stock of different types of badges.

1 Create a spreadsheet with the following data:

Product Code	Product Group	Product Description	Quantity in stock	Price per badge	Total Value of stock
123SX	Sussex	Westbourne	52	2.56	
458SX	Sussex	Chichester	213	3.76	
179KT	Kent	Sandwich	122	2.98	
234AY	Cardiff	Cardiff	277	1.78	
864CY	Conway	Conway	145	0.98	
190DE	Dundee	Dundee	90	1.94	
999FK	Fife	Fife	55	0.87	

2 Calculate the total value of stock per badge and the total value of stock for all the badges.

3 For the data extract calculate the minimum, maximum and average value of all stock.

4 Sort the Product Group into alphabetical order.

5 Print the spreadsheet data and formulas.

6 Save the spreadsheet as **Badge Stock**.

7 The Sales Department requires a database to record badge types and dates of promotion. Create the database with the following fields: Product Code, Product Group, Product Description, Date of Promotion.

8 Integrate the relevant data from the Badge Stock spreadsheet and add the following promotion dates:

11/09/2002	13/08/2003	30/03/2003
01/01/2003	09/09/2003	12/12/2003

9 Save the database as **Promotion**.

10 Search for all Sussex badges and print out only the Product Group, Product Description and Date of Promotion. Save the query as **Sussex Badges**.

11 Search for all badges between 01/01/2003 and 12/12/2003.

12 Create the following memorandum:

MEMORANDUM

TO:	Alice Forman
FROM:	Simon Samson
DATE:	12/12/2003
SUBJECT:	Current Stock Levels

Below are the current stock levels which you requested:

13 Copy the spreadsheet data into the memorandum.

14 Embolden the heading MEMORANDUM.

15 Change the left and right margins to 2.75 cm.

16 Save the memorandum as **Stock memo**.

Consolidation 2

1 Boris Badges requires a database to store contact details for its suppliers. Create a database to store the following data:

ABX Supplies	123 The Street	Southampton	Hants	SO98 1AA	Mr A Pickle
Ace Metals Ltd	97 Canada Drive	Portsmouth	Hants	PO11 1XX	Mr G Neilson
Wire Metals Ltd	45 Ace Trading Estate	Southampton	Hants	SO11 1ZZ	Mr M Bragg
1A Alloys Ltd	1A Ace Trading Estate	Portsmouth	Hants	PO99 999	Mr L Darling
H D George Plc	23 Bowers Close	Portsmouth	Hants	PO87 1AA	Mrs A Smith
AD Trainer Ltd	Freemans Trading Estate	Portsmouth	Hants	PO98 2ZZ	Mr G Martin
GF Metals Ltd	England Grove	Southampton	Hants	SO87 1ZZ	Mr H Eating
Ace Metals Ltd	Saints Trading Estate	Southampton	Hants	SO88 1AA	Ms F Channel

2 Save the database as **Metal Suppliers**.

3 Type in the following text:

Supply of Metal Sheets for Badge Pressing

Dear

Further to our recent telephone conversation please can you confirm the delivery period for the supply of metal sheets.

Please could you also confirm the price as of 1st December 2003.

I look forward to your reply.

Yours sincerely

Paul Jones
Purchase Manager Boris Badges

4 Centre the heading and change the font size to 12.

5 Embolden the heading.

6 Save the text as **Suppliers text**.

7 Create a mail-merged letter using the Suppliers text and the Metal Suppliers database.

8 Print the letters.

9 A spreadsheet is required to record the increases in Badge prices in December 2003. Type in the data and calculate.

Badge Type	Badge Name	Price at 30/11/2003	Percentage increase	New Price 01/12/2003
Kent	Sandwich	1.21	5%	
Kent	Folkestone	3.54	8%	
Sussex	Bognor Regis	3.22	2.40%	
Sussex	Chichester	2.9	1%	
Hampshire	Alton	1.45	7.90%	
Hampshire	Havant	4.76	6.50%	
Kent	Chatham	3.99	0.90%	
Kent	Maidstone	3.86	11%	

10 Print the spreadsheet.

11 Print the formulas.

12 Format all data to 2 decimal places.

13 Insert a row at row 1 and add the title Badge Increases December 2003.

14 Save the file as **Badge Prices December 2003**. Exit the Microsoft Excel application.

Consolidation 3

Task 1

The Marketing Manager of Boris Badges requires a Sales presentation for a new range of badges for dog clubs.

1 Create a six-slide PowerPoint presentation to promote the new badge. Your presentation should include:
- three different slide layouts
- a minimum of two clip art images
- a bulleted list
- transitions between slides
- three slides to use preset animation
- a printout all the slides as handouts.

2 Save the file as **Dog Club Sales Presentation**.

3 Add a new slide to the presentation giving details of a contact address for Boris Badges.

4 Print out the additional slide.

Task 2

1 Move your taskbar to a new position on the screen. Produce a screenshot to show the new position.

2 Produce a screenshot displaying an image using Image Preview.

3 Create a shortcut to the Dog Club Sales Presentation.

Task 3

1 Create the following letter:

Mr Ian Smyth

22 The Lane

West Nutland

Bognor Regis

PO99 1XX

Dear Mr Smyth

Thank you for your enquiry regarding the new range of dog badges available from 1 January 2004.

Please find enclosed a brochure detailing this exciting new product.

I look forward to receiving your order.

Yours sincerely

Peter Smyth

2 Add an address for Boris Badges.

3 Change the font to Times New Roman and the size to 12.

4 Add the reference NEW! Badges for Dog Clubs. Make this bold and size 14.

5 Add the date.

6 Save the file as **Enquiry 1 Dog Badges**.

7 Print the file.

Section 3 | Using Windows

You will learn to

- Describe the terms GUI and 'user friendly'
- Operate view and navigate functions using pointer devices, click operations, keyboard, scroll bars, zoom, magnification, whole page, print preview
- Show and hide toolbars, menus, keyboard shortcuts
- Create a desktop shortcut
- Respond to error messages and prompts
- Describe the term 'multi-tasking' and how it can be used

Information: Microsoft Windows

Microsoft Windows does not require large amounts of text to be typed in to operate because it uses a graphical user interface (GUI) to function. A GUI uses icons for program commands and files. An icon is a small picture that represents the programs or files on your computer desktop.

Before Microsoft introduced the Windows operating system the interface between the user and the computer was text based. In order to load files and enter commands the user had to type in the commands; it did not use icons to represent the commands. The problem with using a text-based system is that you have to remember the commands in order to load and manage your files. It was very easy to make typing mistakes, which could produce incorrect results or failure to perform the command you required.

The advantage of a GUI is that it does not rely on text to operate. You do not need to remember a list of commands or have technical knowledge to perform basic tasks. It is much easier to move a mouse pointer onto a picture that represents the program or function you want to use, and click the mouse button, than it is to remember a sequence of text commands.

The Windows operating system is much easier to use than a text-based system such as MSDOS (Microsoft Disk Operating System). As it is easier to use we can say it is 'user friendly'.

Information: The desktop

A desktop is so called because all the tools, which you require to produce your documents, are accessible from here, just like having all your pens and paper available on your desk at home or in the office. Do not be concerned if the desktop shown in Figure 3.1 looks different from your desktop, as the appearance will depend on how your computer has been set up. You can change these settings, such as the background colour or the size of the text and icons. The desktop has some basic components. →

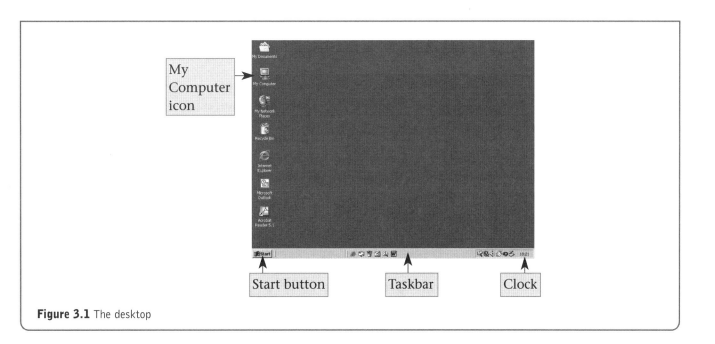

Figure 3.1 The desktop

Information: Taskbar

The default location for the taskbar is at the bottom of the screen. It has the Start button on the left-hand side and the system clock on the right-hand side. You may see additional icons, for example an icon for setting the volume 🔊 or one representing your virus protection software.

The taskbar is also used to display the different documents or programs you have open at the same time, and is a convenient place to switch between these programs and files. When you open a program you will see that a button for the program has been placed on the taskbar. If you have selected more than one program you will see additional buttons on the taskbar.

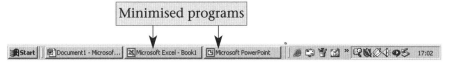

Figure 3.2 The taskbar

You can click on these buttons to switch between programs.

| Task 3.1 | Changing the appearance of the taskbar |

You can customise the appearance of the taskbar. If you wanted, for example, to create more space on the taskbar you could remove the clock, which is set as a default on the right-hand side of the taskbar.

Method

1	Right-click on a blank area of the taskbar.
2	Select **Properties** from the pop-up menu.
3	Click on the **Show clock** checkbox to remove the tick.
4	Click on **Apply**.

Task 3.2 — To add a toolbar on the taskbar

A toolbar comprises a series of icons that the user can select to perform common tasks. By placing a toolbar on the taskbar the user can conveniently select these tasks. There are several toolbars available; the default toolbar is the Quick Launch toolbar, which has icons for Show Desktop, Internet Explorer and Outlook Express. Here is how to place the Quick Launch toolbar on the taskbar.

Method

1	Right-click on the taskbar.
2	Select **Toolbars**.
3	Select **Quick Launch**.
4	You will see the icons for Quick Launch on the taskbar. If they are not all shown on the taskbar you can resize the toolbar by moving the cursor to the left-hand side. The cursor will change to a double-headed arrow. Hold the left mouse button down and drag to the required size.

Task 3.3 — To delete a tool from the taskbar

Try it out!

Identify the icons on your taskbar.

Method

1	You can remove a tool from the taskbar by right-clicking on the icon and selecting **Delete.**

Task 3.4 — Moving the taskbar

Hint:

If you have hidden the taskbar, press Ctrl+Esc to make the taskbar visible.

Method

1	Click and hold the left mouse button down on an empty part of the taskbar.
2	Drag the taskbar to where you want it to go.
3	Release the mouse button.

Task 3.5 — Resizing the taskbar

Method

1	Move the mouse pointer to the edge of the taskbar. You will see a double-headed arrow.
2	Keep the left mouse button down and drag the taskbar to the width you require.

Try it out!

Customise the desktop:

1 Move the taskbar to the top of the screen.
2 Widen the taskbar.
3 Delete the date display from the taskbar.
4 Place the Links toolbar on the taskbar.

Using the Print Screen key on your keyboard print a screenshot of your changes.

Try it out!

Customise the desktop:

1 Move the taskbar to the top of the screen.
2 Widen the taskbar.
3 Delete the date display from the taskbar.
4 Place the Links toolbar on the taskbar.

Using the Print Screen key on your keyboard print a screenshot of your changes.

Caution!

If you delete from a floppy disk the file will not go into the Recycle Bin, it will be permanently deleted.

Information: Tools

 Start button   The Start button is on the taskbar. From here you can start your programs, obtain help on using your files and programs, locate where your files are stored and, when you have finished using the computer, this is where you shut the computer down.

 Mouse pointer   In order to start your programs or open your files you use a pointing device, such as a mouse pointer, to point and click on the icon representing that program or file.

 My Computer   This is a quick way to see the contents of what is stored on your computer.

 Recycle Bin   When you delete a file held on the computer the file is put into the Recycle Bin. Files remain in here until they are either deleted from the bin or are restored at a later date.

 My Network Places   If your computer is part of a network, you use this icon to find out what network resources, such as printers or drives, your computer is connected to.

Information: Using the mouse

To use the tools available on the desktop you need to use a pointer device such as a mouse. Computer mice come in different shapes and colours but typically will have two buttons on the top. Your mouse may also have features such as a scroll wheel in the middle or a third mouse button. These features are additional to what is required to use Windows. Most of the time you will use the left mouse button (unless the mouse has been configured for left-handed use, in which case the right mouse button will be used most).

If the mouse has been set for right hand use then the left mouse button is the most frequently used, if it is set for left hand use the right mouse button will be used most. The mouse enables you to:

• move around the screen
• move objects around the screen
• select and action commands.

The right mouse button is used to access pop-up menus, which are used to access additional commands.

Using the mouse to move around the screen
Move your mouse on the mouse mat and you will see a little arrow move on the screen. This is called a pointer and enables you to move to different locations on the screen. For example, if you move the mouse to the left a corresponding signal is sent to the computer and the mouse pointer moves to the left. The mouse moves in the direction that you move it on the mouse mat.

Task 3.6 — Use the mouse to move objects around on the screen

This method is called drag and drop because you use the mouse pointer to select the object and drag it to a new location where you drop it into its new position.

Method

1   Move your pointer onto an icon and hold the left mouse button down. As you move the mouse, still keeping the left button down, you will see that the icon moves with it.

2   Release the left mouse button and there will be one of two results. The icon will either have moved to the position you moved the mouse pointer to or it will have gone back to its original position.
     Note: It will go back to its original position if the properties, i.e. how the desktop is set up, have previously been set to automatically align the icons. This would override your attempt to move the icons. The icons would only move to a new position if you first changed the properties of how the icons are arranged on the desktop.

Task 3.7 — Use the mouse to select and activate commands

Method 1

This will involve using a single mouse click.

1   Click once on the **Start** button. A pop-up menu will appear with a list of options you can choose from.

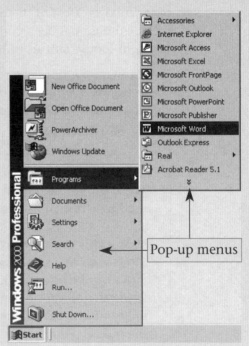

Figure 3.3 Pop-up menus

Hint:

If you accidently click on a button and a pop-up menu appears press the **Esc** key to hide it from the display.

Information: A menu

A menu is simply a list of choices available to the user when you select an option. Menus can either be pop-up menus (see Figure 3.3) or pull-down or drop-down menus, which are menus selected from the bottom of the screen or pulled down from the top of the screen. Figure 3.4 shows a pull-down menu from a Microsoft Excel spreadsheet.

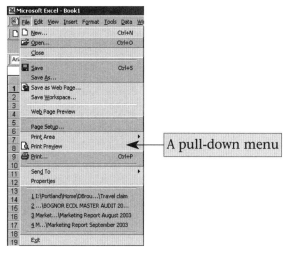

A pull-down menu

Figure 3.4 A pull-down menu

Method 2

Here you will use a double mouse click to select and activate commands.
Note: You can select and activate commands by pressing the left mouse button quickly twice (double click).

1   Move the mouse pointer onto the **My Computer** icon

2   Double-click on the icon with the left mouse button. A window similar to the one shown in Figure 3.5 should appear.

Figure 3.5 Window

If you do not see this window but see only the **My Computer** icon highlighted, it is because you have not double-clicked on the left mouse button quickly enough.

3 If you are having difficulty with this you can perform the same actions as a double-click by moving the pointer onto the icon and then right-click with the mouse. A pop-up menu will appear.

Figure 3.6 Menu

4 Move the mouse pointer onto **Open** and click once with the left mouse button.

Information: Minimise, Maximise, Close and Restore buttons

On the **My Computer** menu you will see that on the right-hand side

of the title bar there are three buttons 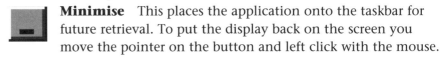 which are

the Minimise, Maximise and Close buttons.

Minimise This places the application onto the taskbar for future retrieval. To put the display back on the screen you move the pointer on the button and left click with the mouse.

Maximise This enlarges the window so it fills the screen. You can also enlarge the window by double-clicking on the title bar.

Close This will close the window.

Restore button The Restore button allows you to restore the size of the window to what it was before you maximised it.

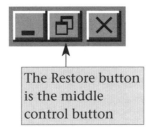

The Restore button is the middle control button

Figure 3.7 Restore button

Things to do

1 Close the Excel spreadsheet by a single left mouse click on the Close button. Microsoft Word is the main window displayed on the screen.

2 Minimise the Microsoft Word window. You will see the Word button displayed on the taskbar and the desktop shown as a full screen. Click on the Word button on the taskbar. Microsoft Word will be displayed on the screen.

3 Close Microsoft Word.

Task 3.8　Using the Restore button

Method

1　Open **My Computer**.
2　If My Computer is displayed as a full screen, click on the Restore button.

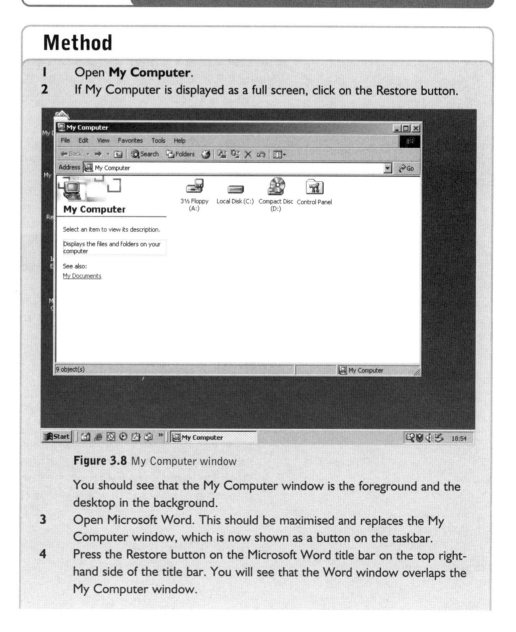

Figure 3.8 My Computer window

You should see that the My Computer window is the foreground and the desktop in the background.

3　Open Microsoft Word. This should be maximised and replaces the My Computer window, which is now shown as a button on the taskbar.

4　Press the Restore button on the Microsoft Word title bar on the top right-hand side of the title bar. You will see that the Word window overlaps the My Computer window.

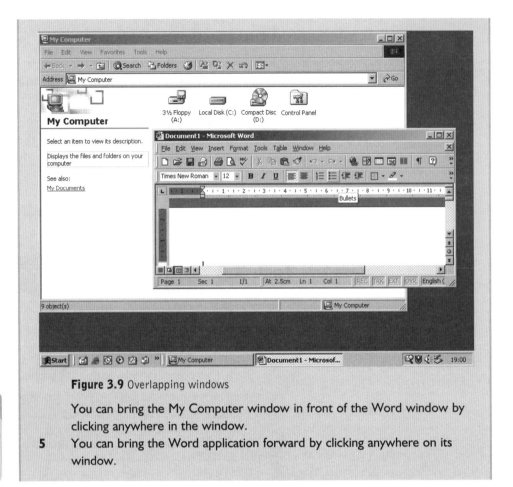

Figure 3.9 Overlapping windows

Hint:

Use Alt+Tab to switch to the last window you have used.

You can bring the My Computer window in front of the Word window by clicking anywhere in the window.

5 You can bring the Word application forward by clicking anywhere on its window.

Task 3.9 | Resizing a window

You can resize windows which are displayed on the screen. The following method shows you how to resize the **My Computer** window.

Method

1 Double-click on the **My Computer** icon.
2 The My Computer window will be displayed.
3 If you move the mouse pointer to any of the four sides, the mouse pointer will change to a double-headed arrow. Hold the left mouse down and drag the window across to the desired position.
4 When you have resized the window release the left mouse button. This will change the window size to where you had resized it.

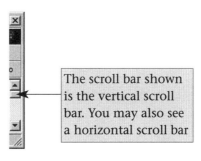
Things to do

The following are the ways in which to use the scroll bar.

- To scroll one line at a time, click an arrow.
- To scroll continuously, click on the scroll bar and hold the left mouse button down and drag it. The position of the scroll bar indicates your position within the window. If the scroll bar is at the top of the window, for example, you are situated at the beginning of viewing the contents of the window.
- To scroll one window at a time, click in the bar.

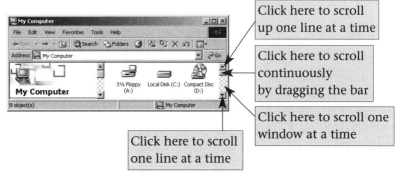

Click here to scroll up one line at a time

Click here to scroll continuously by dragging the bar

Click here to scroll one window at a time

Click here to scroll one line at a time

Figure 3.11 Using the scroll bar

Using print preview and the magnifier

When using an application you may want to view how your document is displayed on the page layout prior to printing it out. You can use the Print Preview button, which is located on the Standard toolbar. When you select the Print Preview button you will see the following screen, at the top of page 94.

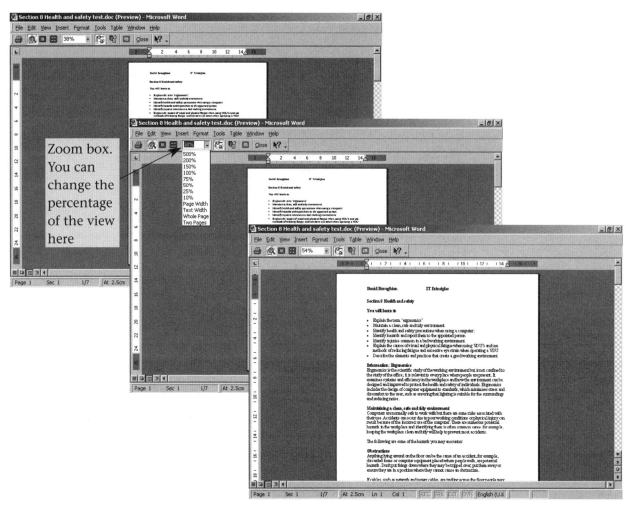

Figure 3.12 Print preview and changing preview page

This screen shows the layout of the text on the page but the text is too small to read. This is because the current view selected is 38% of the actual size of the document. You can alter this view size by selecting the arrow next to the Zoom box, where the percentage is shown, and selecting a new view size.

Alternatively, you can increase the view size by clicking in the Zoom box and typing in your preferred view size. In Figure 3.12 the percentage has been increased to 54% and you will see that the text is larger.

Changing the preview

There are other buttons for previewing your document.

 Printer   After proofreading your document you can print by clicking this icon.

 Magnifier   If you click on this button the screen will be magnified by the percentage shown in the Zoom dialogue box.

Click on this button to see a magnifying glass pointer on your document. You will need to click on the document for the new zoom percentage to take effect. To switch to your previous view, click on the document.

 One Page   By selecting this button you will see your document one page at a time.

Multiple Pages By selecting this button you will see a box appear with multiple pages showing.

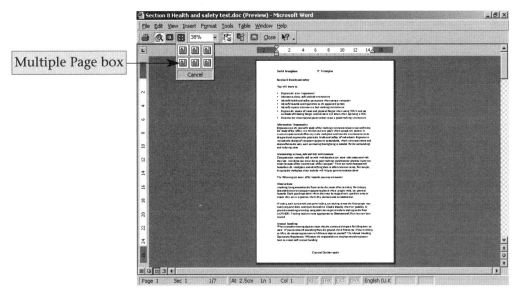

Multiple Page box

Figure 3.13 Multiple Page box

Click and hold your mouse button down to highlight the number of pages which you want to view at any one time. In the example shown, four pages have been selected. To activate the multiple pages selected click on the left mouse button.

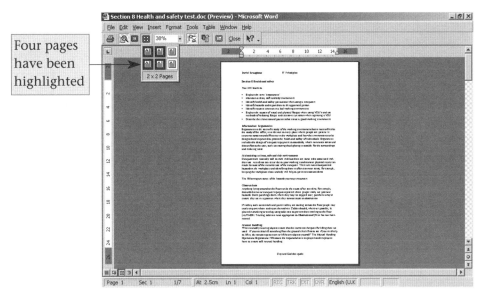

Four pages have been highlighted

Figure 3.14 Pages for viewing

Zoom box   You can change the percentage of the view here.

View Ruler   By selecting this button the horizontal and vertical ruler bars are displayed.

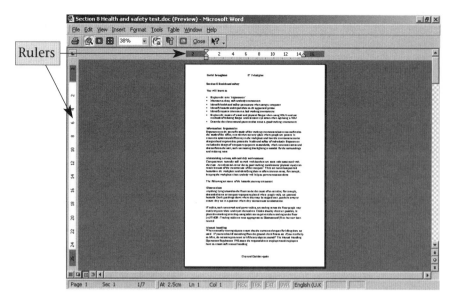

Figure 3 15 Ruler bars

Note: If you do not see the ruler displayed click on **View**, then **Ruler**.

Shrink to Fit When you click on this button your document will shrink to one page. If you wanted to cancel this operation then you can select **Edit** from the menu bar, then **Undo**.

Full Screen Click on this button to obtain a full screen view of your document. To close the full screen and return to normal view, click on **Close Full Screen**.

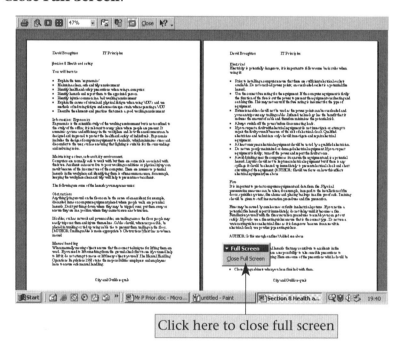

Click here to close full screen

Figure 3.16 Closing full screen

Information: Viewing files

There are different ways in which you can view the files stored on your computer. These can be accessed via the View menu or by using the appropriate icon.

This is the method to follow for choosing an option for viewing files.

Method

I   Either double-click on **My Computer** or select **Windows Explorer** from the **Start** button on the taskbar.
2   Click on **View** on the menu.
3   You will see a pull-down menu. Click on one of the following options to change the view:
   ● **Large icons** Large pictures representing the folders and files.
   ● **Small icons** Small pictures representing the folders and files.

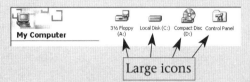 

Figure 3.17 Large icons and small icons

   ● **List** This displays both the folders and the files in columns but the difference with small icons view is that all the folders are shown before the files.

Figure 3.18 List

   ● **Details** Folders are displayed first and then the files. This view contains details on the filename, size, type, and when modified (date and time).
   ● **Thumbnails** You will find this additional view in Windows Explorer. It gives a small picture. If the file is a graphical image, for example a wedding photo, this will show a small view of the photo. This is particularly useful when you wish to view the several files without having to load the program.

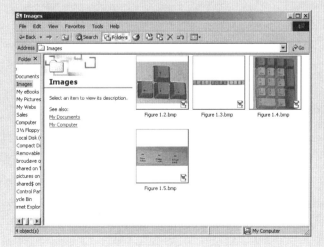

Figure 3.19 Thumbnails

Task 3.11   Previewing an image

Here you will preview an image in folders other than My Pictures.

Method

1   Double-click on **My Computer**.
2   Select the drive and then the folder on which the images are stored by double-clicking on the drive and the folder which contains your pictures.
3   Select **View**.
4   Select **Customize This Folder**.

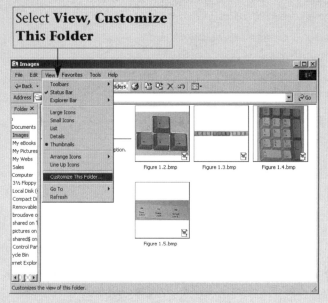

Figure 3.20 Customising a folder

5   You will then see the **Customize This Folder Wizard**.

Figure 3.21 Customize This Folder Wizard

6   Click on **Next**.

7   Select the option **Choose or edit an HTML template for this folder**.

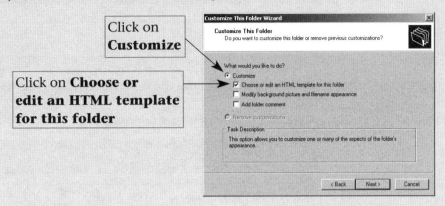

Click on **Customize**

Click on **Choose or edit an HTML template for this folder**

Figure 3.22 Choosing an option

8   Click on **Next**.

9   Click on the **Image Preview** option.

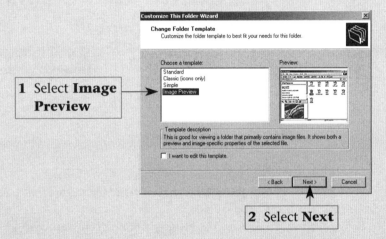

1 Select **Image Preview**

2 Select **Next**

Figure 3.23 Selecting image to preview

10   Click on **Finish**.

Hint:

If you make changes to how your folders are viewed and then decide you don't want to accept them, then as long as you haven't clicked the **Finish** button you can always click **Cancel** and none of the changes will be implemented. This can be a useful hint to remember when experimenting with many of the change properties options in this section.

Task 3.12 — To preview a picture in more detail

Method

1   Double-click on **My Computer**.
2   Double-click on the drive and the folder containing the image you want to preview.
3   Click on the image you want to preview.

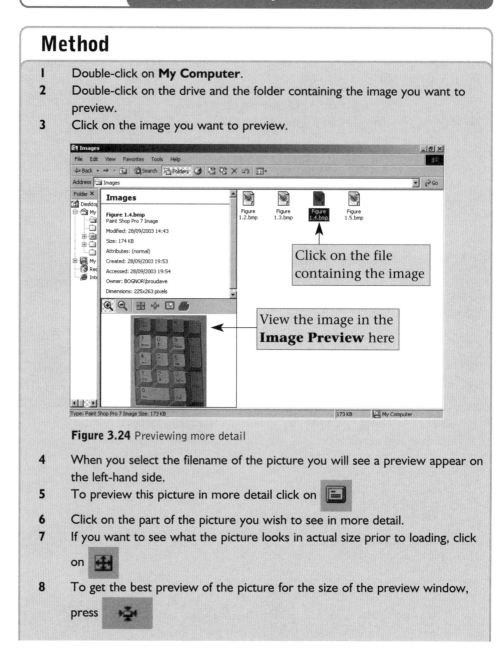

Figure 3.24 Previewing more detail

4   When you select the filename of the picture you will see a preview appear on the left-hand side.
5   To preview this picture in more detail click on 🔲
6   Click on the part of the picture you wish to see in more detail.
7   If you want to see what the picture looks in actual size prior to loading, click on 🔲
8   To get the best preview of the picture for the size of the preview window, press 🔲

Things to do

Open Windows Explorer and view your folders in:
- Large icon view
- Small icon view
- Details view
- Thumbnails

You can customise the desktop by displaying or hiding the taskbar.

Task 3.13   To hide the taskbar

Method 1

1   Click on **Start** on the taskbar.
2   Move the mouse pointer to **Settings**.
3   Move the pointer to **Taskbar and Start Menu Properties**. You can also get
     to this point by right-clicking on a blank area of the taskbar and then selecting
     Properties.
4   Click on the **Auto hide** checkbox.
5   Click on **OK**.

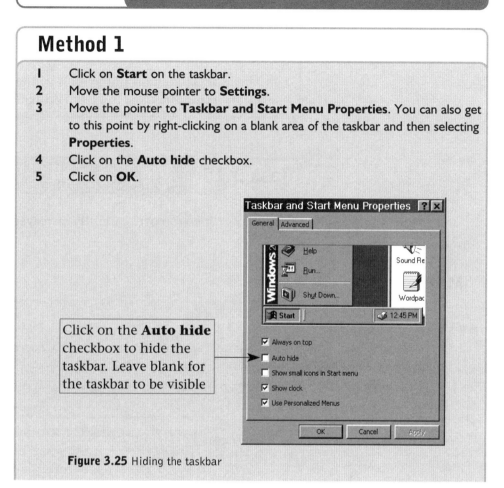

Click on the **Auto hide**
checkbox to hide the
taskbar. Leave blank for
the taskbar to be visible

Figure 3.25 Hiding the taskbar

Method 2

1   You can temporarily hide the taskbar by moving to the edge of the taskbar.
     Your pointer will change to a double-headed arrow.
2   Keep the left mouse button down and drag the taskbar down out of view.

Task 3.14   To display the taskbar

Method

1   Click on **Start** on the taskbar.
2   Move the pointer to **Settings**.
3   Move the pointer to **Taskbar and Start Menu Properties**.
4   Clear the Auto hide checkbox by clicking next to **Auto hide**.
5   Click **OK**.

> ## Information: Viewing toolbars within an application
>
> When you use an application all the available toolbars are not all displayed on the screen. This is because they would take up too much room and you would have little space available in the working area to create your documents.
>
> In Microsoft Word most of the tools you require on a regular basis are available in the Standard and Formatting toolbars.

Task 3.15 | Viewing toolbars

To display or hide toolbars currently displayed on the screen follow this procedure.

Method

1   Select **View** from the menu bar.
2   Select **Toolbars**.
3   If the toolbar is currently displayed on your screen it will have a check against it. If it is not currently displayed it will have the name of the toolbar only.

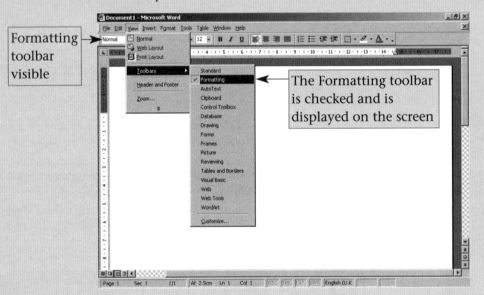

Figure 3.26 Formatting toolbar

4   To add or remove a toolbar click on the toolbar name.

Information: Keyboard shortcuts

You can access most of the commands in Windows by using the keyboard rather than the mouse. The advantage of using a keyboard shortcut is that it is quicker than using the menus.

You can use the following common shortcut keys in Windows.

Keys	Result
Alt and underlined letter in the menu bar	Actions the corresponding command on the menu, e.g. in Word, Alt + F will give a pull-down menu for File options
F1	Displays the Help files
Ctrl+F4	Closes the current program you are using
Ctrl+Esc	Selects the Start menu
Alt+Tab	Switches to the last window you have used
Ctrl+C	Copies the selected item into the clipboard
Ctrl+F	Find
Ctrl+G	Go to
Ctrl+H	Replace
Ctrl+O	Opens an existing file
Ctrl+N	Opens a new file
Ctrl+P	Print the current file
Ctrl+S	Saves the current file
Ctrl+V	Pastes the selected item from the clipboard
Ctrl+X	Cuts the selected item to the clipboard

You can also use keyboard shortcuts in dialogue boxes. Examples include:

Keys	Result
Esc	Cancels the current task
Alt and underlined letter in the menu bar	Carries out the command which is highlighted in the menu
Enter	Selects the highlighted button
Shift+Tab	Move backwards through the options which are displayed
Ctrl+Shift+Tab	Move backwards through the tabs of the menu
Tab	Move forwards through the options
Ctrl+Tab	Move forwards through the tabs of the menu

Information: Create a desktop shortcut

If you are using a program or file on a regular basis you can create a shortcut to this on the desktop. When you double-click the desktop shortcut icon Windows will shortcut direct to that location. Using a shortcut reduces the time and the number of key presses required to load the file or program.

There are several ways in which you can create a shortcut. You can:

- put a shortcut on the desktop
- create a shortcut in a folder
- create a new submenu in the **Programs** menu on the **Start** menu.

Task 3.16 — Create a shortcut on the desktop

Here you will create a shortcut to the Excel spreadsheet

Method

1   Double-click on **My Computer**.
2   Double-click on the drive which contains the Excel spreadsheet. If you are not sure where the file is located you can create a shortcut in the folder, as in Task 3.17.

Task 3.17 — Create a shortcut in a folder

Method

1   Double-click on **My Computer** and select the drive where the folder is located by double-clicking on the drive location. Locate the folder where you want to place a shortcut and double-click on the folder.
2   Select the **File** menu.
3   Select **New**.
4   Click on **Shortcut**.

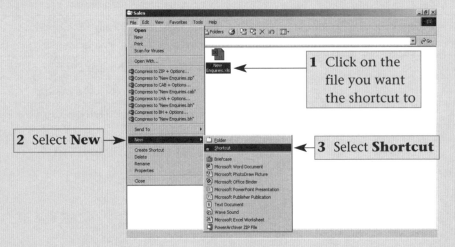

Figure 3.27 Create shortcut in a folder

Method

1   Click on **Start**.
2   Select **Settings** and click on **Taskbar & Start Menu**.
3   Select the **Advanced** tab.

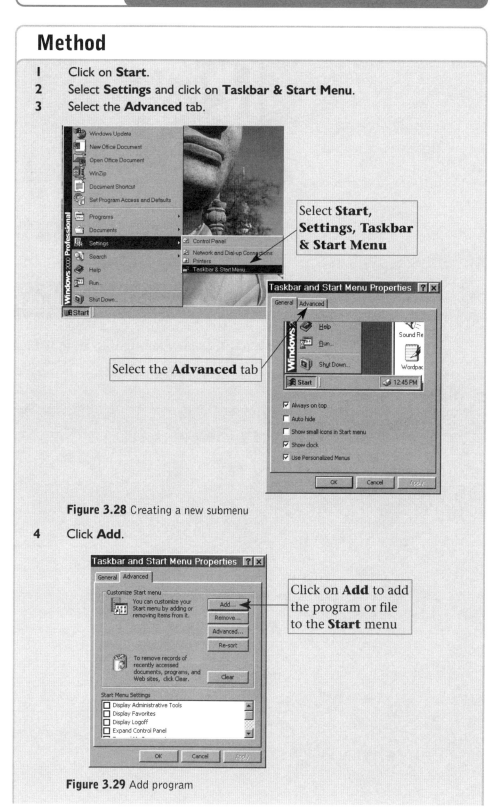

Select **Start, Settings, Taskbar & Start Menu**

Select the **Advanced** tab

Figure 3.28 Creating a new submenu

4   Click **Add**.

Click on **Add** to add the program or file to the **Start** menu

Figure 3.29 Add program

5   The **Shortcut** wizard will be displayed.

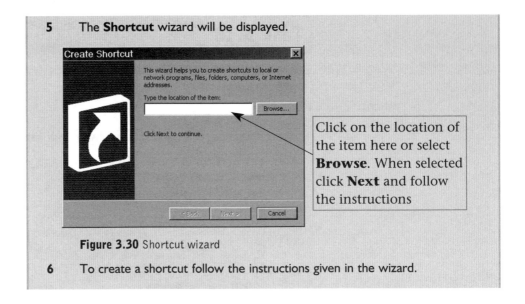

Click on the location of the item here or select **Browse**. When selected click **Next** and follow the instructions

Figure 3.30 Shortcut wizard

6   To create a shortcut follow the instructions given in the wizard.

Task 3.19 | To create a shortcut to a file

Here you will create a shortcut to an individual file.

Method

I	Double-click on **My Computer**.
2	Double-click on the drive with the folder containing the file.
3	Double-click on the folder.
4	Right-click on the file.
5	Click on **Send to**.

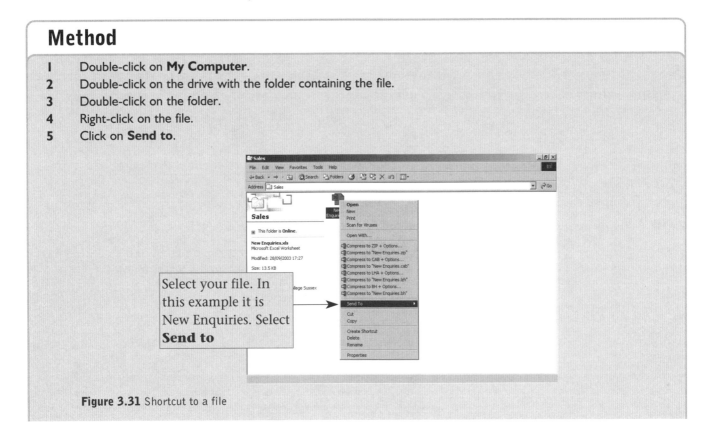

Select your file. In this example it is New Enquiries. Select **Send to**

Figure 3.31 Shortcut to a file

6   Click on **Desktop (Create Shortcut)**.

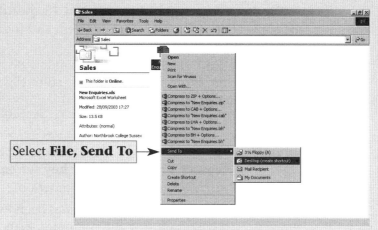

Figure 3.32 Create shortcut

You should now see a shortcut to your file on the desktop.

7   To activate the shortcut, double-click on the icon.

8   If you want to change the name of the shortcut, right-click on the shortcut, select **Rename** and type in a new name for your shortcut. This will rename the shortcut but it will not affect the file to which it relates.

Information: Error messages and prompts

In Windows you may encounter some error messages on the screen because a problem has occurred with the Windows software or there are errors relating to the hardware or the user has not followed the correct procedures. Your response will depend on the message shown, if any, or the lack of response from the computer. Some examples of errors you might encounter are described below and details of how to correct them.

Problem 1   No error message and no response when you use the mouse or keyboard

To solve

1   Press the **Ctrl**, **Alt** and **Delete** keys all together.

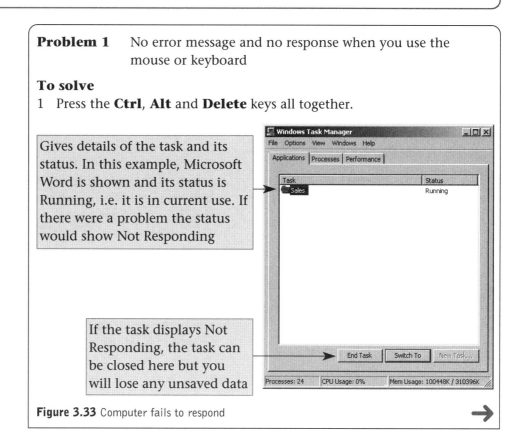

Gives details of the task and its status. In this example, Microsoft Word is shown and its status is Running, i.e. it is in current use. If there were a problem the status would show Not Responding

If the task displays Not Responding, the task can be closed here but you will lose any unsaved data

Figure 3.33 Computer fails to respond

2 You will see the window as shown in Figure 3.33. If the application is not working the status is shown as **Not Responding**. In Figure 3.33 the application does not have a problem and the status is therefore shown as **Running**.

3 Click on the **End Task** button. The window disappears. Try to reload the application. If this fails you may need to close further tasks by repeating each of the three steps.

Problem 2	The error message, **Non-System disk or disk error replace and strike any key when ready,** is displayed when you switch the computer on
To solve	A non-system floppy disk has been left in the floppy disk drive on starting the computer. Remove this disk and press any key on the keyboard.

Problem 3	The error message, **Windows was not properly shut down**, is displayed when you switch the computer on
To solve	Run **Scandisk** to check your hard disk for errors. If Scandisk does not run automatically select:

    1 **Start**
    2 **Programs**
    3 **Accessories**
    4 **System Tools**
    5 **Scandisk**

Scandisk is covered in more depth in Section 6 on 'Maintaining your Computer'.

Problem 4	When saving files the error message, **The disk in the destination drive is full**, appears
To solve	The destination where you are trying to save your file has run out of space. Check the drive and remove any files that are no longer required. **Caution!** Do not remove any files unless you are certain of their content – they may be system or application files whose removal would lead to failure of the operating system or application. You need to remove some files in order to create more space for the new file. If you are copying onto a floppy disk you can insert a new disk and click on **Retry**.

Problem 5	The error message **Not enough memory** is displayed
To solve	The computer is running out of memory. You may have too many windows open at the same time (multi-tasking), or you may be using image files which can take up a lot of memory, and you have run out of available memory. Close down some of the windows to free up some memory. You may have insufficient physical memory and you need to upgrade the amount of memory in the computer.

Problem 6	The error message appears, **You have placed a large amount of data on the clipboard. This data may take up quite a bit of memory and could degrade system performance if left on the keyboard**
To solve	If you have finished with the data you have placed on the clipboard, then click **No**. If you want to use what you placed on the clipboard in another application, click **Yes**. If you have applications running which you are not using close them down to increase the memory.

Information: Troubleshooting

If you experience a problem using Windows 2000 you can troubleshoot the problem in the following way:

1 Select **Start**.
2 Select **Help**.
3 Select **Contents** tab.
4 Select **Troubleshooting and Maintenance**.
5 Select the Troubleshooting and Maintenance subject required.

Information: Multi-tasking

You should see one window displayed on the screen, the **My Computer** window. Windows however allows you to have more than one application open at the same time; this is called multi-tasking. It is a useful feature which enables you to switch quickly and easily from one application to another.

In the following task you will open two applications – Microsoft Word and Microsoft Excel.

Task 3.20 | To multi-task

Method

Here you will open Microsoft Word.

1 Click on **Start**.
2 Select **Programs**.
3 Move the mouse pointer onto Microsoft Word and left-click.

Here you will open Microsoft Excel.

1 Click on **Start**.
2 Select **Programs**.
3 Move the mouse pointer onto Microsoft Excel and left-click.

As soon as you open Microsoft Excel, this screen will replace Microsoft Word on the screen display. Microsoft Word is still open however – it has been placed on the taskbar.

→ Practise your skills 1

1 Type in the following text:

MEMORANDUM

To: Alan Smith
                David Jones
                Paula Hammond

From: Pierre Aaron

Ref AS/M0I

10th October 2002

NEW PROMOTIONAL CATALOGUE

This is to confirm that the Spring edition of our marketing literature is now available. Please will you ensure that you use this catalogue, with immediate effect, when you visit your customers. Please return any unused catalogues to reception for recycling.

Will you please point out to your customers the special promotion of sports badges as shown on page 5 of the catalogue.

Thank you.

---

2 Preview the document with a magnification of 150%.
3 Preview the document in full screen.
4 Save the file as **Marketing Memo 1**.
5 Create a shortcut to this file and place it on the desktop.
6 Preview the file details.
7 Add the file to the Start menu.

→ Check your knowledge

1 Which view would you use to find out the size of a file?
2 Toolbars cannot be hidden. True or False?
3 Why would you run Scandisk?
4 What happens when you press Ctrl, Alt and Del altogether?
5 What is the purpose of the taskbar?
6 What should you do to create a submenu on the Start menu?
7 What is multi-tasking?
8 The computer displays a message that it is low on memory, what should you do?
9 What is a Thumbnail?
10 What is the shortcut key for Print?

Has a Tutor seen your blue RECORD
OF PROGRESS card recently?

IF NOT ASK A TUTOR TO CHECK
YOUR PROGRESS NOW

Section 4 | Managing files and folders

You will learn to

- Describe what makes an effective directory structure
- Create folders and sub-folders
- Maintain folders and directory structure
- Within a directory structure, manipulate files, folders and sub-folders, multiple files:
  - ☐ Copy
  - ☐ Move
  - ☐ Delete
  - ☐ Cut and paste
  - ☐ Drag and drop
- View the attributes and properties of directories, folders and files
- Identify common filename extensions used to describe types of files
- Use the search and advanced search functions
- Recover deleted files

Information: Managing your files and folders

When files are saved on the computer it is important to remember where you have saved them! Organising your files on a computer is the same as in a manual system. If in a manual system you filed everything in the same drawer without subdividing it in logical sections, the individual papers would be difficult to find. In a well-organised manual filing system information can be found easily because it has been sorted in a logical way and subdivided into sections. When storing your files on a computer you should adopt the same basic principles of a good manual filing system.

Do not store all your files on the drive of your computer without first planning your filing and devising a logical system. For example, you may group your files in a certain way. You may want to place all your word processing files in one location and all your spreadsheet files in another. To do this you would create one folder to store the word processing files and another folder for the spreadsheet files. Within these folders, the files stored could be further subdivided. In the word processing folder, for example, sub-folders could be created, one for reports, one for memorandums, and one for letters. This is a hierarchical filing system. It is easier to find information which has been stored in an efficient filing system consisting of folders, sub-folders and files.

> ## Information: Case study
>
> A new Administrative Assistant has been appointed at Boris Badges. One of their first tasks is to organise the folders and files stored on the office computer. The tasks include:
>
> - using Windows Explorer
> - creating new folders and sub-folders
> - naming a folder
> - selecting and copying single files and multiple files.
> - deleting folders and files.

Task 4.1	Accessing Windows Explorer

Method 1

1 Click on the **Start** button on the desktop.
2 Move the pointer onto **Programs**.
3 Select **Windows Explorer**.

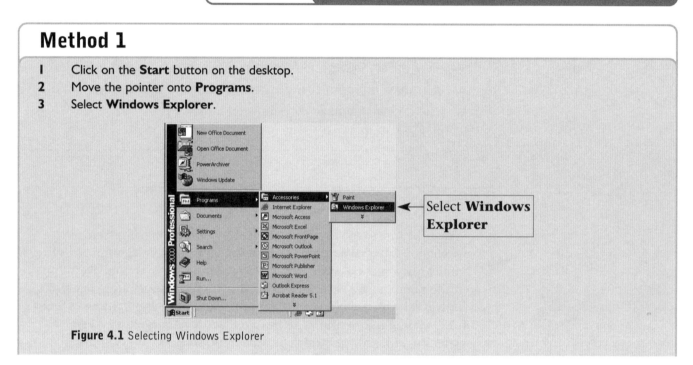

Figure 4.1 Selecting Windows Explorer

Method 2

1 Right-click on the **Start** button.
2 A pop-up menu will appear, select **Explore**.

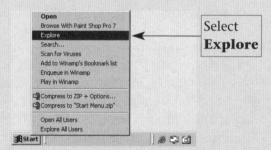

Figure 4.2 Select Explore

The Explorer window will appear. On the left-hand window the drives and the folders are displayed. On the right-hand windowpane the contents of the drive or folder selected are shown.

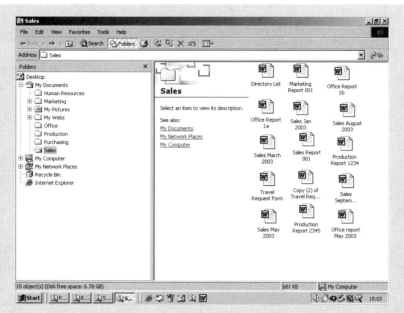

Figure 4.3 Contents of a folder

By looking at this Boris Badges' Administrative Assistant can see that files have not been filed in a logical manner. Some folders have been created but there are files which should be filed in the folders.

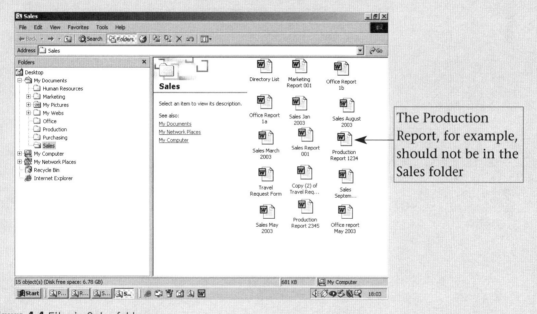

The Production Report, for example, should not be in the Sales folder

Figure 4.4 Files in Sales folder

The company has experienced a number of problems because they have not managed their files and folders correctly. Some files have been deleted because different users have used the computer and have deleted files saved in their folders which should have been saved in another user's folder. The main problem however is the time wasted because users have to search to find where the files have been saved.

Task 4.2 | Create folders

The Assistant's first task is to create new folders for each of the separate departments.

Method

1 Select **Windows Explorer**.
2 Click on **File**.
3 Move the mouse pointer to **New**.
4 Click on **Folder**.

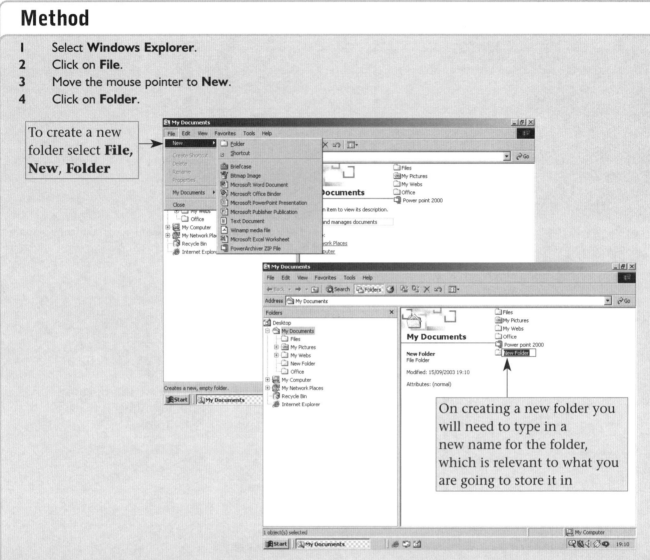

To create a new folder select **File, New, Folder**

On creating a new folder you will need to type in a new name for the folder, which is relevant to what you are going to store it in

Figure 4.5 Creating a new folder

5 **New Folder** is displayed.
6 Key in the name for the folder. Ensure the name given for the folder is relevant to the files which you are going to store in it. Do not, for example, save the files as 1, 2, etc. as it will be difficult to remember what 1 and 2 relate to and which folders are contained in them.

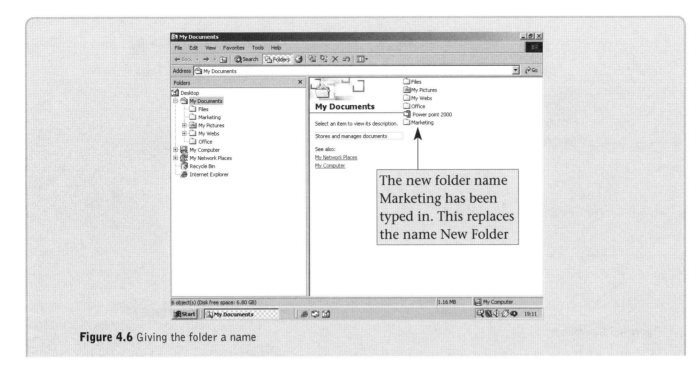

Figure 4.6 Giving the folder a name

The new folder name Marketing has been typed in. This replaces the name New Folder

Information: Sub-folders

A sub-folder is a folder within a folder. Folders used to be called directories and sub-directories but as Windows was developed they were renamed to folders and sub-folders. Sub-folders are useful because you can organise your work more efficiently by grouping similar files together under a general folder.

In the left-hand windowpane of Windows Explorer the drives and folders are displayed hierarchically and in the right-hand pane the contents of the selected folder is shown.

A plus sign beside the folder is used to highlight that the folder has sub-folders contained within it. For a filing system to be efficient you should be consistent in storing files in the correct folder or sub-folder

Information: Case study – creating sub-folders

Having created folders for each of the separate departments the Administrative Assistant has decided that the best way to organise the office files is to create sub-folders for each of the department folders under the My Documents folder. In Figure 4.7 a Marketing sub-folder has been created containing further sub-folders for Images, Inventory and Sales Forecasts.

To the left of these sub-folders are lines showing the link to the Marketing folder. You can see that the Marketing folder icon is displayed as an open folder and the contents of that open folder, i.e. the sub-folders Images, Inventory and Sales Forecasts, are displayed in the right-hand windowpane.

This is a hierarchical structure. If someone, for example, wants images created by the Marketing Department on the office computer, they do not have to guess where it might be stored or have to search on the computer for it. Provided the file is saved in the correct place the user knows that to retrieve the file they need first to look at the My Documents folder, and then look under the department, for example Marketing, and next any other relevant sub-folder, for example Images. For such a system to work however, users must be consistent in storing files into the correct folder or sub-folder. →

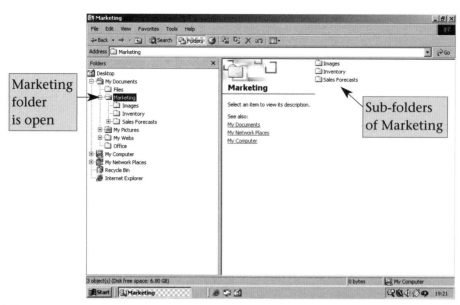

Figure 4.7 Sub-folders

In Figure 4.8 it can be seen that sub-folders have been created in the Sales Forecasts folder for the sales regions: North, South, East and West. To retrieve sales forecasts for the North region you would find them stored under:

My Documents: Marketing: Sales Forecasts: North

Figure 4.8 Sales forecasts sub-folders

In the lower screenshot the sub-folder North is open. In the left-hand windowpane you can see that the folder icon displays an open folder, the contents of which are displayed in the right-hand windowpane, i.e. in this example the sub-folder North contains two files called October Sales Forecast and November Sales Forecast.

Task 4.3 — To select an individual folder or file

Method

1   Select **Windows Explorer**.
2   Choose your preferred view.
3   If you are selecting files from within a folder, double-click on the folder where the files are stored.
4   Click on the file to select it.

Task 4.4 — To select multiple consecutive files

Method

1   Repeat the previous steps 1 and 3. You do not need to select view unless you want to change the current view.
2   Click on the first of the files you want to select.
3   Press and hold down the **Shift** key.
4   With the Shift key held down, click on the last file that you wish to select. The files will be highlighted.

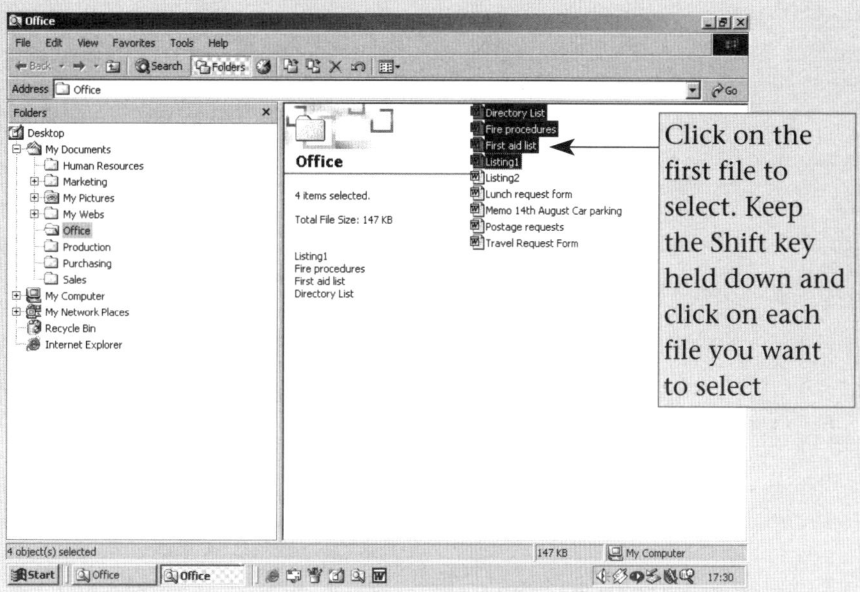

Click on the first file to select. Keep the Shift key held down and click on each file you want to select

Figure 4.9 Selecting multiple consecutive files

<table>
<tr><td>**Task 4.5**</td><td>**To select multiple non-consecutive files**</td></tr>
</table>

Method

1 Press and hold down the **Ctrl** key on the keyboard.
2 Click on each of the files or folders you want to select. You will see that they are highlighted.

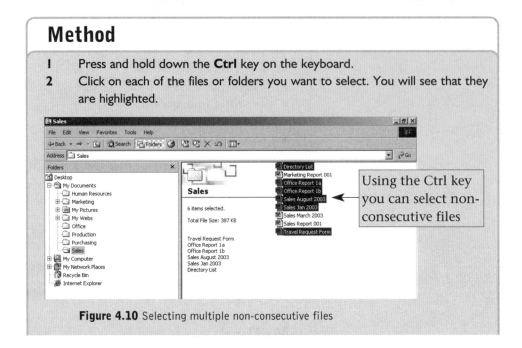

Figure 4.10 Selecting multiple non-consecutive files

<table>
<tr><td>**Task 4.6**</td><td>**To select all of the files displayed in the window**</td></tr>
</table>

Method

1 Click **Edit** on the menu.
2 Click on **Select All**. You will see that all of the files in the window have been highlighted.

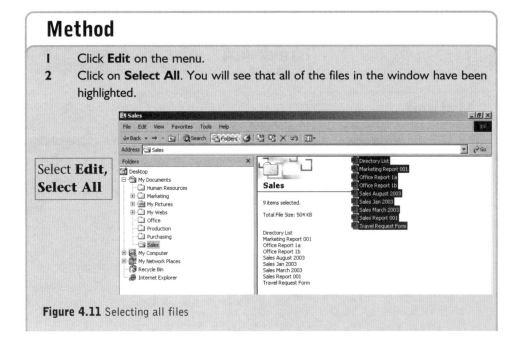

Figure 4.11 Selecting all files

Information: Case study – copying folders or files

The folder Inventory has been created in the Marketing folder to hold the Excel spreadsheet relating to an inventory of the equipment held in the Marketing Department of Boris Badges. The Assistant wants to copy this folder to other department folders.

Task 4.7	How to copy folders or files

There are several methods of doing this.

Method 1

I   Select **Windows Explorer** or double-click **My Computer** on the desktop, select the drive where the folders or files are located by double-clicking on the drive. In our example the Inventory sub-folder is located in the Marketing folder.

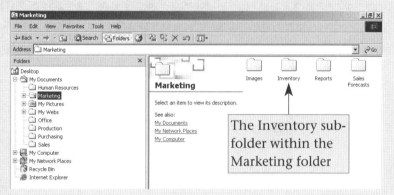

Figure 4.12 Selecting a sub-folder

Decide on which folders or files you want and highlight by using the selection method for either a single file, consecutive file, non-consecutive file or all files as displayed in the window.

2   Go to **Edit** on the menu bar.
3   Click on **Copy**.

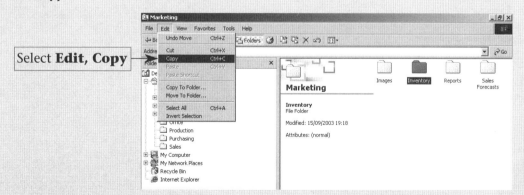

Figure 4.13 Copying folder

4   Click to the new location where you want the copy to be placed.
5   Click on **Edit** on the menu.
6   Click on **Paste** on the menu. The file will be copied to the new location.

Note: If you want to copy this file to more than one location after the first copy, you can omit steps 1–4 as the file will still be available to paste from the clipboard. If you shut down the computer and later want to make multiple copies using this method, you will need to repeat all the steps for the first copy.

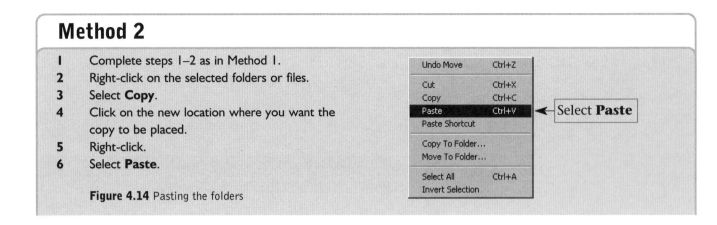

Method 2

1	Complete steps 1–2 as in Method 1.
2	Right-click on the selected folders or files.
3	Select **Copy**.
4	Click on the new location where you want the copy to be placed.
5	Right-click.
6	Select **Paste**.

Figure 4.14 Pasting the folders

Method 3

Here you will use Drag and Drop using the right mouse button.

1	Select the required folders or files.
2	Hold down the right mouse button. The selected folders or files will be highlighted.

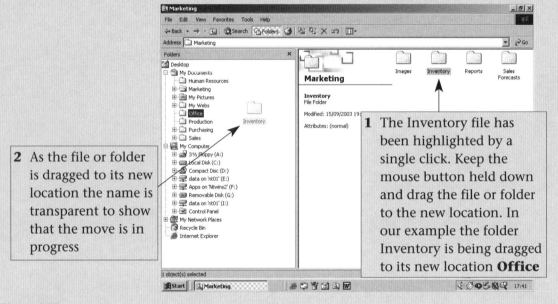

Figure 4.15 Drag and drop

3	Drag the file to the required position.
4	Release the mouse button, a menu will appear.
5	Click on **Copy Here** to create a copy in the destination folder.

Figure 4.16 Copy Here

Method 4

Here you will copy a file in the same folder.

I   You can create a copy of the file in the same folder if, for example, you need a backup copy of the file. Follow either method I or 2. When the file is pasted in it will be named **Copy of** followed by the original filename.

Method 5

Here you copy file(s) to a folder.

I   Select the file(s) to copy.
2   Select **Edit**.
3   Select **Copy To Folder**.

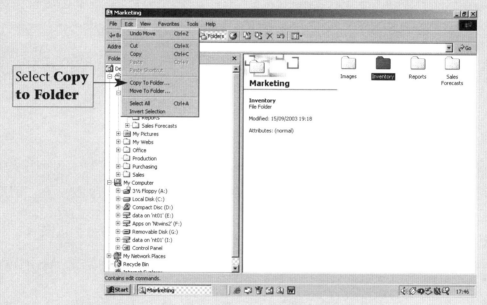

Figure 4.17 Copying a file to a folder

4   In the **Browse For Folder** select the folder location you wish to copy the file(s) to.

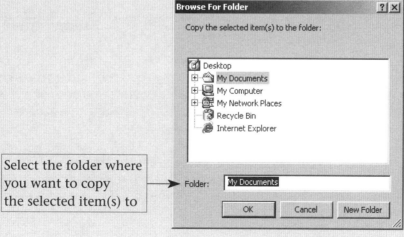

Figure 4.18 Selecting folder to copy items to

> **Information:** Case study – moving files or folders
>
> The Boris Badges Administrative Assistant wants to cut the file **Sales Report Toothbrush Inc. 10th October 2002**, which has been incorrectly filed in the Purchasing folder, and paste it into the Sales folder.

Task 4.8   How to move folders or files

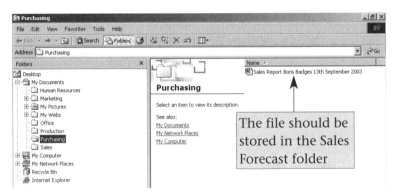

Figure 4.19 Selecting file to move

Method 1

Here you will use Cut and Paste to move a file or folder.

1 Double-click on **My Computer** on the desktop and select the drive in which the folders or files are located by double-clicking on the drive.

2 Click on the file or folder to move.
   Note: If you select a folder, the files contained in it will also move when you cut and paste it.

3 Select **Edit** from the menu.

4 Select **Cut** from the menu.

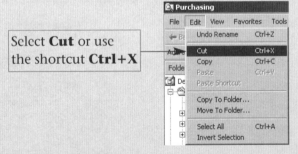

Figure 4.20 Cutting a file

5 You will notice that the icon fades. The selected files or folders remain displayed on the screen but are now on the clipboard. This is a temporary storage area.

6 Select the folder where you want your selection to move to.

7 Select **Edit**.

8 Select **Paste**.

The original selection has moved from the clipboard to the new location and is no longer displayed in the original location.

Method 2

Here you will use Drag and Drop using the left mouse button.

I Select the folders or files to move.
2 Hold down the left mouse button.
3 Keep the mouse button held down and drag the file to the new location.
4 Release the mouse button.

Method 3

You will use Drag and Drop using the right mouse button.

I Select the folders or files to move.

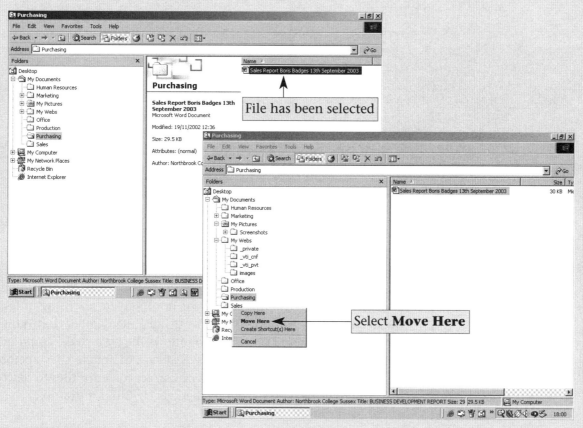

Figure 4.21 Moving file to new location

2 Right-click on the selected folders or files. These will be highlighted.
3 Keep the mouse button held down and drag to the new location.
4 Release the mouse button. A menu will be displayed.
5 Click on **Move Here**.

Method 4

Using Move To Folder to move file.

1 Select the file(s) to be moved.
2 Select **Edit**.
3 Select **Move To Folder**.

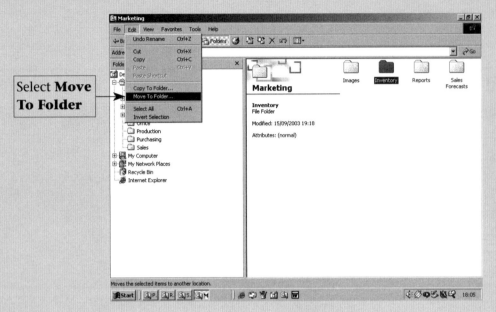

Select **Move To Folder**

Figure 4.22 Moving file to folder

4 In the **Browse For Folder** window select the folder position you want the file(s) to be moved to.

Information: Deleting folders or files

Whether you are deleting a single file or multiple files there are some simple rules to follow. The first rule is not to delete anything unless you are absolutely sure that it can be deleted. Remember that Windows is made up of files and deleting a Windows file by mistake could make your system unusable. Another rule is always to double check before you delete making sure you select the correct folder or files to delete. Once you have deleted files from the Recycle Bin, for example, they cannot be retrieved.

Task 4.9 Deleting folders or files

Method 1

1 Select a single file or folder or select multiple files or folders using the methods described earlier.
2 Press the **Delete** key on the keyboard.
3 You will be prompted to confirm that you want to delete the selection.
4 Check that you really want to delete the selection before you click on **Yes**. If you have made a mistake and do not want to delete the file then click on **No**.

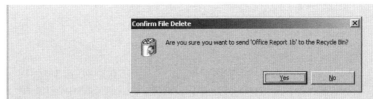

Figure 4.23 Make sure you want to delete

Method 2

1   Right-click on the files you want to delete.
2   Click on **Delete**.

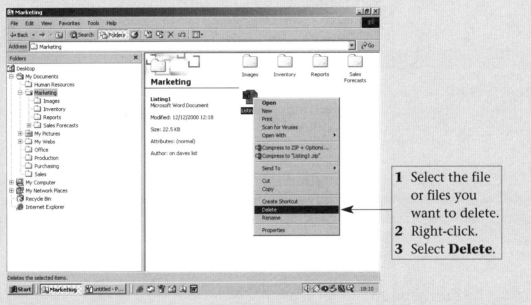

Figure 4.24 Deleting a file

3   You will be prompted to confirm you want to delete the selection.
4   Select **Yes** if you are sure the highlighted files are those you want to delete or **No** if they are not.

Method 3

Here you will delete all the folders or files displayed in the window.

1   Select the location containing the folders or files.
2   Click on **Edit** on the menu.
3   Click on **Select All**. All the files in the window will be highlighted.
4   Check you have selected the files you want to delete!
5   Press **Delete** on the keyboard.
6   You will be prompted to confirm you wish to delete the selection.
7   Select **Yes** if you are sure the highlighted files are the ones you want to delete or **No** if they are not.

Information: Attributes and properties of folders and files

File properties give information about the file selected and file attributes give information of how the file is to be used by the operating system.

File properties

The Properties window gives information on your selection:

- **Type of file**   This tells you what type of file it is. In Figure 2.98 for example, the file type is a Microsoft Excel spreadsheet.
- **Opens with**   This displays the application associated with the file or folder.
- **Size**   This displays the size of the file or folder.
- **Size on disk**   This displays the actual amount of disk space the file or folder has used.
- **Created**   This gives the date and time the file or folder was created.
- **Modified**   This gives the date and time the file or folder was modified.
- **Accessed**   This gives the date and time the file was last accessed.

File attributes

- **Read only**   If there is a check mark shown here, it means that the file can be read but not written to, i.e. you cannot edit it. This prevents any changes being made to the file and it also prevents any accidental deletions of the file.
- **Hidden**   If there is a check mark displayed here it means that the hidden attribute is on and you will not be able to see the file unless you know its name.

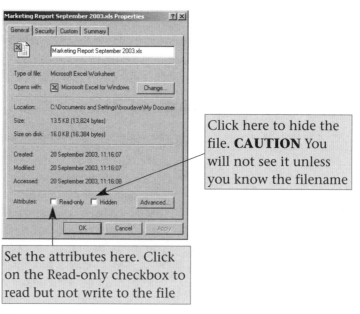

Click here to hide the file. **CAUTION** You will not see it unless you know the filename

Set the attributes here. Click on the Read-only checkbox to read but not write to the file

Figure 4.25 Properties and attributes

Information: Advanced attributes

Advanced file and index attributes

There is an option to set advanced attributes for files held on your computer, but some caution must be exercised if you use this feature. You can, for example, encrypt files and folders but in doing so only the user who encrypts the file or folder can access the content. Options include:

Folder is ready for archiving

If you see a check mark here it indicates if the file(s) or folder(s) selected are to be archived or not. Some programs use this feature to determine which files are to be backed up. If there is more than one file or folder selected the check mark means that all files or folders will have the archive attribute set. A filled box indicates that some, but not all, of the folder(s) or file(s) have the attribute set.

For fast searching, allow indexing service to index this folder

The advantage of indexing files or folders is that it enables faster searching and, in addition to searching its properties and attributes, you can also search for text within the folder or file.

Compress or encrypt attributes

Compress contents to save disk space

Compression is used to save on overall disk space. This option may be used to determine which folders or files, if any, are compressed. The default is that folders and files are not compressed unless the checkbox is selected. If the check mark is set for compression you will be prompted to compress the files, but note that files that have been compressed cannot be encrypted. If there is a fill box when multiple files are selected, this indicates that some, but not all, files are compressed. If there is a check mark it indicates that all the files are compressed.

Encrypt contents to secure data

Check mark this box if you want to encrypt a folder or file.

With multiple files a check mark indicates that all files selected are encrypted and if there is a fill box it means that some, but not all files selected, are encrypted.

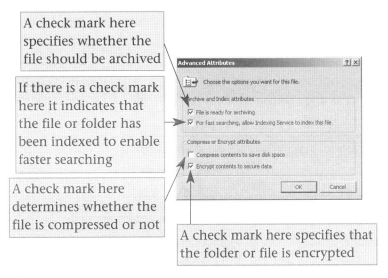

A check mark here specifies whether the file should be archived

If there is a check mark here it indicates that the file or folder has been indexed to enable faster searching

A check mark here determines whether the file is compressed or not

A check mark here specifies that the folder or file is encrypted

Figure 4.26 Advanced attributes

Caution!

If you encrypt the folder or file you restrict who has access to it. If the folder or file is moved or copied however, you may be able to decrypt it, but this depends on the method used.

Method

I   Right-click on the file or folder you want to view the properties or attributes of.

2   Select **Properties** from the menu.

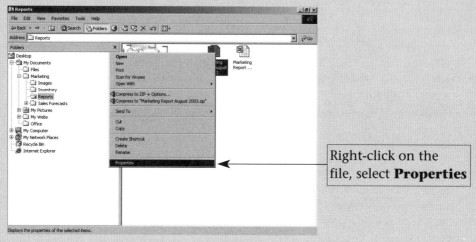

Right-click on the file, select **Properties**

Figure 4.27 Selecting properties

Information: Filename extensions

Filename extensions are used to describe the following types of files: word processing, spreadsheet, database, presentation, rich text image.

File extensions played an important roll in identifying the file type in operating systems prior to Windows 2000. A Windows 2000 file does not need a file extension type to indicate what type of file it is; you can call the file what you want to call it.

A file extension refers to the three characters which follow the dot after the filename. These can be useful to identify the type of file but are not used as much as they were. The development of software has increased the number of file extensions significantly. Shown below are some of the common filename extensions you may see:

Extension	Description
$$$	Temporary files
bak	Backup files
doc	Word document
hmtl	Hyper Text Markup Language
msg	Program message
ppt	PowerPoint
rtf	Rich text format
sys	System file
xls	Excel spreadsheet

Some common graphic files include:

Extension	Description
bmp	Bitmap image file
gif	Graphic Interchange File
jpeg	Joint Photography Experts Group
png	Portable Network Graphic file
tif or tiff	Tagged Image File Format

Some common sound files include:

Extension	Description
wav	Waveform sound
aud	Audio file
mid	Musical Instrument Digital Interface
ram	Metafile (Real Audio)
ra	Real audio

Some common video files include:

Extension	Description
avi	Audio Video Interleave file
mov	Movie QuickTime for Microsoft Windows
mpg/mp3	Moving Pictures Expert Group

Try it out!

Identify three more file extensions not shown in the above list.

Information: Search and advanced search functions

Search and advanced search functions include wildcards to locate files and folders by date, name, content.

If you cannot remember where a file is located you can search for it either by using the search facility within Windows or you can find and replace text within an application such as Word or Excel.

Task 4.11 To search for files on the desktop

Method

1   Click on **Start** on the taskbar.
2   Select **Search**.
3   Move the mouse pointer to **Search** and then **For Files or Folders**.

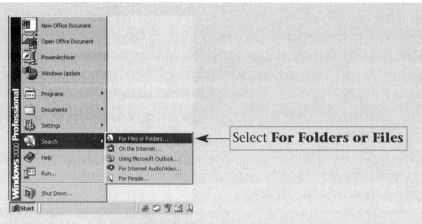

Select **For Folders or Files**

Figure 4.28 Searching for files and folders

4   Type in the file or folder name you require to find in the **Search for files or folders named** dialogue box.
5   In the **Containing text** dialogue box, type in some of the text contained in your file.
6   Select the drive where the file is contained.
7   Click on **Search Now**.

You can also refine your search by specifying searches by **Date**, **Type**, **Size** and **Advanced Options**.

Type the name of the file or folder to find here

If you know some of the text contained in the file, type it in here

Select the drive to search

Search by either **Date, Type, Size** or **Advanced Options**

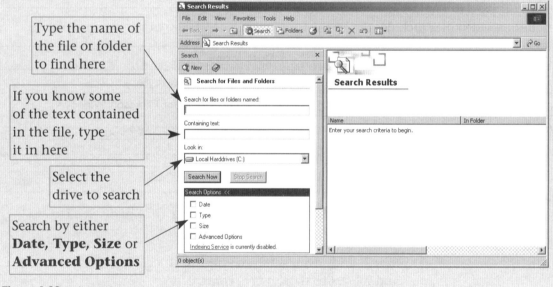

Figure 4.29 Refining a search

Task 4.12   To search for a folder or file

Method 1

1   In the **Search for files or folders named** dialogue box, type in the file or folder you want to find.
2   In the **Look in** dialogue box (as shown in Figure 4.30), select the drive(s) where you think the files or folders, which you wish to locate, are stored.
3   Click on **Select Now**. This will display the results in the left-hand windowpane.

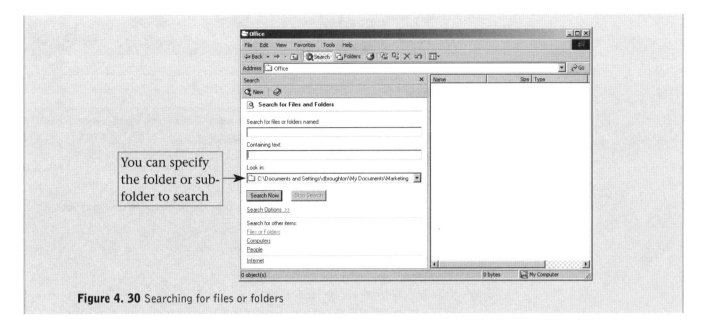

You can specify the folder or sub-folder to search →

Figure 4. 30 Searching for files or folders

Method 2

1   In the **Search for files or folders named** dialogue box, type in the file or folder you want to find.
2   If you know some of the text contained in the file, type the text in the **Containing text** dialogue box.
3   Click on **Select Now**. This will display the results in the left-hand windowpane.

Information: Case study – finding files

The Administrative Assistant wants to find the file Boris Badges. They know the file contains the text Pen Promotion so have entered this in the **Containing text** dialogue box. They have searched for this file by looking in the My Documents folder, as shown in the **Look in** dialogue box, but have not entered a date in the **Search options** dialogue box as they do not know when the file was created.

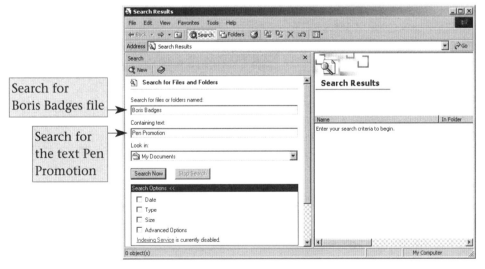

Search for Boris Badges file →

Search for the text Pen Promotion →

Figure 4.31 Searching for files

The Assistant can refine the search further by selecting the search options in the **Search Options** dialogue box. She can combine these search options. For example, she can search by date and by file type.

Task 4.13 To search by date

Method

1   In the **Search for files or folders named** dialogue box (as shown in Figure 4.31), type in the file or folder required.
2   In the **Look in** dialogue box select the drive(s) where you think the files or folders, which you want to locate, are stored.
3   Click in the **Date** checkbox.
4   Below the Date checkbox is a dialogue box. Click on the arrow and you will see three options:
    ● files Modified
    ● files Created
    ● files Last Accessed
5   Select one of these options.
6   You have the option to refine your search by selecting in the checkbox:
    ● in the last months
    ● in the last days
    ● in between
7   Select one of these options.
    Next to these dialogue boxes is an arrow. Select this and a pop-up calendar will be displayed (Figure 4.32). Click on the date. You can scroll through the calendar by clicking on either the right or left arrow.

Either type in the date here or select the down arrow. A pop-up calender will appear. Click on the date to select it. If you need to select a different month click on either the left or right arrow in the month heading to select a different month

Figure 4.32 Searching by date

Task 4.14 **To search by type**

You can search for files by their file type.

Method

1	In the **Search for files or folders named** dialogue box (as shown in Figure 4.31), key in the file or folder you require.
2	In the **Look in** dialogue box, select the drive(s) where you think the files or folders, which you want to locate, are stored.
3	Click in the **Type** checkbox. The default is for **All Files and Folders**.
4	To specify a type, click on the pull-down arrow and select the file type.

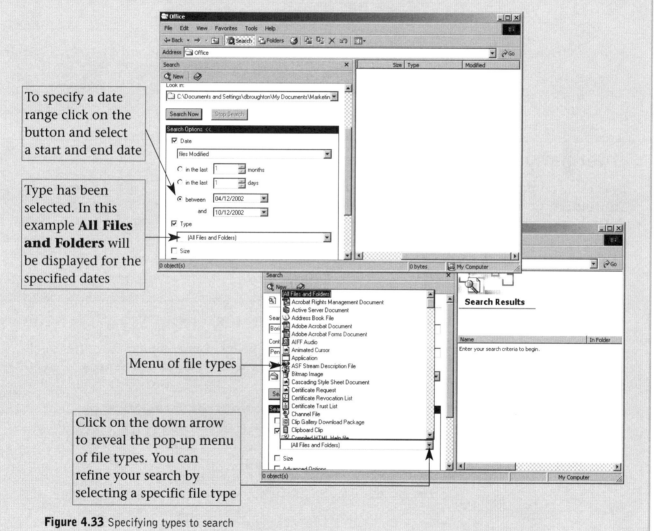

To specify a date range click on the button and select a start and end date

Type has been selected. In this example **All Files and Folders** will be displayed for the specified dates

Menu of file types

Click on the down arrow to reveal the pop-up menu of file types. You can refine your search by selecting a specific file type

Figure 4.33 Specifying types to search

Task 4.15 **To search by size**

Method

1	You can search for files by their file size by selecting the **Size** checkbox.
2	To define the range of your search select either **at least** or **at most**.

3 Select the file size in KB by using the up or down arrow.
In Figure 4.34 the search selected is for files with at least 150 KB.

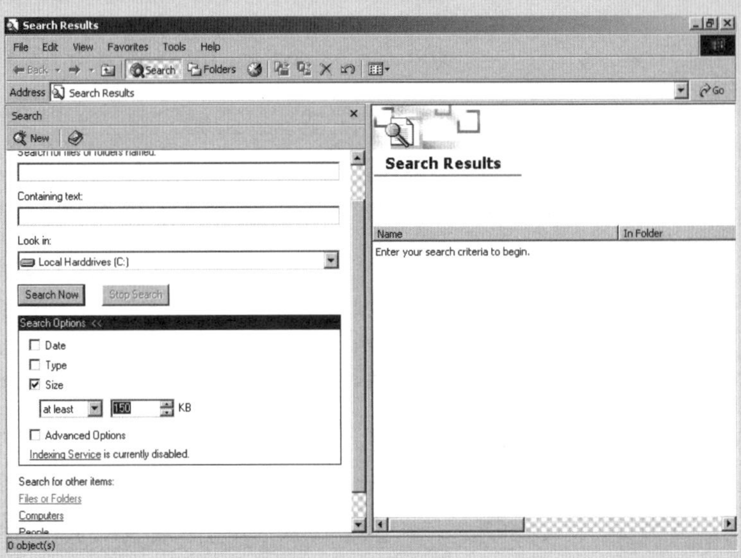

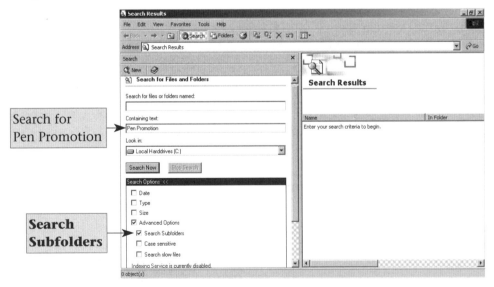

Figure 4.34 Searching by size

Information: Advanced options

By clicking on the **Advanced Options** checkbox you may further refine your search by **Search Subfolders**, **Case sensitive** and **Search slow files**. The **Search slow files** in the Advanced Options of search files relates to files which are stored on removable storage media, such as magnetic tape or optical disk, used to back up files. Backing up data onto this type of media may require the files to be copied first to a faster storage medium before the data stored can be searched.

Information: Case study – using advanced options to search for file

The Administrative Assistant wants to find a file containing the text Pen Promotion. On the Search Options they have selected the C drive and selected the **Advanced Options** and **Search Subfolders** (Figure 4.35).

Figure 4.35 Using advanced options

Information: Using wildcard searches

If you do not know the exact spelling of a file and you want to avoid keying in the whole filename, you can use wildcards. You can use the asterisk (*), which represents one or more characters. In Figure 4.36, in the **Search for files or folders named** dialogue box, *.doc has been keyed in. This will search for all files with a .doc extension.

You can also use a question mark to represent a single character in a filename. If you typed in, for example, tes?.doc in the dialogue box the search would find a file named test.doc but not a file named testing.doc.

A wildcard (the asterisk) has been used to represent all files or folders. In this example the search criteria is for all files with the .doc file extension

The search criteria in this example specifies to search for the files or folders in the My Documents folder

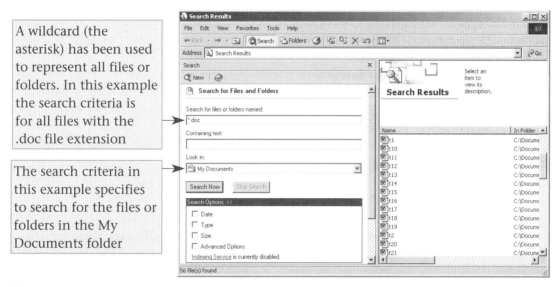

Figure 4.36 Wildcard searches

In Figure 4.37 the wildcard has been used to search for all files starting with Scan with the .sav file extension.

Search for all Scan files with the .sav extension

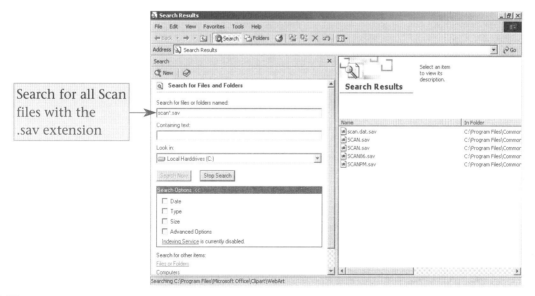

Figure 4.37 Using .sav extension to search

Information: To find and replace text within an application

You may want to find text within an application or you may want to find text and then replace it with something different. You will create a document in Microsoft Word, keying in the text below and saving it to a certain location. In the task that follows you will search to find the document file.

BORIS BADGES
21 Byards Avenue
Boham
West Sussex
RH1 2YP

21 November 2002

Dear Mr Action

New! Chester range of badges

Thank you for your recent enquiry regarding the Chester range of badges. I think you will agree that these are a valuable addition to our current range. I have enclosed a brochure for your attention which includes the latest prices.

We look forward to receiving your order.

Yours sincerely

Libby Smith-Jones
SALES DEPARTMENT

Enc

Task 4.16   Using Find to search for text

Method 1

I   Go to **Edit** on the menu bar.

2   Select **Find**.

Select **Edit, Find**

Figure 4.38 Using Find

3   Key in the **Find what** dialogue box the text you wish to find, e.g. Badges.

4   Click on **Find Next**.

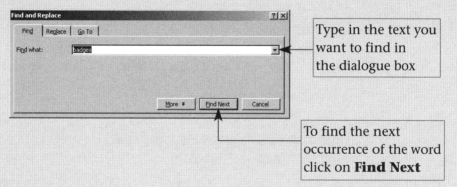

Type in the text you want to find in the dialogue box

To find the next occurrence of the word click on **Find Next**

Figure 4.39 Find what dialogue box

5   Repeat this process until you find the text you want. If you want to replace the text, click on **Replace** and type in the text to replace.

Method 2

Here you will find a file using Go To.

1   Go to **Edit** on the menu bar.
2   Select **Find**.
3   Type in the **Find what** dialogue box the text you want to find, e.g. Badges.
4   Click on **Go To**. You will have the option of either entering the page number in the **Enter page number** dialogue box, or make a selection in the **Go to what** box.

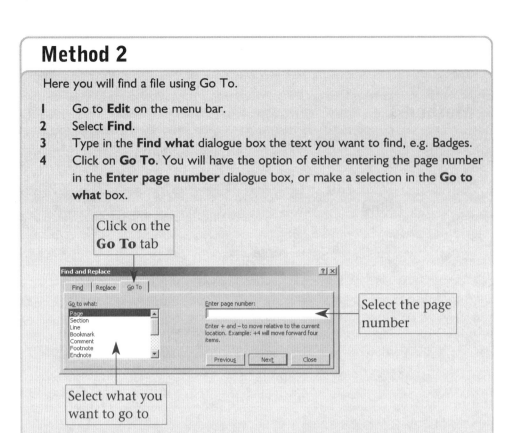

Figure 4.40 Selecting where to go to find file

Method 3

Here you will use Find and Replace.

1   Go to **Edit**.
2   Select **Replace**.
3   Key in the **Find what** dialogue box the text you want to find, e.g. Badges.

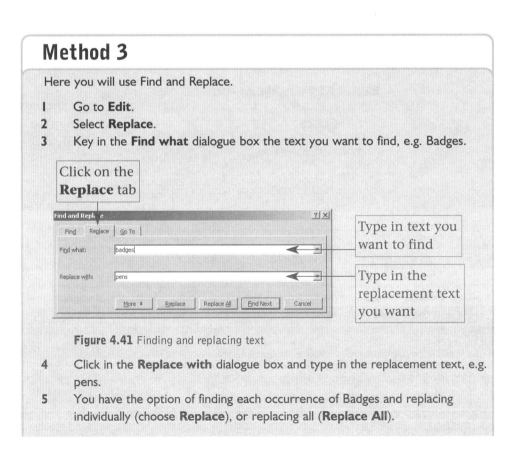

Figure 4.41 Finding and replacing text

4   Click in the **Replace with** dialogue box and type in the replacement text, e.g. pens.
5   You have the option of finding each occurrence of Badges and replacing individually (choose **Replace**), or replacing all (**Replace All**).

Information: How to recover deleted files

If you have deleted a file by mistake you can recover the file from the Recycle Bin. This may not always be the case however, as the Recycle Bin can be configured to automatically empty as soon as anything is sent to it. Always err on the side of caution when you empty the Recycle Bin, as once it is empty you will not be able to recover anything that was sent to it.

If you have deleted a file or folder but want to recover and restore it, the following task shows you how to do it.

Task 4.17 | Restoring a file

Method 1

1 Go to **Edit** on the menu bar.
2 Select **Undo delete**.

To undo delete select **File, Undo Delete**

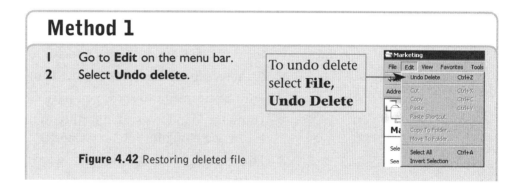

Figure 4.42 Restoring deleted file

Method 2

This involves restoring an item from the Recycle Bin.

1 Double-click on the **Recycle Bin** on the desktop.
2 Either right-click on the item to be restored and press **Restore** or highlight the multiple items to restore, and click on **Restore** on the display. To select more than one file to be recovered, highlight the file by clicking on each file whilst holding down the Ctrl key.

If the file(s) you want to restore is located in a deleted folder, Windows will recreate the folder first and then restore the file or files into the restored folder.

To restore files or folders select the item(s) you want to restore and click on **Restore**

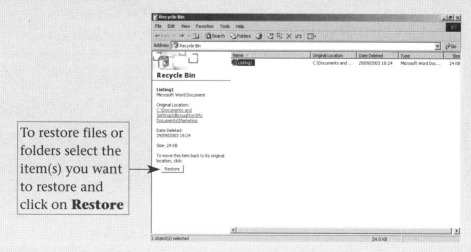

Figure 4.43 Select items to restore

→ Practise your skills 1

1 Create a folder called **City & Guilds**.

2 Create a sub-folder of the City & Guilds folder called **Unit 1**.

3 Load Word.

4 Move the file Marketing Memo 1 (previously created) to Unit 1 sub-folder.

5 Create a new folder called **Notes**.

6 Copy the Marketing Memo 1 file to the Notes folder.

7 Create a new sub-menu in the Programs menu on the Start menu and position it in the City & Guilds folder.

→ Practise your skills 2

1 Create a new folder called **Chester Range**. Copy the Marketing memo 1 file from the Notes folder into the Chester range folder.

2 Create a sub-folder in the Chester Range folder called **Badges**.

3 Print a screenshot to show you have created the sub-folder.

4 Using the Windows search facility to find the Marketing memo 1 file by searching for the text 'Chester'.

5 Print a screenshot showing your search criteria.

6 Delete the Marketing memo 1 file from the Notes folder.

7 Make the Marketing memo 1 file read only.

8 Print a screenshot to show that you have made the file read only.

→ Check your knowledge

1 What is an attribute?

2 What is a wildcard?

3 Gif is an Graphic Internet File. True or False?

4 What does * denote when you use wildcards?

5 What does a + sign represent in Windows Explorer?

Section 5   Computer networks

You will learn to

- Describe and give examples of networks: wide area network (WAN), local area network (LAN), workstation, client server, peer-to-peer network
- Describe the advantages and disadvantages of networking computers
- Access shared data and configure rights of other users to own files
- Describe methods of maintaining confidentiality and privacy over a network
- Explain what is needed in terms of hardware and software to connect to the Internet
- Describe what is meant by the terms 'freeware' and 'shareware'
- Describe the main uses of commonly used software packages: Internet browser
- Describe and give examples of: URL, ISP, Internet/Intranet, protocol
- Describe the legal issues concerning software copyright, licensing, multi-licensing
- Use a browser to locate a website and download information to a hard disk
- Select, open and save email attachments in selected folders

Information: Standalone computers

A standalone computer is one which is not connected to any other computer but can work independently from other systems. Increasingly computers are networked together in order to share information either in the same building (local area network) or over a wider geographical area (wide area network). A computer (workstation) on the network is linked either to similar computers in a peer-to-peer network to share resources or linked to a server which distributes services throughout the network.

Information: Wide area networks (WANs) and local area networks (LANs)

There are different types of computer networks which can be defined in terms of the geographical area they cover:

- Local area networks (LANs)
- Wide area networks (WANs)

Local area network (LAN)
A local area network describes the connection of computers via cabling or wireless technology within a small geographical area, up to a distance of one kilometre. LANs are located in a small location, typically in a single building.

→

Information: Case study

The sales of Boris Badges continue to rise. At a recent meeting of the Board of Directors the decision was made to expand the company by opening a new factory located on the outskirts of town on the industrial estate. At this meeting it was agreed to develop the existing computer network in the company to cater for this new development.

The existing IT system used within Boris Badges consists of a number of standalone computers and a local area network. In the General Office standalone computers are used but throughout the rest of the company a network is in operation.

Requirements of a network

Workstation

A computer which is connected to a network is called a workstation. Workstations do not normally have their own storage facilities, but instead are connected to a central file server. The file server stores the operating system, the application programs and the data, and distributes them to the rest of the network; this is called a distributed system.

Client server

A client server is a computer which is used to distribute programs and services, such as managing the printer, to the 'client', which is a workstation. Servers can be dedicated to particular functions, such as a print server. The workstation has its own processing capability, but the files and programs are stored on the file server.

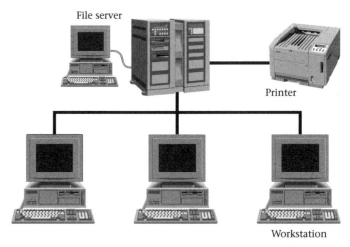

Figure 5.1 A local area network

Peer-to-peer network

A client-server network has a dedicated server, which distributes services to the clients on the network. In a peer-to-peer network however there is not a dedicated server, instead all computers and devices, such as printers within the network, are joined together and communicate with each other. The advantage is that it is simpler since you do not need a dedicated server, but the disadvantage is that it is slower than a client-server system.

Information: Networking computers – advantages and disadvantages

Using a network has considerable advantages over using standalone computers.

- Sharing is the most significant advantage. In the case of Boris Badges, using standalone computers in the General Office makes it difficult to share data. If a file is required on more than one computer, for example, it has to be copied onto a floppy disk or other storage medium and physically transferred onto the other computer. If the data has to be amended the process of transferring the changes onto the other computers has to be repeated. This is time-consuming and is an inefficient way of sharing data. Another disadvantage of using standalones is that because data is not shared data, it could be duplicated and it is difficult to keep track of any amendments made.
- By using a client-server network within the General Office, files can be stored on the main server and all users within the office can access these resources. This is more efficient, less time-consuming, and is beneficial to team working, as all staff can communicate with each other and share resources.
- Using a file server reduces the software cost, as programs held on the file server can be shared by all the workstations. It is easier to maintain integrity of data as all users can access the same data. This centralisation is also beneficial in that it is easier to control the security of programs and files.
- Networks have distinct advantages compared with standalone systems, however there are some disadvantages. This includes the initial cost to install the network and the need for technical knowledge to maintain it.
- Another disadvantage is that if the main server develops a problem this can affect the whole network system.

Information: Shared data

Networks connect workstations together to enable data and resources to be shared. Files may be configured to allow access by all users or restricted to specified users. Access to these files may be restricted to read only; users can load the files but not change them.

Accessing shared data

Files shared on the network are stored on the network server, which the network administrator gives users rights to access and use according to their individual user rights. To access shared data, you need to single-click on the shared drive.

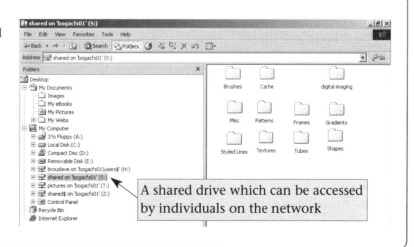

A shared drive which can be accessed by individuals on the network

Figure 5.2 A shared drive

You can configure the rights of your own files so that other users can use them. You can set the rights so that others can read the files but not change them or you can give them full access to the files.

Method

I   Select the folder to share.

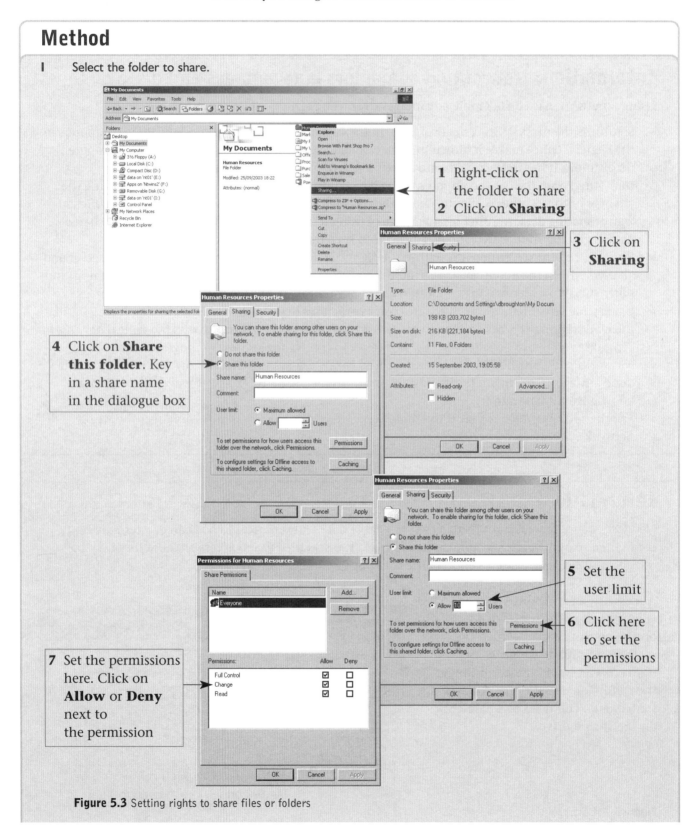

1 Right-click on the folder to share

2 Click on **Sharing**

3 Click on **Sharing**

4 Click on **Share this folder**. Key in a share name in the dialogue box

5 Set the user limit

6 Click here to set the permissions

7 Set the permissions here. Click on **Allow** or **Deny** next to the permission

Figure 5.3 Setting rights to share files or folders

Connecting to the Internet

To connect to the Internet you will need the following hardware and software:

Computer

Older computers, which have a minimum specification of a 486 processor with Windows 95 and have 8 MB RAM memory, can access the Internet, however if your computer is as old as this you should upgrade it, as the processing speed will be slow. A computer older than two years may require upgrading to take advantage of faster processing speeds and updates on the operating system. You can upgrade the RAM by installing additional memory modules.

Modem

A modem (**mo**dulator-**dem**odulator) is required to convert digital signals, which the computer sends (modulates), into analogue signals, which telephone lines use (demodulates). Another modem is required to convert the analogue signals back into digital signals.

Modems can be either internal or external to the computer but they are usually internal. The speed at which modems send and receive data is measured in bits per second. There are different speeds of modems but a typical speed is 56 Kbps, however this does not mean that you will receive data at this rate. This is because if data is being sent at a slower speed your modem will receive the data at that speed.

Telephone line connection

You need a telephone line for connecting the modem to the Internet.

Internet Service Provider (ISP)

An ISP is a company which provides both the software and the connection to the Internet, either for a fee or free, excluding phone charges whilst connected. To connect you to their server the ISP provides a username and password. They provide additional services such as web-hosting facilities for your web pages, email services and links to information resources.

Web browser

A web browser is a software program that allows users to read and browse for information on the World Wide Web. Examples include Microsoft Internet Explorer and Netscape Navigator.

Information: Broadband – ADSL (Asymmetric Digital Subscriber Line)

Broadband or ADSL (Asymmetric Digital Subscriber Line) enables voice and fast transmission of data over a telephone line. There is no dial up process required as with standard modems because the connection is 'always on', i.e. it is on all the time your computer is switched on. Broadband requires an ADSL modem or router to connect to the service.

Disadvantages:

- The cost of installation and ongoing monthly subscription charges.
- The computer is potentially at risk from unauthorised access because the connection is on when the computer is on. To prevent unauthorised access make sure the computer has sufficient firewall protection.

Information: Intranet and Internet

The Internet is a world-wide network of computers, which uses telecommunications links to connect individuals, businesses, governments and other organisations and institutions together to share information. Information that is stored on the computers connected to the Internet is called the **World Wide Web**.

The Internet is a vast external network of computers. The Intranet is an internal network of computers which use Internet software to share information, but does not have to be connected to the Internet to do so. The Intranet is used to store company information and documents on a web server which individuals can then access using a web browser.

Accessing the Internet

A web page can be accessed on the World Wide Web by keying in its address if you know it; if you don't you can use a search engine to find the information you want.

URL (Uniform Address Locator)

You find information on the Internet by typing the URL (Uniform Address Locator) in the address bar of your web browser. The URL is the address of the web page. An example is http://www.msn.co.uk.

The **http (Hyper Text Transfer Protocol)** refers to the communications protocol which is being used to transfer information across the Internet; this is the most common protocol. The protocol is the method by which data is transferred from one computer to another and is used for error checking. When data is sent via telephone lines the danger is that some errors may occur in the transmission. The protocol checks for errors between the sender and receiver computers and reports errors so data can be sent again.

The **WWW** refers to the World Wide Web. The World Wide Web consists of the millions of web pages on the Internet.

The next part of the URL refers to the domain name of the organisation, the individual or the Internet Service Provider (ISP) which hosts the website. In our example **msn** refers to Microsoft.

The next part of the URL in our example, **.co**, refers to the type of organisation. The **co**, or **com**, refers to a commercial organisation. There are different abbreviations to represent different types of institutions, for example **.ac** signifies an academic institution and **.gov** a government body.

The last part of the URL represents the country. In our example **.uk** is the United Kingdom.

Search engines

Search engines, such as Google, Altavista or Yahoo!, are programs which are accessed via the Internet and are used to find information from a vast database of websites. You type in keywords to search for information on a chosen subject and the search produces a list of relevant websites with a brief description of their contents. You can then click on any of the links displayed to go directly to the web page containing that information.

Searches should be specific otherwise your search will return thousands of web pages. You can further restrict the amount of pages received by limiting your search to only UK sites.

Internet browser

Microsoft Explorer is an Internet browser which allows a user to access the World Wide Web to locate information on a vast range of subjects which, subject to copyright, can be downloaded.

Microsoft Internet Explorer is the browser we will use. The opening window displays:

- Title bar at the top
- Menu bar
- Standard buttons
- Address bar
- Web page

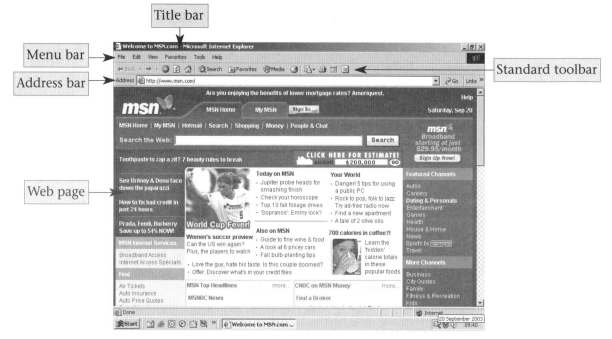

Figure 5.4 Microsoft Internet Explorer homepage

Task 5.2 To use a browser

Here you will use a browser to locate a website and download information to a hard disk.

Method

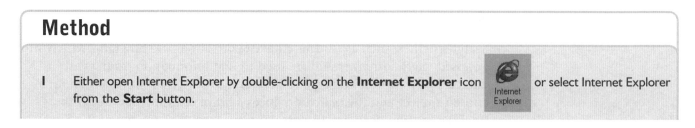

I Either open Internet Explorer by double-clicking on the **Internet Explorer** icon or select Internet Explorer from the **Start** button.

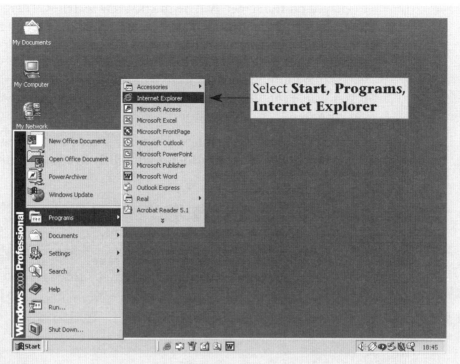

Figure 5.5 Opening Internet Explorer

2   Click in the address bar and key in the name of the website you want to access. An example is: http://www.msn.co.uk. You will see a web page similar to the one shown below.

3   On this page search the web for the information of your choice by clicking in the **Search the Web** dialogue box shown on the web page in Figure 5.6.

4   To complete the search for the chosen topic, either press **Enter** or click on the **Search** button.

Click into the search box and type in what you want to search for. When you have typed your search criteria press the Enter key once

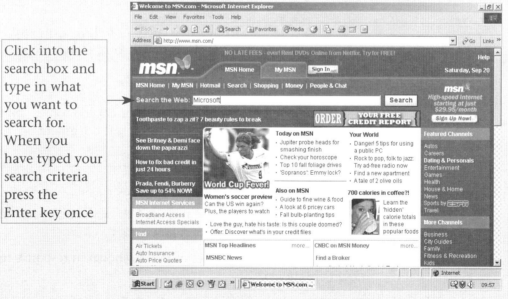

Figure 5.6 MSN dialogue box

In our example we searched the web for Microsoft and this has produced a number of results. The search results are underlined in blue. This links to another web page containing information relating to the chosen topic. When you click on a link, which may be text or a graphic, the link navigates to the URL address of the web page, which is hidden from view.

Displayed on the screen will be the first few searches. There may be many thousands of results which match your original search criteria. So, it is important when you make your initial search to try to be specific with your search criteria in order to narrow the results of your search. For example, if you search for 'holidays' it's likely you will get thousands of results, whereas if you search for 'holidays in Bognor Regis' you will narrow your search and get fewer results to choose from.

On the page, only the first few results are shown with a brief description of their content. To look at further results click on the Next link, as shown in Figure 5.7.

Click on a link which matches your search. You can scroll through the results to find the best match

Click on NEXT to find more sites which match your search criteria

Figure 5.7 Search results

When you find a relevant web page for your chosen topic, you can save this page in a similar way to saving other Microsoft documents.

Try it out!

Load your web browser and enter the URL www.msn.co.uk in the address bar. Enter a search for 'Planet Mars'.

How many 'hits' (the number of results shown in response to your search) are shown?

Click on five different links. Does the information from the pages which you find displayed match your search?

Task 5.3   Saving a web page

Method

1   Go to **File** on the menu bar.
2   Click on **Save As**.

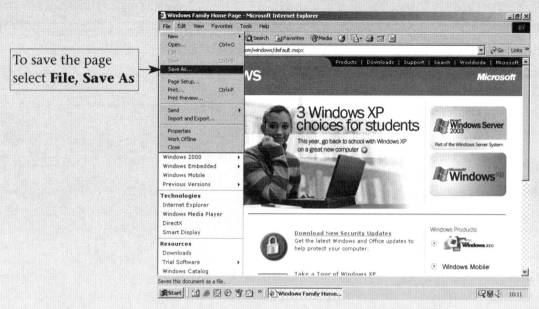

> To save the page select **File, Save As**

Figure 5.8 Saving a web page

3   Select where you want to save the page in the **Save in** dialogue box.
4   Key in the name for your document in the **File name** dialogue box.
5   In the **Save as type** dialogue box there are a number of choices. To save the complete web page, for example, select **Web Page, complete (*.htm,*.html)**.
6   Click on **Save**.

> Select the file type here

Figure 5.9 Selecting page to save

You can select text and graphics on a web page by highlighting text with the mouse, or right-clicking on a picture. Once you have made your selection you can copy and paste this selection into other programs (Figure 5.10).

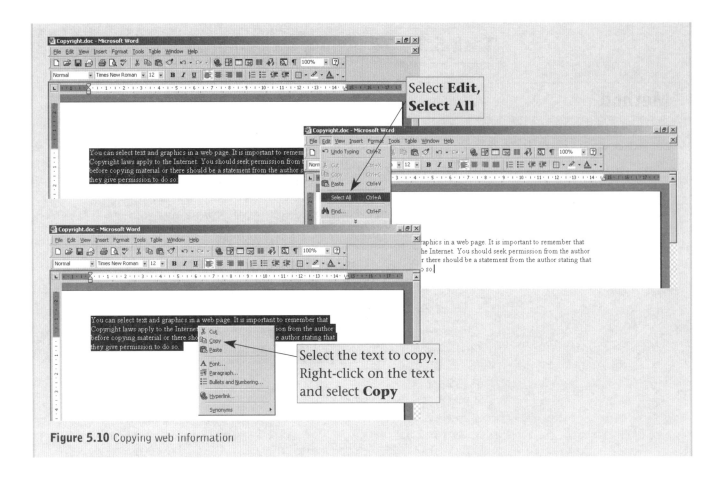

Figure 5.10 Copying web information

Task 5.4 — To print web pages

You will print a web page displayed on the screen.

Caution!

Information stored on the Internet may be subject to copyright. You should not reproduce any text or images which are subject to copyright unless you receive permission from the author to do so.

Method

1	Go to **File** on the menu bar.
2	Select **Print** and click to print.

Task 5.5 — To bookmark a web page

If you find a web page you want to revisit you can add this to your Favorites list. This will make it easier to locate the web page in the future. It is a shortcut to the page. You will now add a web page to your Favorites list.

Method

1	Go to **Favorites** on the menu bar.
2	Select **Add to Favorites** and click on it.

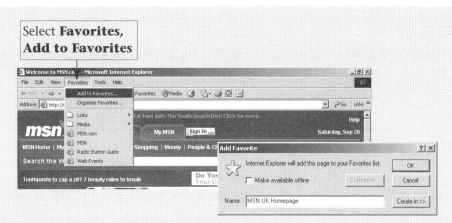

Figure 5.11 Adding a web page to Favorites

3 Either accept the description in the **Name** dialogue box or give a new description and then click on **OK**.
4 If you click on **Favorites** the page is shown in the Favorites list. Next time you want to visit this page you just go to Favorites and click on the Favorite page to link to it.

Figure 5.12 Web page added to Favorites list

If you have a lot of favourites you may want to organise them into folders.

<table>
<tr><td>**Task 5.6**</td><td>**To organise favourite web pages into folders**</td></tr>
</table>

Method

1 Go to **Favorites**.
2 Select **Organise Favorites**.

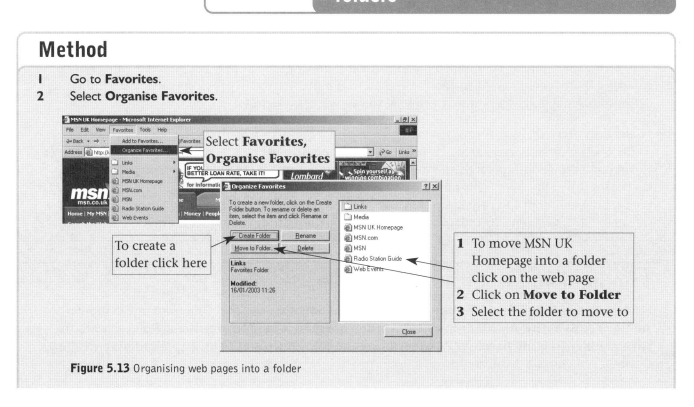

Figure 5.13 Organising web pages into a folder

3	To create a new folder for your favourites click on **Create Folder** and give the folder a name and click on **OK** to enter the name.
4	To move a favourite to a folder click on the web page in the Favorites list and click on **Move to Folder**. Click on the folder you wish to move to.
5	To accept the move click on **OK**.

Information: Freeware and shareware

Freeware describes software which can be used and copied at no cost, however because it is copyrighted it must not be used as part of another program. Freeware is not the same as free software.

Shareware is software which is distributed on a trial basis for a limited period, usually 30 days. The user can try the software for free during the trial period but must purchase it, if they want to continue using it, after the trial period expires.

Information: Copyright, licensing, multi-licensing

Copyright
Information on the World Wide Web is subject to copyright which you must not infringe. If you reproduce text or a photo on your website without obtaining the permission of the author, you will have broken copyright laws and may be prosecuted.

Software licences
In the purchase of software you are purchasing only a licence to use the software according to an End User Licence Agreement. By accepting the terms and conditions of the licence.

If you break the terms of this agreement, for example by copying the disk when it is not permitted, you are committing an offence of computer theft.

Software licences vary. Here are examples of different types of licence:

Single licence
This allows the software to be installed on one computer only. You must not copy the program onto another computer.

Site licence
This permits software to be installed on a specified number of machines. The software must not be copied on more computers than those specified in the site licence. These licences vary regarding the definition of site, so be careful that you read the agreement carefully.

Multi-user licence
A client-server network is a single network version of the software program which is stored on the server. When purchasing software for the network you purchase a copy for the server and then a multi-user licence for the number of clients running on the network. This software allows up to the limit specified in the licence conditions and denies access to any additional clients. If more clients are required to use the software than your licence permits you need to upgrade the existing multi-user licence.

Information: Electronic mail

Electronic mail (email) is an electronic method of sending messages and data from one computer to another across a network. Electronic mail is faster and more secure than post and you can send the same message to many people without incurring the costs. Microsoft's email applications are called Outlook and Outlook Express.

Here you open Microsoft Outlook in order to send an email.

Method

1   Click on **Start**.
2   Go to **Programs**.
3   Select **Microsoft Outlook** or double-click on the Microsoft Outlook icon

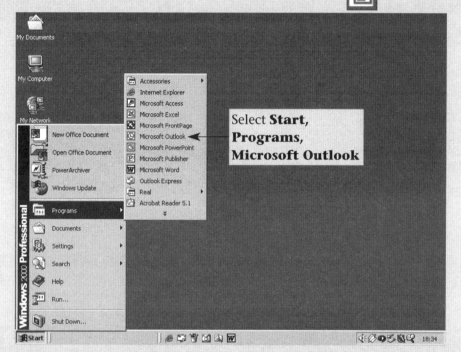

Figure 5.14 Selecting Microsoft Outlook

When opening Microsoft Outlook the following screen will be displayed:

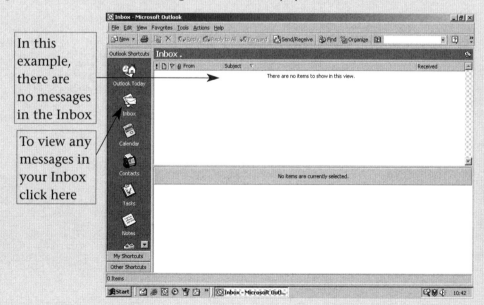

Figure 5.15 Microsoft Outlook window

The Inbox window should be displayed on the screen. If you do not see the same window as shown, click on **View** in the menu bar and move to Current view and click on **Messages**.

Task 5.8   To send an email

With Microsoft Outlook open you will now send email.

Method

I   Click on **New**. The following screen will be displayed.

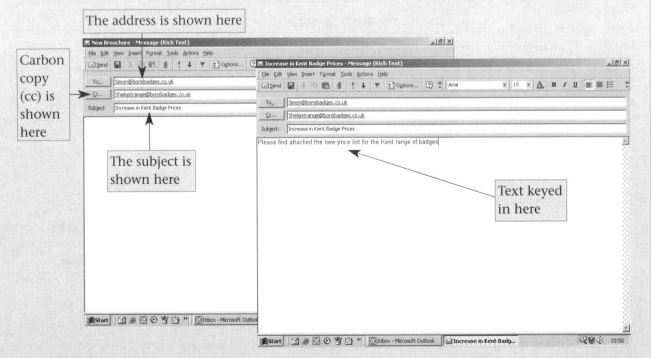

Key in the email address of the person or persons you want to send the email to

Key in the email address of the person or persons you want to send a copy to

Key in the subject of the email here

Type in your text here

Figure 5.16 Message window

2   In the **To ...** dialogue box key in the email address.
3   In the **Cc ...** dialogue box key in the email address of the person you want the email to be copied to.
4   In the **Subject** dialogue box key in the subject of the email.
5   Finally, type your text in the windowpane.
     Figure 5.17 shows an email address, carbon copy, subject entered and text added in the windowpane.

The address is shown here

Carbon copy (cc) is shown here

The subject is shown here

Text keyed in here

Figure 5.17 Adding the recipient(s), subject details and text to email

Information: Attachments

An attachment is a file which has been appended to the electronic message. The attachment can be a variety of file formats, including, for example, a word-processed file, database file, music file or video file. When the recipient receives the attachment with the email they can, provided they have compatible software, load the file which has been sent.

Task 5.9   To send an attachment

Sometimes you need to send an attachment with the email. This is how to do it.

Method

I   Key in the email address, carbon copy (if required), subject and text.

2   Click on the paper clip to attach a file.

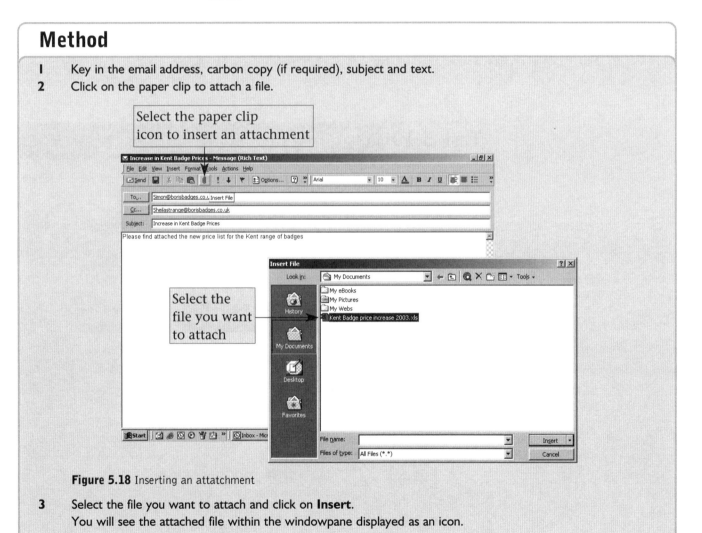

Figure 5.18 Inserting an attatchment

3   Select the file you want to attach and click on **Insert**.
You will see the attached file within the windowpane displayed as an icon.

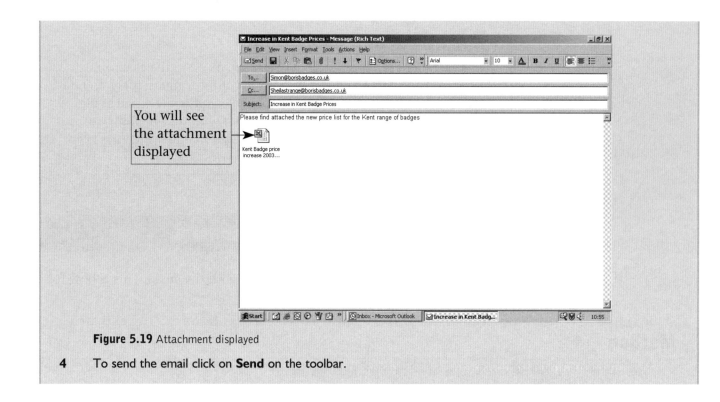

You will see the attachment displayed

Figure 5.19 Attachment displayed

4   To send the email click on **Send** on the toolbar.

Task 5.10   To open an email

Method

I   Select the message by double-clicking anywhere on the message title in your Inbox.

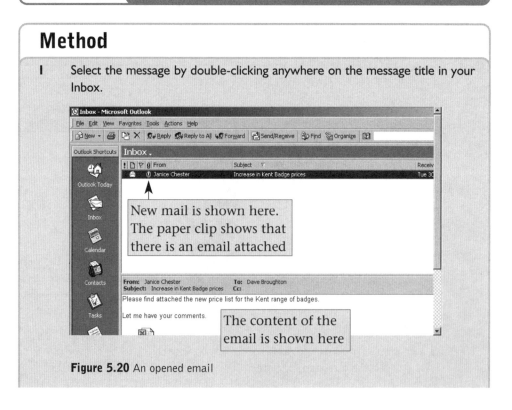

New mail is shown here. The paper clip shows that there is an email attached

The content of the email is shown here

Figure 5.20 An opened email

Task 5.11   To open an attachment

When you receive email it will be displayed in the Inbox. The paper clip indicates that there is an attachment with the message.

Method

I   To open the attachment, double-click on the attachment icon or right-click on the icon and select **Open** (Figure 5.21).

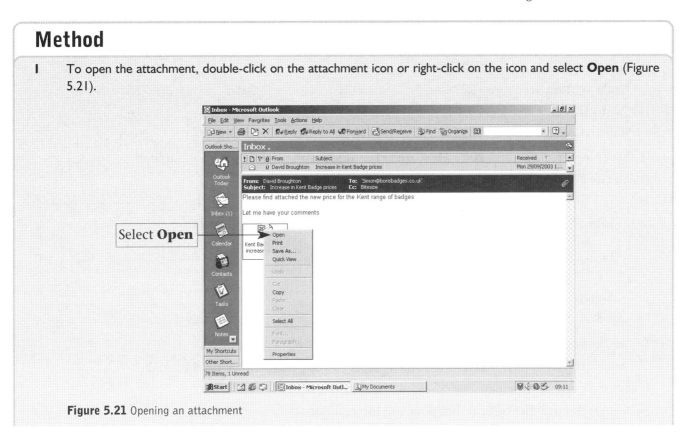

Figure 5.21 Opening an attachment

Task 5.12   To save an email

Saving an email message is the same as saving any document in Microsoft Office.

Method

1   Select **File** from the menu bar.
2   Select **Save As** and give the document a name.
3   Click **OK**.

Task 5.13   To save an attachment

Method

1   Right-click on the attachment.
2   Select **Save As** from the File menu and give the file a name.
3   Click on **Save**.

→ Practise your skills 1

1 Create a new folder called **Sales**.

2 Set the permissions for this folder to allow other users to access it.

3 Enter the following information into a spreadsheet:

Sales 2003 Bosham Range of Badges Number of Sales

Salesperson	January	February	March	April
Sally Won	1254	3568	4809	5000
Paula Winton	2222	6421	9642	7532
David Drive	6911	9132	8123	2143
Roberto Duarte	3311	1325	7511	2368

4 Save the spreadsheet as **2003 First quarter sales**, and save it in the Sales folder.

5 Create a new mail message and key in the following text:

> John
>
> Please find attached the quarterly figures you requested.
>
> Simon

6 Address the email (your tutor will provide you with a suitable address).

7 Attach the 2003 First quarter sales spreadsheet to your email and send the email.

8 Print a copy of the email.

9 Search the Internet to find the following information:

a Where is Bosham situated and which king lived there?

b Who invented the hovercraft?

c Who invented judo?

d Which is the world's longest river?

e What is the lifespan of a giraffe?

10 Add the web page containing the answer to 9e to your favourites.

→ Check your knowledge

1 What is the difference between a WAN and a LAN?

2 What is a workstation?

3 What is a client server?

4 What are the advantages and disadvantages of network computers?

5 How would you protect the confidentiality of someone's information on a network?

6 What is required for connecting to the Internet?

7 What do the following mean: URL, ISP, Intranet, protocol?

8 What is an Internet browser?

9 What do you understand by copyright?

10 What does cc mean on an email message?

Consolidations 4–5

Consolidation 4

Jane Hooper has joined Boris Badges in the office and she requires new folders to be created for her administration work.

1 Create a new folder called **Jane Hooper**.

2 Create a sub-folder in the Jane Hooper folder called **Memos**.

3 Create the following memorandum and save the file as **Memo1** in the Memos sub-folder.

Memorandum

To: Andy Lines

CC: Sarah James

From: Paul Murray

Date: 10/01/2004

Re: New member of staff

I would like to introduce Jane Hooper who has joined the Office Team as from Monday 19th January 2004.

4 Set the attributes of Memo1 to read only.

5 Create a shortcut to the file on the desktop.

Consolidation 5

1 Go to the Heinemann site at www.heinemann.co.uk

2 Bookmark the page as a Favorites.

3 Print the web page.

4 Copy a selection of the text into Microsoft Word and save the file as **New text**.

5 Open Microsoft Outlook and type in the following message:
Please find the attached file New text.

6 Attach the file New text and send to one person in your class group.

7 Rename the file New text to **Changed text** and send the file as an attachment with the following email message to three people in your group.
Please find the attachment Changed text.

8 Search for books on ICT on the Heinemann site.

9 Bookmark a different page as a Favorite.

10 Copy a selection of the text into Word and add a new title for the text.

11 Print out a selection of text from the web page and email this to four people in your group.

Maintaining your computer

You will learn to

- Identify cleaning procedures related to IT equipment
- Install input and output devices for use
- Select a printer for use as a default printer
- Configure a printer for economy

Information: Maintenance and health and safety

It is important that you regularly clean and maintain your computer equipment. Otherwise it will look dirty and may become a hazard. Dirty equipment distracts from the rest of the environment, if that itself is kept clean. Lack of maintenance may also increase the chances of things going wrong with the equipment.

The following information aims at helping to improve the appearance of the working environment and minimising the failure of equipment.

Maintaining hardware – Cleaning

Keeping computer equipment clean creates a good impression and reduces the likelihood of faults.

How often you clean the equipment will depend on the working environment. Hardware, such as the computer case, should not need frequent cleaning. A once-a-month inspection and clean should be enough, whereas the computer screen will need cleaning every day or every week depending on the environment.

The following provides a guide on keeping clean the external parts of the computer and the peripherals.

Keyboard

The keyboard is used most of the time so must not be neglected. Remember to inspect and clean it regularly. Lack of maintenance can lead to an accumulation of dust building up between the keys, which can result in the keys sticking together. You can minimise this by using a dust cover when the keyboard is not in use and making sure that you have clean fingers, as any dirt will transfer onto the keys as you type.

You should **not**:

- eat near the keyboard as the crumbs may fall between the keys
- drink near the keyboard, as spilt drinks are not only a potential safety hazard but can cause problems with the keyboard which are very difficult to rectify.

To clean the keyboard, turn the keyboard over and gently tap on the back. This should dislodge most of the dust and debris which has fallen between the keys. To remove any stubborn debris lodged between the keys you can purchase specialised tools which use compressed air to gently remove the debris.

Clean the keys by using a cotton bud or cotton wool dipped into a proprietary cleaning solution and wiping the surface of the keys. *Do not* use water to clean the keyboard. *Do not* use excessive amounts of fluid and make sure the keys are dry before use.

Think safety!

Switch the computer off.

Mouse

Inside the mouse there is a ball which moves as the mouse is moved across the surface of the mat. This ball makes contact with rollers inside the mouse housing which converts these movements into electrical signals which in turn controls the mouse pointer on your screen. The problem is that when you move the mouse tiny amounts of dust can enter the mouse housing and eventually be transferred onto the rollers. If this happens the mouse will not function properly and the pointer on the screen may not respond accurately to movements of the mouse.

Think safety!

Before cleaning the mouse, unplug it from the back of the computer.

Turn the mouse upside down and you will see a ring on the underside. Move this ring anticlockwise – sometimes there is an arrow to indicate the direction to turn the ring – and carefully remove the ring. Be careful when you remove the ring as the mouse ball will fall out!

Inside the mouse you will see rollers. Any debris on these rollers can be picked off with some tweezers. Make sure all of it is removed, otherwise it will result in poor mouse performance. When the debris is removed you can use a cotton bud dipped in a proprietary cleaner and gently wipe the rollers. Make sure this fully dries out before reassembling the mouse. To reassemble the mouse place the ball back in the mouse housing and replace the ring turning it clockwise to secure it. Reattach the mouse cable to the mouse port at the back of the computer.

Computer case

Don't forget to clean the computer case. It should not need to be cleaned as regularly as other hardware; once a month should be sufficient.

Think safety!

Make sure the computer is switched off and unplugged.

The computer case houses the internal components of the computer, such as the processor, hard drive, memory and graphics, and helps keep these components cool.

If there isn't enough air circulation the internal components could overheat and malfunction. Try to avoid placing the computer too close to walls or furniture as this will block and restrict the ventilation slots, leaving insufficient air to circulate to cool the computer. If dust accumulates, particularly at the back of the computer around the fan housing, it could further restrict ventilation.

If your computer case requires cleaning, use an acrylic cleaner. Do not spray the fluid directly onto the case because of the risk of the fluid entering the inside of the computer case. Spray the cloth first and then wipe the case clean.

Visual display unit (VDU)

A dirty VDU screen may contribute to eyestrain. The screen requires cleaning more frequently than other hardware because the high voltage used within the monitor attracts static electricity and dust will stick more readily to the screen surface.

Use anti-static wipes to clean the surface, as these will help to reduce the amount of dust drawn towards the screen surface. Also, do not forget to clean the rest of the monitor. Do not spray any cleaning solution directly onto the monitor as this will clog up the ventilation slots located at the back.

Printer

Clean the exterior of the printer in the same way as the computer case. The inside of the printer should not normally require cleaning, however if it is required, it can be cleaned with a lint-free cloth.

Installing peripherals to the computer

After unpacking the system unit, keyboard and mouse read the manufacturer's instructions prior to connecting the peripherals. The next section will show how to connect and install common peripherals.

Information: Computer ports

Peripherals, such as the mouse and keyboard, are connected to the computer via ports; you must be familiar with these ports, as you need to know the differences when you connect the peripherals.

Parallel port – also referred to as the LPT port (line terminal printing)
A parallel port is commonly used to connect printers but can be used to connect other external peripherals such as scanners and external drives. It has a 25-pin connection but is less frequently used now since the introduction of the universal serial bus (USB) port.

Serial port – COM port (COMmunications port)
A serial port is used to join external peripheral devices to the computer such as the mouse, plotter or printer. It has either 9 or 25 pins but you can join the two different sized connections together by using an adapter.

USB (universal serial bus) port
The universal serial bus (USB) port has been designed as a standard external port which allows different peripherals, such as modems, scanners and printers, to connect to the computer. It supports fast data transfer rates and you can connect up to 127 devices to a computer. →

PS2 port

This type of connector is used for the mouse and for the keyboard.

Other ports include the monitor port which connects from the video card to the monitor and the game port, to which a joystick or similar device is attached.

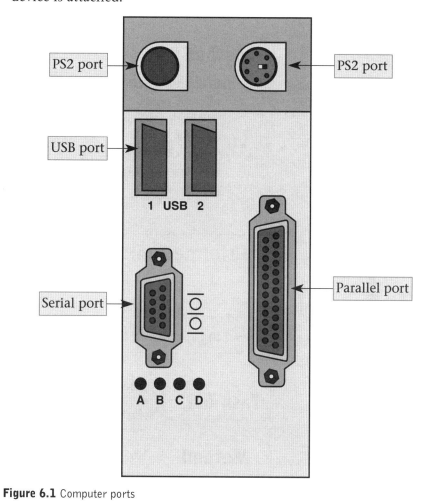

Figure 6.1 Computer ports

When you are familiar with the different types of ports and where they connect together follow the instructions for each of the peripherals below to install them.

In order for a printer to work print cartridges and printer drivers have to be installed.

Task 6.1   Installing printer

In order for the printer to operate

- remove any protective packaging inside the printer
- connect the cables to the printer.

Method

1. Connect the USB or the parallel cable to the printer and connect the cables from the printer to the computer. The printer cable is frequently sold separately from the printer, so do not forget to purchase one if it is not included!
2. Connect the power lead to the printer and when connecting these cables take care not to force them together as this could damage the cable or the port.

Information: Loading paper

For inkjet and laser printers fill the paper tray with paper, ensuring the paper is positioned correctly; the printer will have paper guides, which you can adjust. Do not place too much paper in the tray as this will lead to paper jams.

Hint:

Do not open any sealed package containing printer cartridges until you are ready to install them, as if left unsealed the ink will dry out quickly. Printer cartridges are expensive; you can extend the life of the cartridge by using draft or economy print for drafts and using print preview to proofread documents on screen prior to printing.

Task 6.2   To install ink cartridges

Method

1. Open the printer lid. Keep your fingers clear because the printer cradle will move across as soon as the lid is opened. The lid should stop in the middle of the printer and the compartment where you install the print cartridges will be exposed.
2. Remove the strip which covers the copper contacts of the cartridge. Do not touch these copper or gold contacts as this can damage the ink cartridge.
3. Insert the cartridges into the cartridge compartment. An arrow may be visible which indicates the cartridge alignment.
4. Make sure the cartridge is firmly pushed in and close the printer lid.

Hints:

- For all types of printers ensure you have a spare cartridge ready, it is frustrating when printing a document and the cartridge runs out!
- If using an inkjet printer do not throw your cartridge away until you have a cartridge ready to replace it as the majority of inkjet printers have both a colour and a black ink cartridge, and will only function if both cartridges are present.

Method

1   Install the printer driver for your printer. Insert the CD or disks supplied with the printer. The disk should run automatically. Follow the instructions on screen. If the software does not run automatically:
2   Click on **Start**.
3   Click on **Settings**.
4   Select **Printers**.
5   Double-click on **Add Printer**. The **Add Printer** wizard appears.

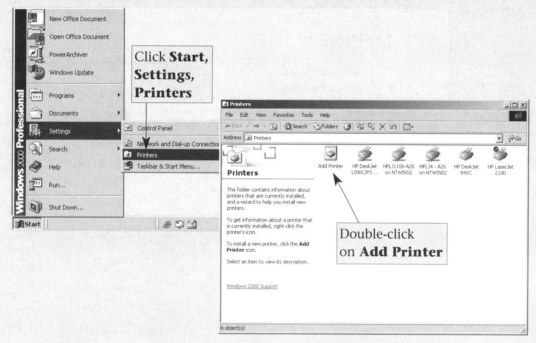

Figure 6.2 Installing printer driver

6   Click **Next**.

Figure 6.3 Add Printer Wizard

7   Follow the instructions on screen.

Task 6.4   How to align the printer cartridges

When the cartridges are installed you may need to align them to achieve best performance. When you align a printer cartridge a test page is printed showing different alignment of lines. Select the best pattern of alignment and confirm this selection by choosing the matching alignment as shown on the screen.

The steps required to align a cartridge can vary depending on the printer type. Printer software should include a toolbox for alignment of cartridges, which is usually found on the taskbar or within the Start menu.

Method

1   Click on **Start**.
2   Select **Settings**.
3   Select **Printers**.
4   Right-click on the printer you want to align.
5   Select **Properties**.
6   Select **Services** (this can vary according to different printers).

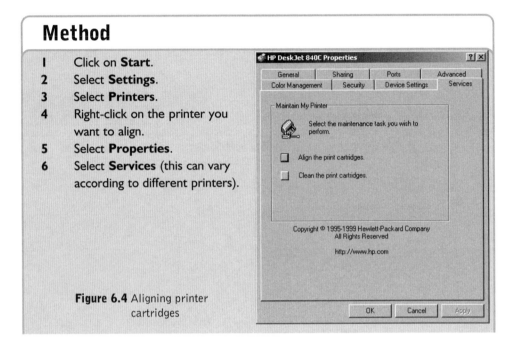

Figure 6.4 Aligning printer cartridges

Task 6.5   Installing laser printer cartridges

Method

1   Switch on the printer and lift the lid.
2   Laser cartridges, like inkjet cartridges, have a plastic strip, which must be removed before installing the cartridge in the printer. Do not remove the strip until you are ready to install it in the printer, as spilt toner can be very messy to clean up!
3   Remove the old cartridge and wipe away any visible excess powder.
4   Insert the cartridge into the printer housing. The cartridge inserts only one way, indicated by an arrow. Do not force the cartridge in.
5   Close the printer lid.

Information: Selecting a default printer

In the case of computer networks, computers can share resources such as printers; you should therefore set a default printer for the computer. There may be several printers available on the network and setting a default printer specifies which printer you will use from the list of available printers. The default printer will print your documents unless you change the default and select a different printer as the default.

Task 6.6 | To select a default printer

Method

1   Click on **Start**.
2   Select **Settings**.
3   Select the printer you want to use as the default and right-click on the printer icon.

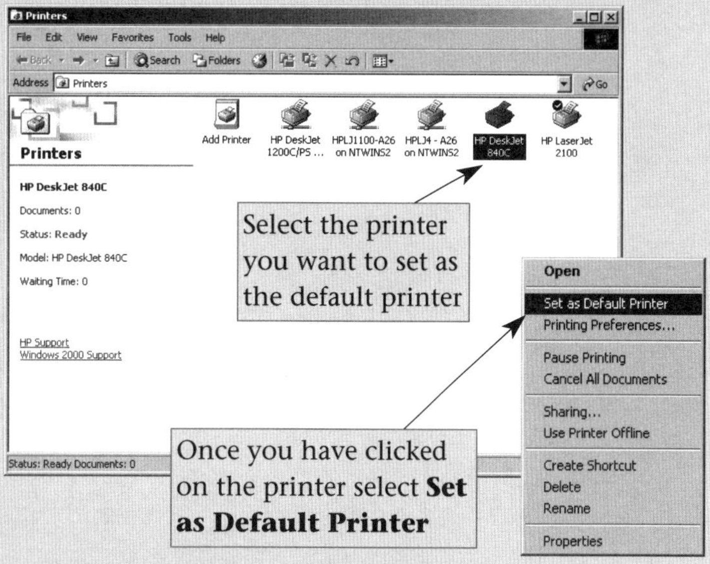

Select the printer you want to set as the default printer

Once you have clicked on the printer select **Set as Default Printer**

Figure 6.5 Selecting and setting default printer

4   A menu will be displayed, left-click on **Set as Default Printer**.

Information: Configure a printer for economy printing

Whilst the price of printers has fallen significantly in recent years ink cartridge prices remain relatively expensive. You can however prolong the life of your ink cartridge by selecting, for those printouts which do not require best quality, the draft or economy (eco) setting for the printer. Draft setting will produce a good copy but it uses less ink, and so will prolong the life of the ink cartridge.

To configure printer for economy

Method

1. Click on **Start**.
2. Select **Settings**.
3. Select **Printers**.
4. Right-click on the printer icon.
5. Select **Printing Preferences**.

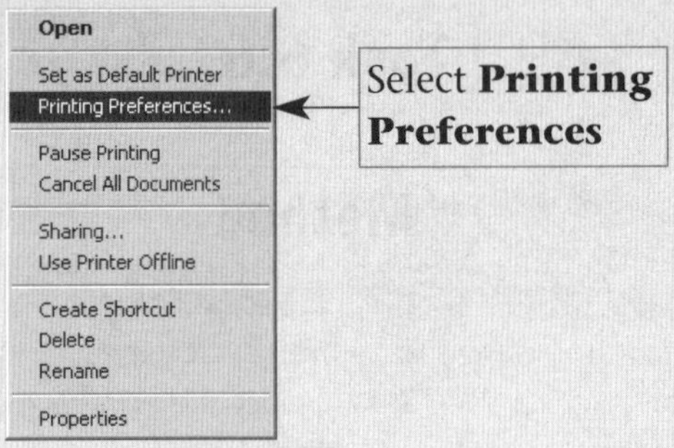

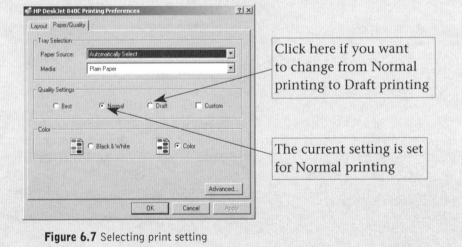

Figure 6.6 Configuring printer

6. Select the **Paper/Quality** tab.
7. Click on **Draft** to change to Draft setting. This will remain on the Draft setting until you change by repeating the steps above and selecting a different printing preference.
8. Select **Apply**.

Figure 6.7 Selecting print setting

Information: Orientation

When you print a document you have the option of printing in portrait or landscape.

Portrait layout

Landscape layout

| Task 6.8 | To select the orientation of the printer and the page order |

Method

1   Click on **Start**.
2   Select **Settings**.
3   Select **Printers**.
4   Right-click on the printer icon.
5   Select **Printing Preferences**.
6   Select **Layout** to change the orientation. Click on either the **Portrait** or **Landscape** button.
7   To change the order in which pages are printed select **Page Order** and click on either **Front to Back** or **Back to Front**.

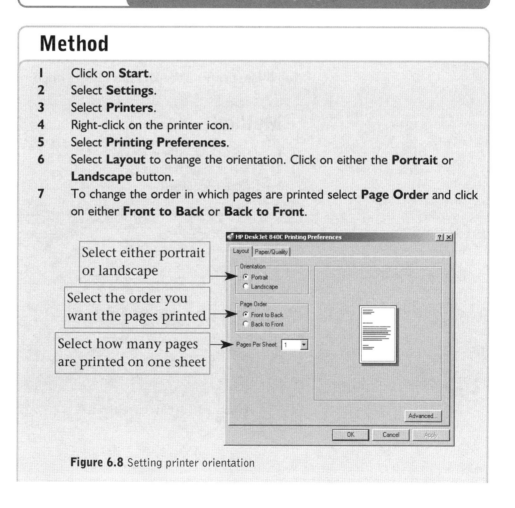

Select either portrait or landscape

Select the order you want the pages printed

Select how many pages are printed on one sheet

Figure 6.8 Setting printer orientation

Task 6.9   To configure your printer for black and white printing

Method

1   Click on **Start**.
2   Select **Settings**.
3   Select **Printers**.
4   Right-click on the printer icon.
5   Select **Printing Preferences**.
6   Select **Black & White** under the Color setting.
7   Select **Apply**.

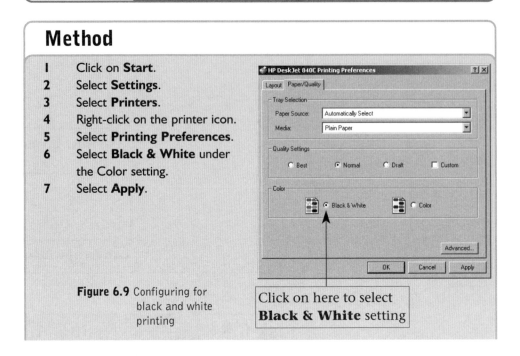

Figure 6.9 Configuring for black and white printing

Click on here to select **Black & White** setting

Task 6.10   Setting the printer to collate

To collate printouts, select Microsoft Office application.

Method

1   Go to **File** in the menu bar.
2   Select **Page Setup**.
3   Click on **Collate**.

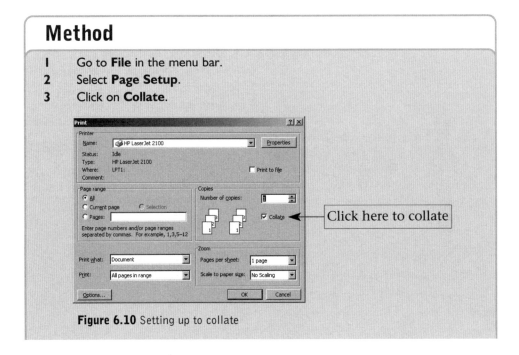

Click here to collate

Figure 6.10 Setting up to collate

Method

1 Click on **Start**.
2 Select **Settings**.
3 Select **Printers**, right-click on the required printer.
4 Select **Printing Preferences**.

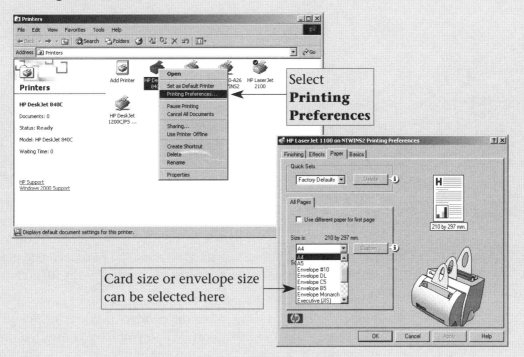

Figure 6.11 Setting printer for printing envelopes or card

5 Select **Paper**.
6 Select the envelope or card size required.
7 Click on **OK**.

Task 6.12 **Set up paper size**

Here you will set up the paper size within the Microsoft Office application.

Method

1 Select **File** from the menu bar.
2 Select **Page Setup**.
3 Select **Paper Size**.
4 Select the pull-down arrow to scroll for paper sizes.
5 Select the envelope size.
6 Click on **OK**.

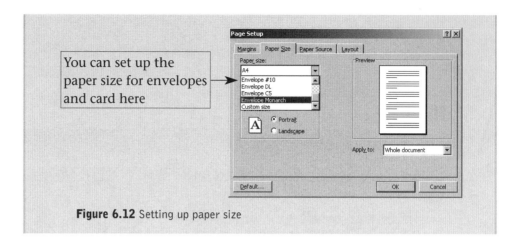

You can set up the paper size for envelopes and card here

Figure 6.12 Setting up paper size

Information: Installing a mouse

Ensure the power is switched off before checking the type of mouse connection you have. The commonest type of connection used is the PS2. This plugs in to the mouse port. Next to the port there is usually a diagram of the mouse to aid identification so as not to confuse it with the keyboard port. The end of the mouse connection and the port may also be colour coded.

Serial ports are either 9-pin or 25-pin connections. The serial mouse has a 9-pin connector which plugs into the serial port at the back of the computer. If there is only a 25-pin serial port available you can join this to a 9-pin connector by using a 9-pin to 25-pin adapter.

When connecting the mouse to the computer port make sure it is properly aligned. Do not force the connector as this will bend the pins and damage the mouse or port. When you have connected the mouse to the mouse port switch on your computer.

Windows should automatically detect that new hardware has been added. If the mouse has special features, make sure you install the additional software drivers, otherwise the features will not operate. Insert the disk supplied by the manufacturer and follow the instructions on screen.

Task 6.13 Configure your mouse

After installing your mouse you can change the way the mouse operates. The following is how you can change your mouse settings.

Method

I	Click on **Start**.
2	Select **Settings**.
3	Select **Control Panel**.
4	Double-left-click on the mouse icon.

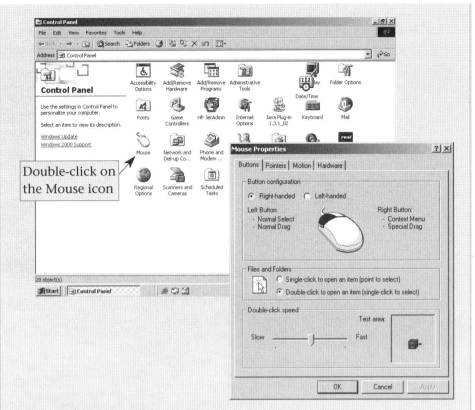

Figure 6.13 Changing mouse settings

5 You will see the mouse properties window has four tabs: **Buttons**, **Pointers**, **Motion** and **Hardware** (Figure 6.14).

Buttons

6 To change the button configuration to left-handed or right-handed select the appropriate box.

7 If you wish to change the way in which files are opened, i.e. with a single or double click, you can change it under **Files and Folders**.

8 To control the double-click speed of your mouse, move the slider under **Double-click speed**, and test click within the test area to view the changed speed.

9 When you have made your changes click on **Apply**.

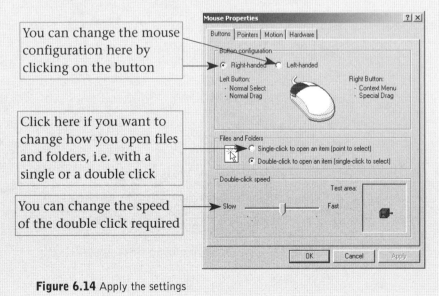

Figure 6.14 Apply the settings

Pointers

10   You may customise the mouse pointer by selecting **Pointers** in the Mouse Properties window and selecting the appearance of the pointer for different conditions.

Select **Pointers** to customise how the mouse pointer is displayed on the screen

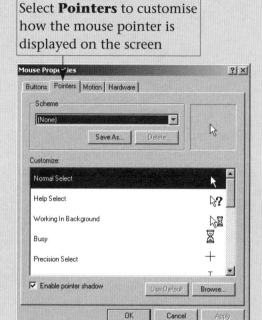

Figure 6.15 Customising the mouse pointer

Motion

11   Select the Motion tab in the Mouse Properties window. You can adjust how quickly the pointer moves by left-clicking on the slider and holding down the button and releasing it to the speed desired. You can also alter pointer acceleration by clicking on either **None** (for no acceleration), **Low**, **Medium** or **High**.

12   Click **OK** when you have made the changes you require.

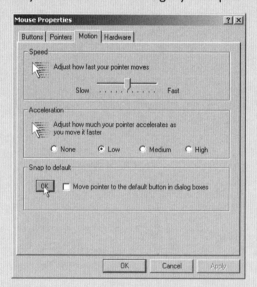

Figure 6.16 Setting the speed

Hardware

Select the **Hardware** tab to choose the mouse type and to troubleshoot any mouse problems.

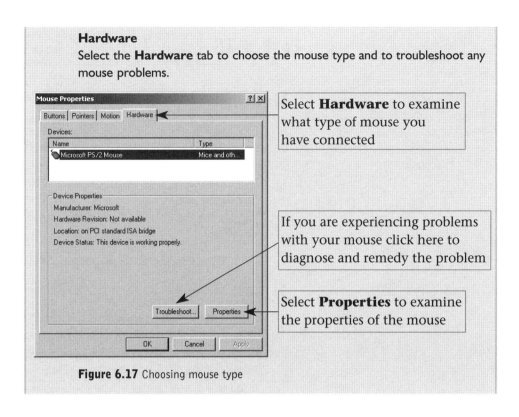

Select **Hardware** to examine what type of mouse you have connected

If you are experiencing problems with your mouse click here to diagnose and remedy the problem

Select **Properties** to examine the properties of the mouse

Figure 6.17 Choosing mouse type

Task 6.14   Installing a keyboard

Method

1   Examine the keyboard connection and the keyboard port on the computer. Both the cable and keyboard port may be colour coded for easier identification of the connection. There may be a picture of a keyboard next to the keyboard port.

2   Determine what type of keyboard connection you have. It will either be a PS2 connector (previously described) or a 5-pin Din connector. If the connector on the keyboard is different to that on the computer, you can purchase an adapter to join them together.

Figure 6.18 Din connector

3   Use caution when you connect the keyboard to the keyboard port. The two connections need to be aligned properly; there is often an arrow on the port and cable to assist in alignment. Do not force the connections together as this will bend the pins and damage the keyboard beyond repair.

4   Switch the computer on, Windows should automatically detect that the keyboard has now been connected to the computer. If the keyboard has non-standard features such as an infra-red keyboard, additional drivers need to be installed in order for the keyboard to function properly. Insert the disk supplied by the manufacturer and follow the instructions on screen.

Task 6.15 Installing a visual display unit

Method

1 Plug the monitor lead into the video port.
2 Connect the power lead into the back of the monitor and insert the plug into the socket. Switch on the socket, then switch on the computer and monitor.
3 Windows should detect that it has found the new monitor.
4 The **Add New Hardware** wizard will be displayed on the screen. Follow the instructions. You will be prompted to insert the driver disk included with your monitor.

If the Wizard does not appear on the screen:

5 Select **Start**.
6 Select **Control Panel**.
7 Double-click on **Add New Hardware**.
8 The **Add New Hardware** wizard will be displayed on the screen.
9 Click **Next** and follow the instructions on the screen.
10 Select the appropriate driver from the manufacturer's list. You may not need to do this as your monitor may use a generic Windows driver.

Task 6.16 To install speakers

Method

1 Different types of speaker units are available. Refer to and check any manufacturer's guidelines for specific instructions on how to install your speakers. A diagram may be included to assist you in connecting the speakers to your computer.
2 Choose a good position for your speakers – refer to the manufacturer's manual.
3 Connect the main speaker to the secondary speaker via the cable supplied. The connection may well be colour coded to aid identification.
4 A cable is connected from the main speaker to the audio line-in plug located at the back of the computer. A diagram may show the device which connects to the plug or they may be colour coded. Do not confuse this with the microphone outlet; it is a common error to plug the speakers into the wrong outlet!
5 Connect the speaker power lead to the power socket.
6 Turn on the speakers and your computer and adjust the speakers' settings, on both the speaker and in Windows, to meet your individual requirements.

→ Practise your skills 1

1 Create a maintenance routine for cleaning your computer.
2 Inspect your computer and follow correct procedures when cleaning the:
   - computer case
   - keyboard
   - mouse
   - visual display unit.

→ Practise your skills 2

1 Add a printer and set the printer as the default printer.
2 Align the printer cartridges.
3 Configure the printer for economy printing.
4 Change the print orientation to landscape.
5 Select the paper size to print card.

→ Practise your skills 3

1 Install a mouse on your computer.
2 Configure the mouse for left-hand use.
3 Change the mouse pointer.

→ Practise your skills 4

1 Connect a keyboard to a computer.
2 Connect speakers to the computer.

→ Check your knowledge

1 What is an LPT port?
2 What is another name for the serial port?
3 USB is Universal Switch Bus. True or False?
4 What is a default printer?
5 Serial ports are either 9 or 26 pins. True or False?

Protecting your computer and customising the desktop

You will learn to

- Describe how to prevent the loss and corruption of data
- Describe the term 'overwrite'
- Explain the terms 'write protection' and 'read-only protection'
- Make backup copies of files and folders
- Use systems tools such as Scandisk and defrag
- Verify a computer desktop configuration, e.g. date and time, volume settings, desktop display settings, desktop default, display options/settings, regional settings, currency
- Describe the advantages and disadvantages of using a screensaver

Information: Preventing loss and corruption of data

Computers should be regularly maintained to ensure that data is secure and reliable. You can undertake preventative measures to protect the security and integrity of data held on your computer. This section outlines some of the steps you may take.

Write protect a floppy

To protect a disk or individual files stored on the disk from being written to, i.e. from being altered or deleted, you can use write protect to prevent any changes being made to the contents. You will be able to read the contents of the disk read-only protection, but not change it.

You can prevent changes being made to your files by either setting the attributes of the file to read only, as discussed in an earlier section, or, if it is a floppy disk, you can make it write protected by moving a small tab located at the corner of the disk.

Write-protect slide
Open to protect disk

Floppy disk

If you move the tab so that a hole is visible the disk is write protected. If you move the tab to close the hole so the disk can be written to, i.e. it will not be write protected, you will be able to edit or delete files stored on it.

Virus checking

A computer virus is a software program which has been written to deliberately create problems on other people's computers. The damage caused varies from annoying simple messages on the screen to corrupting or erasing data held on the hard drive.

Viruses spread from one computer to another in several ways, for example from downloading files from the Internet, from opening e-mail attachments or from loading a virus on an infected disk. Once loaded the virus then spreads quickly and easily to any other computers to which it is attached.

To prevent viruses on your computer install anti-virus software. Make sure that the anti-virus software installed comes from a reputable company, to ensure it is free from viruses! Anti-virus software scans the files stored on your computer for virus infection and will clean or 'disinfect' any viruses it detects. Most anti-virus software has options which you can use to customise which files are checked and how these files are notified and cleaned. The default is the automatic checking of files for viruses, but you can also manually check files individually if required.

Unfortunately there are many different types of viruses and new ones are being created all the time. It is important to ensure that the anti-virus software stored on your computer is kept up to date, otherwise your computer will not be fully protected.

Making backup copies of files and folders

It is important to make backups of your Windows system files and data stored on your disks in case the original files become corrupted or are deleted. Protecting data loss by adopting a systematic approach to backing up your data is preferable to the heartache when important files are lost and the time spent reinstalling software. How often you backup will depend on how often the files are accessed and modified. Files that are in frequent use will require more regular backup than those which are used less often. Your backup routine will therefore vary: some files will require daily backup whereas others may require backing up at weekly or monthly intervals.

There are a number of ways data loss can be prevented. You could, for example, save work and save an additional copy under a different filename in a different location on your disk. If your original file is lost or corrupted you can, depending on the cause of the problem, retrieve the original copy. The problem with storing multiple copies of files on a hard drive is that it will use additional disk space and, if the drive is corrupted, be lost with the original. This can be avoided if data is backed up on another storage medium. You can backup onto a floppy disk, however these have a smaller storage capacity than other storage medium. Use other types of storage which have larger capacity to backup your files, such as a tape backup unit, a CD-R, CD-RW disk or zip disk.

Task 7.1   Backing up files

Backup your files using Windows Explorer and by copying data onto another storage medium, however there are backup utility programs available to make this task easier. In Windows a backup program can be located in **System Tools**.

Method

1   Click on **Start**.
2   Select **Programs**.
3   Select **Accessories**.
4   Select **System Tools**.
5   Select **Backup**.

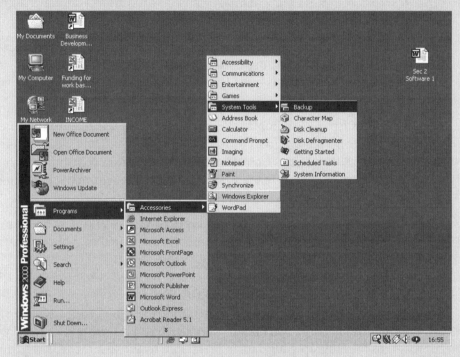

Figure 7.1 Selecting backup

6   This will display the welcome screen. If you do not see the screen as shown in Figure 7.2, click on the first tab, **Welcome**.
7   Select the **Backup Wizard** (Figure 7.2).

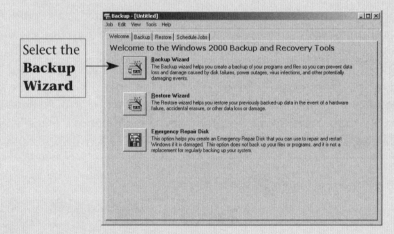

Figure 7.2 Selecting the Backup Wizard

8   Select **Next**.

Select **Next**
to continue

Figure 7.3 Backup Wizard

9   Select what you want to backup (Figure 7.4).

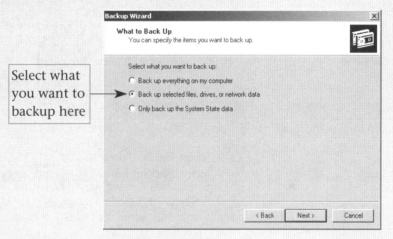

Select what
you want to
backup here

Figure 7.4 Selecting data to backup

10   Select where you want to backup to.

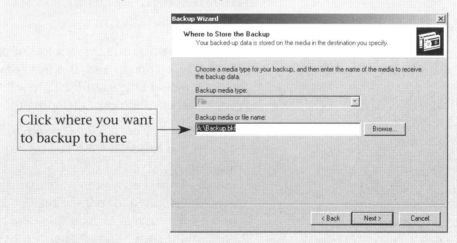

Click where you want
to backup to here

Figure 7.5 Location of backup data

11 Check your selections are correct.

12 If incorrect click on **Back** and make amendments. If correct select **Finish**.

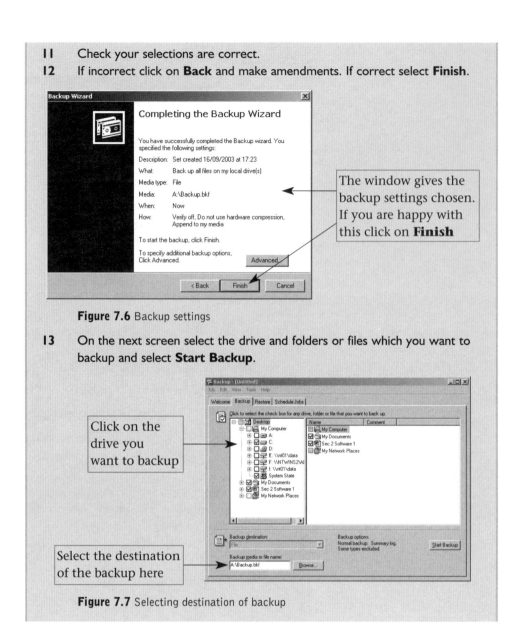

Figure 7.6 Backup settings

13 On the next screen select the drive and folders or files which you want to backup and select **Start Backup**.

Figure 7.7 Selecting destination of backup

Information: Protection from environmental damage

Backups are important to prevent loss of data, but it is also important to protect the computer and data from environmental damage. Larger operations should take additional precautions to protect data from all adverse weather conditions, including the following.

- **Fire**   Keep backups of data stored in a fireproof cabinet or the data should be securely backed up onto a server in a different location.
- **Flood**   Protect data from water damage. Computer equipment should be located in well-maintained buildings and, if located near a water source such as the sea or a river, additional precautions such as flood defences should be in place to protect the equipment in the event of flooding. →

- **Lightning** Lightning can cause power surges which can seriously damage computer equipment. Protect the hardware from these damaging electrical surges by using an UPS, an uninterrupted power supply.

Information: Using system tools

Maintain your Windows software to ensure optimum performance. There are two useful Windows utilities which can be used to check the performance of your computer.

Scandisk
Use Scandisk to check disk drives for errors and to repair any faults identified. If you are having problems with your computer's hard drive, run Scandisk to fix logical or physical errors on the disk to prevent further corruption occurring. As a guideline, the Scandisk utility should be run as part of the maintenance routine at least once every two months to check for data integrity on your hard disk. You can however run the utility more frequently if required.

Disk defragmentation (Defrag)
This is used to arrange the order of data on disk drives. Data may not be arranged sequentially on the drive; it may be held in different places on the disk. If data is held in different locations on the disk it takes time for the disk to spin to that location and the read-write heads of the disk drive to access the data. Data which is adjacent to each other takes less time for the disk to spin to that location and consequently for the read-write head to access it.

Task 7.2 | Using Scandisk

Method 1

1   Right-click on **My Computer**.
2   Select **Explore**.
3   Right-click on the drive you wish to scan.

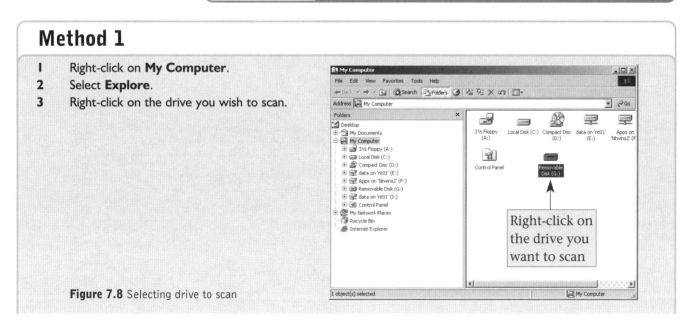

Right-click on the drive you want to scan

Figure 7.8 Selecting drive to scan

3   Select **Properties**.

Figure 7.9 Selecting properties

4   Select **Tools**.
5   Select **Check Now**.

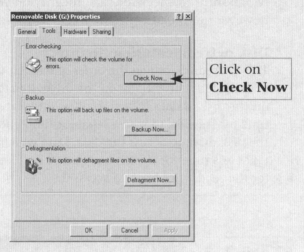

Figure 7.10 Selecting option to check

6   Select your required **Check disk options**

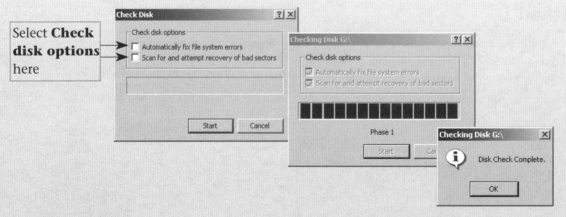

Figure 7.11 Checking the disk

7   When the check is run a status bar showing the amount completed will be displayed.
8   When complete select **OK**.

Method 2

This is the method to use for Windows 95/98, Windows Millennium.

1   Click on **Start** on the taskbar.
2   Select **Programs**.
3   Select **Accessories**.
4   Select **System Tools**.
5   Select **Scandisk**.
6   Click on **Standard** to check files and folders for errors or select **Thorough**, which performs the Standard check and scans the disk surface for any errors.
7   Click on **Start**.

Task 7.3   To defragment the disk drive

Method

1   Double-click **My Computer**.
2   Highlight the hard drive by clicking once on the icon representing the drive.
3   Right-click on the drive.
4   Select **Properties**.
5   Select **Tools**, **Defragment Now**.

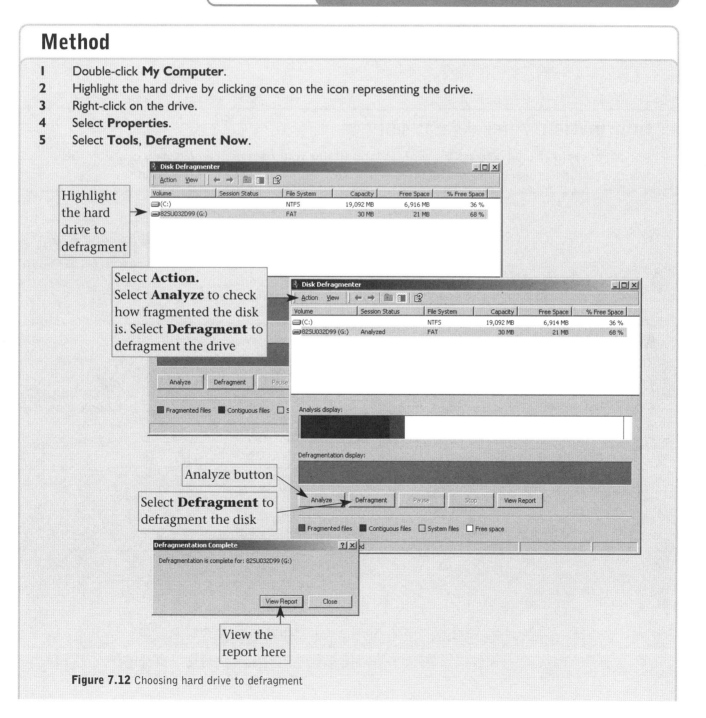

Figure 7.12 Choosing hard drive to defragment

6   To check whether the drive is fragmented select **Action**, then **Analyze**, or click on the **Analyze** button.

7   The colour-coded key displays the status of the files on the display.
When the analysis is complete an Analysis Complete window will appear.

8   To view the report click on **View Report**.

9   To defragment the disk select **Defragment** or you can defragment by selecting either **Action**, **Defragment** or select the **Defragment** button, as shown in Figure 7.12.

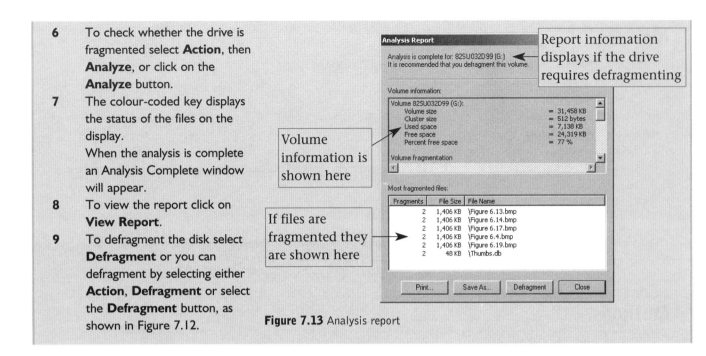

Report information displays if the drive requires defragmenting

Volume information is shown here

If files are fragmented they are shown here

Figure 7.13 Analysis report

Information: Alter default settings

You can alter the default settings for your desktop to suit your own preferences. You can alter the default desktop settings if they are incorrectly set, for example if the time is inaccurate.

Task 7.4	Setting the date and time

This involves changing the clock or date displayed.

Method

1   Click on **Start**.
2   Select **Settings**.
3   Select **Control Panel**.
4   Double-click on the **Date/Time** icon to select the Date/Time Properties. The **Date & Time** tab should appear.

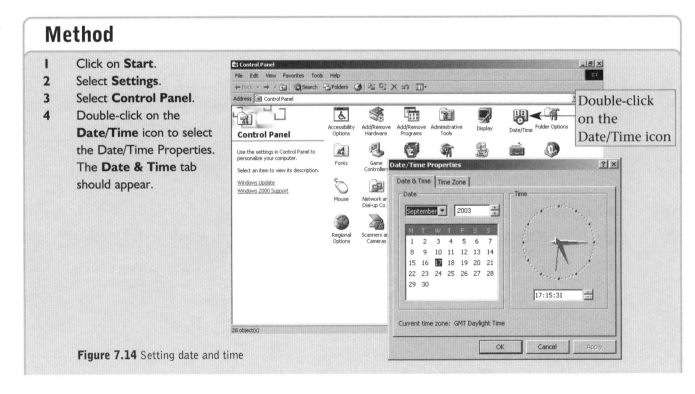

Double-click on the Date/Time icon

Figure 7.14 Setting date and time

5   Adjust the date by clicking on the required date for the day, month and year.

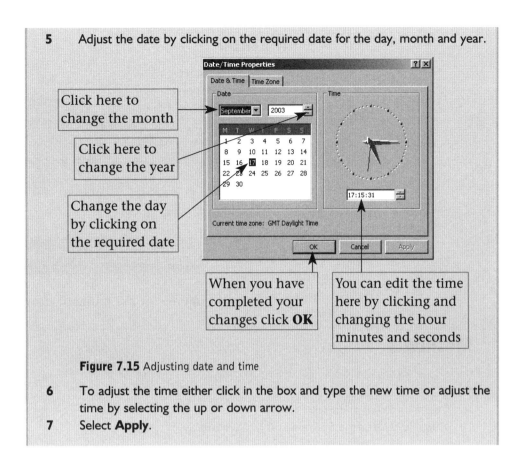

Click here to change the month

Click here to change the year

Change the day by clicking on the required date

When you have completed your changes click **OK**

You can edit the time here by clicking and changing the hour minutes and seconds

Figure 7.15 Adjusting date and time

6   To adjust the time either click in the box and type the new time or adjust the time by selecting the up or down arrow.

7   Select **Apply**.

Task 7.5   To adjust the time zone

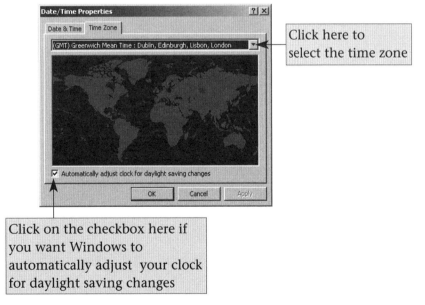

Click here to select the time zone

Click on the checkbox here if you want Windows to automatically adjust your clock for daylight saving changes

Figure 7.16 Adjusting time zone

Method

1	Click on **Start**.
2	Select **Settings**.
3	Select **Control Panel**.
4	Double-click on the **Date/Time** icon.
5	Click on the **Time Zone**.
6	Use the pull-down arrow to select the time zone required.
7	Click on **OK**.

Task 7.6 | Setting the volume

You can set the volume for the sound devices installed on your computer.

Method 1

1	Click on **Start**.
2	Click on **Settings**.
3	Click on **Control Panel**.
4	Double-click on the **Sounds and Multimedia** icon.

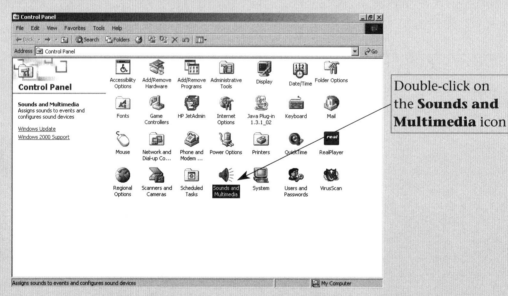

Double-click on the **Sounds and Multimedia** icon

Figure 7.17 Selecting from the control panel

5   Click on the **Audio** tab.

Select the **Audio** tab

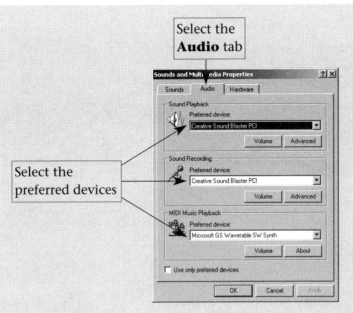

Select the preferred devices

Figure 7.18 Choosing preferred devices

6   Select **Volume**. This is located underneath **Sound Playback**. To alter the volume for each of the sound devices displayed you need to select and change **Volume** beneath each device.

7   You will see **Volume** settings.

8   Move the mouse onto the volume sliders and, holding the mouse button down, move the slider up or down to set your choice.

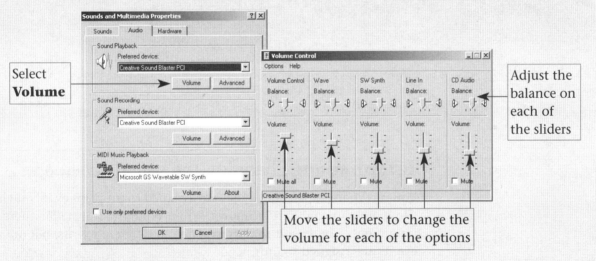

Select **Volume**

Adjust the balance on each of the sliders

Move the sliders to change the volume for each of the options

Figure 7.19 Setting the volume

9   Close the dialogue box by clicking on the **Close** button at the top right of the **Volume Control** menu.

10   Click **OK**.

Method 2

I	Double-click on the **Audio** icon.
2	Click on **Open Volume Controls**.
3	Repeat steps 7–10 above.

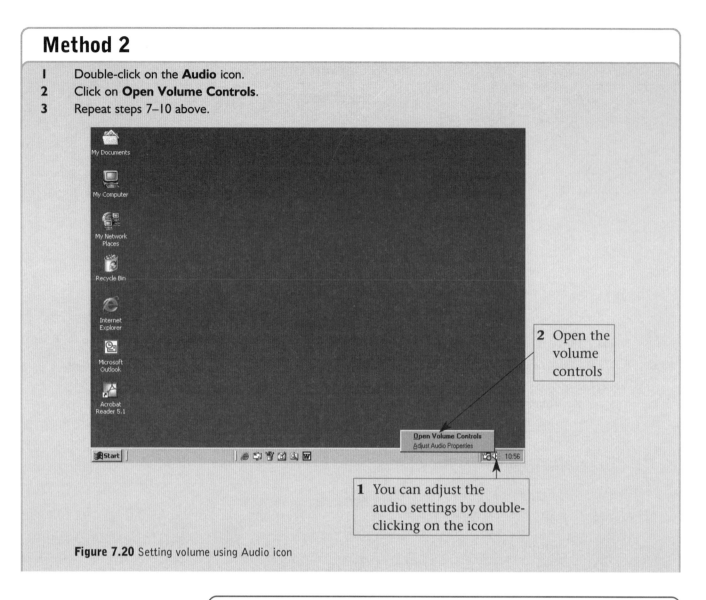

Figure 7.20 Setting volume using Audio icon

Information: Changing the sound scheme

You can change the sounds that are assigned to program events such as Close program and Exit Windows. When Windows is installed there are a number of default sounds assigned to different events, but not all events are assigned sounds.

Task 7.7   **Changing sounds**

A different sound can be assigned to an event or you may select your own sound.

Method

I	Click on **Start**.
2	Click on **Settings**.
3	Click on **Control Panel**.
4	Double-click on the **Sounds and Multimedia** icon.

5   Select the **Sounds** tab.
6   In the **Sound Events** windowpane select the sound event you wish to assign
     a sound to.
7   In **Scheme** select the pull-down arrow to choose a scheme.
8   If the scheme is not shown select **Browse** to search for the sound to use.

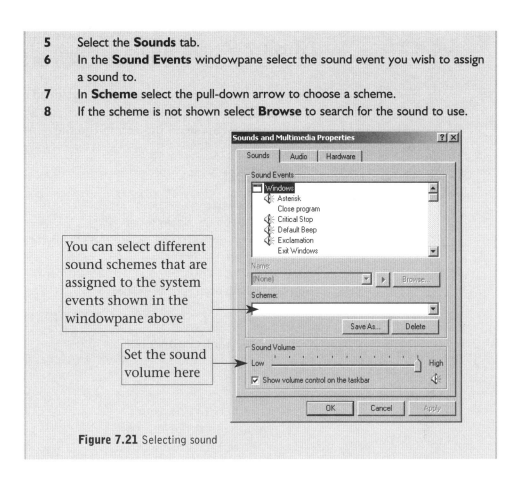

You can select different
sound schemes that are
assigned to the system
events shown in the
windowpane above

Set the sound
volume here

Figure 7.21 Selecting sound

Task 7.8   Setting the desktop display options and settings

Here you will learn to change the display settings on your computer.

Method

1   Click on **Start**.
2   Select **Settings**.
3   Select **Control Panel**.
4   Double-click on the **Display** icon.
     You will see six tabs:
     Background, **Screen Saver**,
     Appearance, **Web**, **Effects**
     and **Settings**.

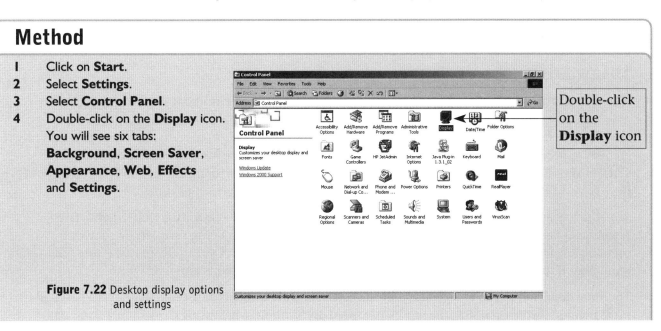

Double-click
on the
Display icon

Figure 7.22 Desktop display options
and settings

You can change the background picture displayed on the screen. There are several default pictures available or you can select your own picture by clicking on **Browse** and selecting the file containing the picture.

Method

1	Follow steps 1–4 above.
2	Click on the **Background** tab.
3	Select a background picture from the list or choose **Browse** to search for a picture.
4	Click on **OK** after you have chosen your preferred background picture or HTML document as wallpaper.

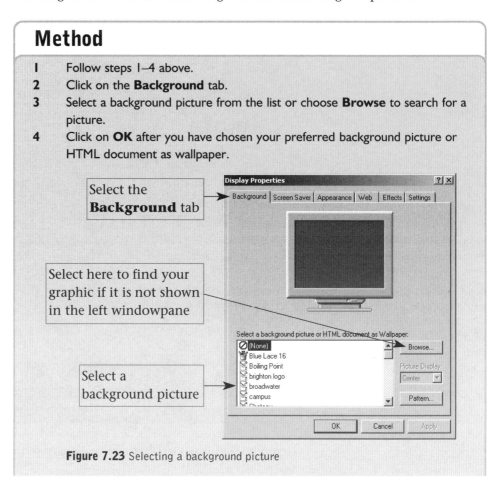

Select the **Background** tab

Select here to find your graphic if it is not shown in the left windowpane

Select a background picture

Figure 7.23 Selecting a background picture

Information: Screensavers

When there has been no input from the keyboard or mouse for a period of time a moving picture may appear on the screen; this is called a screensaver. In older cathode ray tube monitors, an image left on the screen for a long period of time damaged the screen; the image would appear permanently etched on it. Screensavers solved this problem by starting a moving image after a specified period. Current monitors are more technologically advanced, so no longer require screensavers. In addition, they have a sleep mode in which the monitor switches off after a period of time.

Screensavers are now used either to temporarily hide the screen display or for amusement. The screensaver can be password protected to protect the screen details being revealed by someone pressing a key or moving the mouse. If a password is used to protect your screen, make sure you remember it, because the screen will be protected until the password is entered.

There are disadvantages to using a screensaver. Today they are more sophisticated than in the past and use more memory, which can slow the processing speed. In addition, when using CD-writers a screensaver could interrupt the burning process, resulting in errors. When using defragmentation, screensavers can cause the process to halt and start again. Turn off the screensaver prior to running this utility.

Task 7.10 | Selecting a screen saver

Method

1 Click on **Start**.
2 Click on **Settings**.
3 Click on **Control Panel**.
4 Click on the **Display** icon.
5 Select the **Screen Saver** tab.
6 In the **Screen Saver** dialogue box select a screensaver.
7 Click in the **Password Protected** checkbox to assign a password for the screensaver.
8 Click on the **Wait minutes** box for the screensaver to be displayed. Increase or decrease this by either typing in the minutes or using the up or down arrows to change.
9 Click on **Apply**.

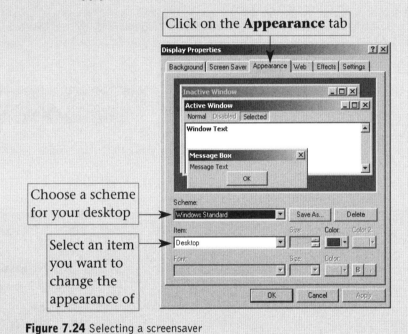

Figure 7.24 Selecting a screensaver

Task 7.11 | Changing the appearance of items

Here you will learn to change the appearance of various items on the desktop, for example the icons, the size and colour of text.

Method

1 Click on **Start**.
2 Select **Settings**.
3 Single-click on **Control Panel**.
4 Double-click on the **Display** icon.
5 Click on the **Appearance** tab.
6 Select the **Scheme** to change.

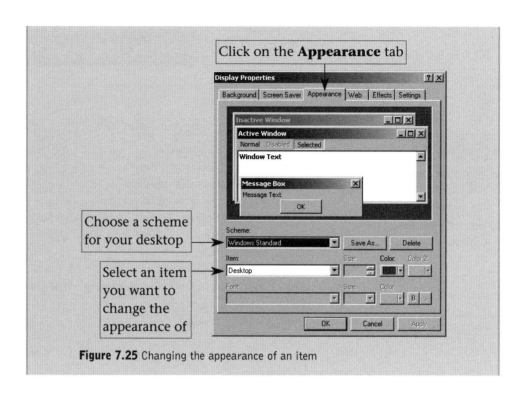

Click on the **Appearance** tab

Choose a scheme for your desktop

Select an item you want to change the appearance of

Figure 7.25 Changing the appearance of an item

Task 7.12   To view desktop as web page

You can set up your desktop to be viewed as a web page.

Method

1   In Display Properties click on **Show Web content on my Active Desktop**.
2   Select **Apply**.

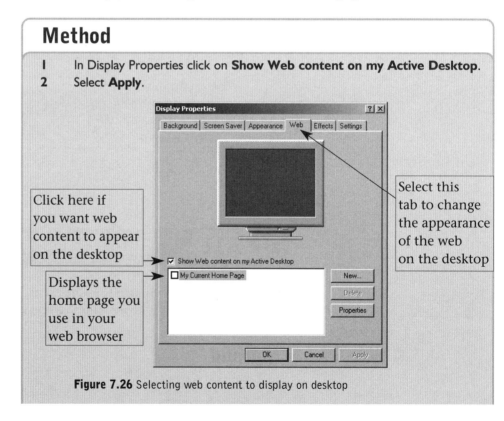

Click here if you want web content to appear on the desktop

Displays the home page you use in your web browser

Select this tab to change the appearance of the web on the desktop

Figure 7.26 Selecting web content to display on desktop

Task 7.13 Altering effects – icons

Here you will use the Effects tab to alter the way some of the icons are displayed, including their size, font and whether the contents are shown as the icon is dragged.

Method

I   In Display Properties click on **Effects**.
2   Make your selections by clicking on the checkboxes.
3   Select **Apply**.

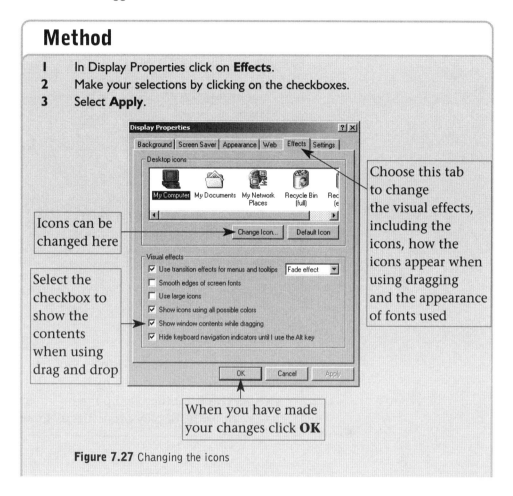

Icons can be changed here

Select the checkbox to show the contents when using drag and drop

Choose this tab to change the visual effects, including the icons, how the icons appear when using dragging and the appearance of fonts used

When you have made your changes click **OK**

Figure 7.27 Changing the icons

Task 7.14 To change settings

You use the Settings tab to change the number of colours used in the display, and the number of pixels displayed in the screen area. It is also used to alter the settings for the graphics adapter used in your computer.

Method

I   In Display Properties click on **Settings**.
2   To change the colours select the number of colours by using the pull-down arrow.
3   To alter the screen size move the slider to increase or decrease the screen area.
4   Select **Apply** to apply the new settings.

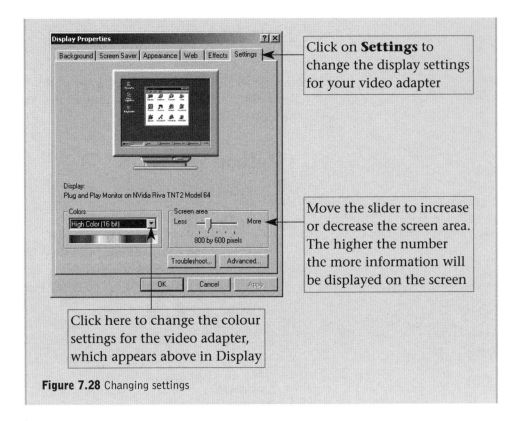

Click on **Settings** to change the display settings for your video adapter

Move the slider to increase or decrease the screen area. The higher the number the more information will be displayed on the screen

Click here to change the colour settings for the video adapter, which appears above in Display

Figure 7.28 Changing settings

Information

You can access the same Display Properties box by clicking the right-hand mouse button in a blank area of the desktop and selecting **Properties** from the pop-up menu. You can then make any changes you want to the display properties as shown in the previous tasks.

Task 7.15   Changing regional settings

The Windows operating system is used worldwide. Within the control panel you can select Regional settings to alter the standard language setting, how numbers, currency, time, date are displayed, and the language setting on the keyboard.

Method

To select regional settings:

1	Click on **Start**.
2	Select **Settings**.
3	Double-click on **Control panel**.
4	Double-click on **Regional Options**.

The standard language
setting here

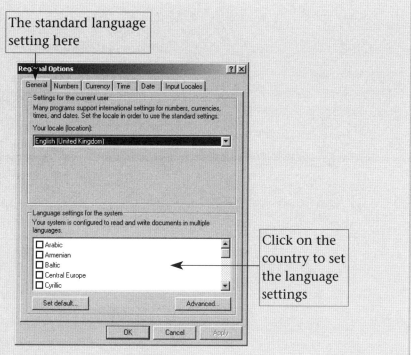

Click on the
country to set
the language
settings

Figure 7.29 Changing regional settings

Use the **General** tab to select the international settings for numbers, currency, date
and time for the country displayed in the Your locale dialogue box. Use the pull-
down arrow to change the country.

Numbers

Use the **Numbers** tab to select how numbers are displayed. Use the pull-down
arrows to make your selections.

Click here to set the
Numbers display

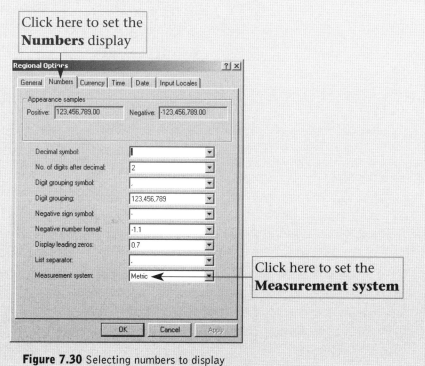

Click here to set the
Measurement system

Figure 7.30 Selecting numbers to display

Currency

Use **the Currency** tab to select how currency is displayed. Use the pull-down arrows to make your selections.

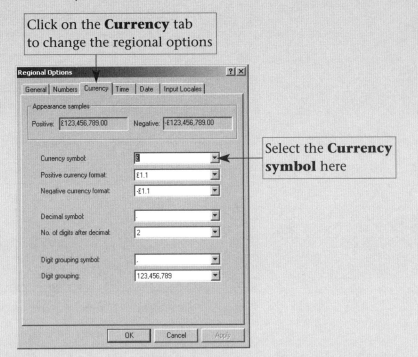

Click on the **Currency** tab to change the regional options

Select the **Currency symbol** here

Figure 7.31 Selecting currency to display

Time

Use the **Time** tab to select the time format. Use the pull-down arrows to make your selections.

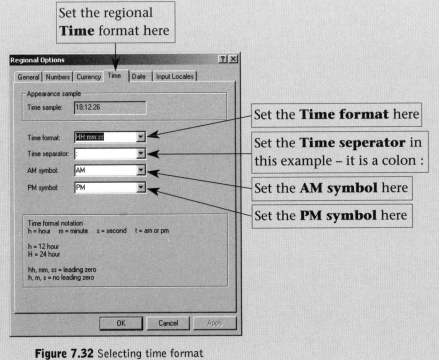

Set the regional **Time** format here

Set the **Time format** here

Set the **Time seperator** in this example – it is a colon :

Set the **AM symbol** here

Set the **PM symbol** here

Figure 7.32 Selecting time format

Date

Use the **Date** tab to select the date format. Use the pull-down arrows to make your selections.

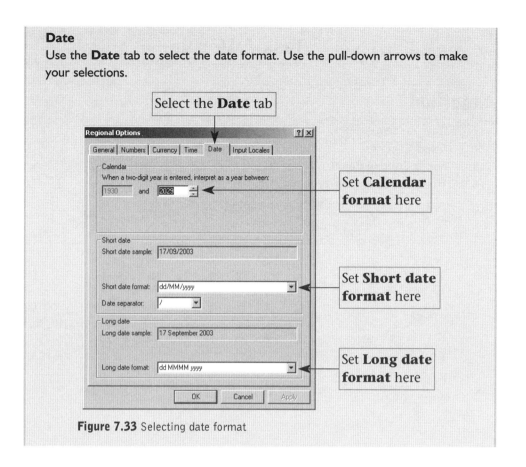

Select the **Date** tab

Set **Calendar format** here

Set **Short date format** here

Set **Long date format** here

Figure 7.33 Selecting date format

Information: Input locales

Windows provides multiple language and keyboard support, which you can select using input locales. The keyboard layout is set as default to the language used but this can be changed if a different keyboard layout is required. If you are working in more than one language you can have more than one input language installed and then switch between these languages by using hot keys.

You may change the key sequence to switch between languages by selecting **Change Key Sequence**.

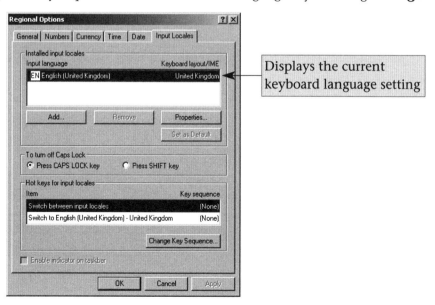

Displays the current keyboard language setting

Figure 7.34 Setting the language

When you have finished making your changes on each regional settings tab, click on **Apply**.

Method

1   Click on **Start**.
2   Select **Settings**.
3   Select **Control Panel**.
4   Double-click on the **Keyboard** icon.

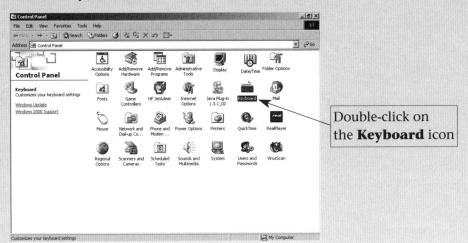

Double-click on
the **Keyboard** icon

Figure 7.35 Changing keyboard properties

Speed

Select the **Speed** tab to change how characters are repeated when you hold down a key and how quick the character is repeated.

You can change the amount of time that passes before a character is repeated when you hold down a key. Click on the slider

You can change how quick the character repeats when you hold down a key

You can change the speed of the cursor blink here

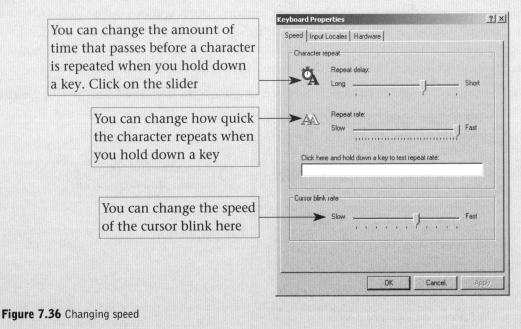

Figure 7.36 Changing speed

Input locales

Select the keyboard language currently installed here for different input locales.

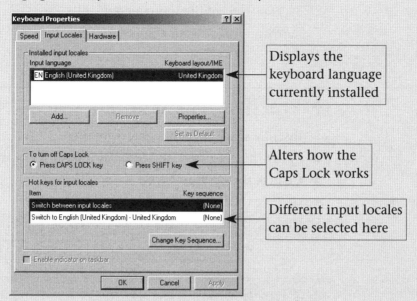

Figure 7.37 Selecting keyboard language

Type of keyboard

You can select the type of keyboard used. The default is a standard keyboard with 101/2 keys, but if a different type of keyboard is required and is attached, select it here.

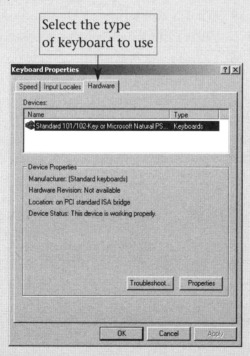

Figure 7.38 Selecting type of keyboard

Note: Confirm your selections by clicking on **Apply**.

→ Practise your skills 1

1 Backup selected files onto a floppy disk.
2 Run Scandisk on your computer.

→ Practise your skills 2

1 Install a screensaver on your computer.
2 Verify the date, time and keyboard settings on your computer.
3 Change the desktop background.
4 Change the icons to large size.
5 Change the speed of the character repeat on your keyboard.

→ Check your knowledge

1 What is a virus?
2 How do you write protect a floppy disk?
3 Describe how to protect data from fire.
4 What is the purpose of the Scandisk utility?
5 What is the purpose of a screensaver?
6 How do you change the display properties?
7 Which storage medium would you use to backup large files?

Has a Tutor seen your blue RECORD OF PROGRESS card recently?

IF NOT ASK A TUTOR TO CHECK YOUR PROGRESS NOW

Health and safety

You will learn to

- Explain the term 'ergonomics'
- Maintain a clean, safe and tidy environment
- Identify health and safety precautions when using a computer
- Identify hazards and report them to the appointed person
- Identify injuries common in a bad working environment
- Explain the causes of visual and physical fatigue when using VDUs and use methods of reducing fatigue and excessive eyestrain when operating a VDU
- Describe the elements and practices that create a good working environment

Information: Ergonomics

Ergonomics is the scientific study of the working environment, but is not confined to the study of the office; it is relevant to every place where people are present. It examines systems and efficiency in the workplace and how the environment can be designed and improved to protect the health and safety of individuals. Ergonomics includes the design of computer equipment to standards which minimises stress and discomfort to the user.

Maintaining a clean, safe and tidy environment

Accidents can occur due to poor working conditions or physical injury can result because of the incorrect use of the computer. There are numerous potential hazards in the workplace and identifying them is often common sense, for example keeping the workplace clean and tidy will help to prevent most accidents.

The following are some of the hazards you may encounter:

Obstructions

Anything lying around on the floor can be the cause of an accident. Don't put things down where they may be tripped over; put them away or ensure they are in a position where they cannot cause an obstruction.

Cables should, wherever possible, be placed in trunking or tied up using cable ties to prevent them trailing on the floor.

Manual handling

When manually moving objects ensure that the correct techniques for lifting them are used. If you need to lift something from the ground check first to see if you need help to lift it; do not attempt to move or lift heavy objects yourself. The Manual Handling Operations Regulations 1992 states the responsibilities employers and employees have to ensure safe manual handling.

Electrical

Electricity is potentially dangerous, so it is important to follow some basic rules when using it:

- Ensure that there are sufficient electrical sockets available. Do not overload power points; an overloaded socket is a potential fire hazard.
- Extension cables should not be used as the power points can be overloaded and you can trip over any trailing cables. Use infra-red technology as it reduces the amount of cable and therefore minimises the potential risk.
- Always switch off the power before disconnecting leads.
- Use the correct fuse rating. If the computer equipment develops a fault the function of the fuse is to cut the power to prevent the equipment overheating and catching fire.
- Do not investigate or attempt to repair electrical faults yourself because of the risk of electrical shock. If there is a fault this should be investigated and repaired only by qualified personnel.
- Each year the electrical equipment must be tested by a qualified electrician.
- Do not use poorly maintained or damaged electrical equipment. If you suspect equipment is faulty, turn off the power and report the fault at once.
- Avoid drinking near the computer. Liquids should not be kept near electrical equipment but if there is any spillage it should be cleaned up immediately to prevent electrical shock and short circuiting of the equipment.

Fire

It is important to protect computer equipment and data from fire. Physical preventative measures can be taken, for example in regard to the installation of fire doors, sprinkler systems, fire alarms and placing backups in a fireproof safe. Training should be given to staff in evacuation procedures and fire prevention.

Fires may be caused by carelessness or faults in electrical systems. Report potential fire hazards immediately; do not delay until it becomes a fire. Familiarise yourself with the fire evacuation procedures to enable you to get out safely. If you do use a fire extinguisher, ensure that it is the correct type. Do not use a water extinguisher on electrical fires as it is dangerous because it can result in electrical shock; use powder type extinguishers.

Other hazards

There are many other potential hazards that may contribute to accidents in the working environment. You have a responsibility to take sensible precautions to prevent accidents from occurring. Here are some of the precautions which should be taken.

- Close filing cabinets when you have finished with them.
- Do not pile objects on top of cupboards.
- Do not run, walk.

- Do not eat or drink near your computer.
- Keep your workstation free from clutter and rubbish.

Remember, you must adhere to health and safety rules at work. If you see a hazard you must report it to the appointed person in the organisation; do not leave it to someone else to do. Employees must co-operate with their employer on all health and safety issues.

Check your knowledge

Look at the following picture below and identify the potential hazards it shows.

Figure 8.1 Potential hazards

Health and safety legislation

Health and Safety at Work Act 1974

The Health and Safety at Work Act 1974 is important regarding health and safety legislation in Britain as it outlines the responsibilities we all have to maintain a safe working environment. Health and safety is not only the responsibility of employers; employees and non-employees also have a duty to report potential hazards to prevent accidents occurring. This Act was strengthened in 1992 by:

- **Management of Health and Safety at Work Regulations (1992)**
  This places a statutory duty on employers, with more than five employees, to carry out a risk assessment within the workplace in order to prevent accidents. The risk assessment must be undertaken by a competent person and include the identification of potential hazards and an examination of whether the current procedures in place at work are adequate for the risks involved. The results of the risk assessment must be formally recorded and reviewed regularly. Training must also be given to employees on health and safety in the workplace.

- **Workplace (Health, Safety and Welfare) Regulations (1992)**
  This legislation applies to many different aspects of basic health and safety and welfare issues in the workplace. It requires, for example, that equipment used in the workplace is in good repair; ventilation and lighting is adequate and suitable; work surfaces, furnishings and fittings are clean and fit for their intended use and that there are adequate washing facilities available. Other issues concerning the welfare of the employees are covered in these regulations.
- **Health and Safety (Display Screen Equipment) Regulations (1992)**
  This places a duty on the employer to provide an analysis of workstations to ensure that they are suitable for their purpose. Employers must plan the work of computer users so that they have regular breaks away from the screen. The Act requires that any employee using display equipment on a regular basis can request from their employer an eye test and glasses if special ones are required. Employees should be provided with information on how to use their workstation and should be given training in its use.

Injuries in the workplace
Visual fatigue
If you work too long at a computer you are liable to strain your eyes and become physically tired. Visual fatigue may be caused by:

- **Brightness and contrast controls adjusted poorly on the monitor** If the screen is too bright or the contrast is incorrectly set your eyes will be strained and this can lead to visual fatigue and headaches.
- **Incorrect monitor height and position** Before you use the monitor make sure it is adjusted so that the top of the monitor is level with your eyes. Tilt or swivel the monitor to attain the correct position to suit you.
- **Reflections on screen** Reflections on the screen can cause discomfort as the user strains to look at the screen display. Reflections can be caused by direct sunlight. To avoid glare, do not place the monitor facing a window. If this isn't possible use blinds or curtains to eliminate glare. Light can be reflected off walls and furniture. Use non-reflective material to minimise the risk of glare.
- **Unsuitable lighting** Poor lighting causes tiredness and eyestrain. Light should not shine directly on to the screen and it should be sufficient for the size of the working area. Diffused lighting is preferable to fluorescent lighting, which causes glare and reflections.
- **Flicker and blur on screen** If the visual display is faulty, what is seen could be blurred or the screen could flicker. Adjust the controls or replace the faulty screen. If the monitor is faulty do not attempt to repair it yourself, as this can be dangerous, even with the power switched off. Only a qualified electrical technician should repair computer monitors.

Physical fatigue
Physical fatigue may be caused by factors such as:

- using the computer without taking regular breaks
- bad posture
- poor heating and ventilation
- excessive noise.

Repetitive strain injury

When working for a long time on your computer without regular breaks you risk straining your muscles, which can result in a painful condition called repetitive strain injury or RSI. The sort of tasks which lead to this condition and stress are keying in data entries repetitively or using the mouse over a long period of time. Avoid RSI by taking regular breaks from the computer to rest your muscles, this will reduce tiredness and achieve more.

Poor posture

Poor posture can lead to discomfort or physical injury. It is important that the monitor, chair, keyboard and desk are correctly adjusted for the individual user. There are ways to avoid problems caused by poor posture.

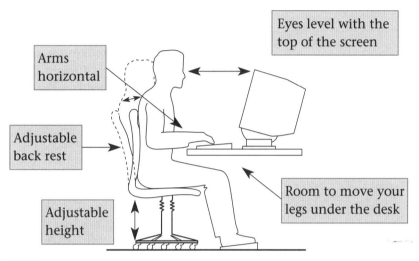

Figure 8.2 Correct posture

- Ensure there is sufficient legroom under the desk. Do not store items under the desk which may obstruct leg movement.
- A footrest may be helpful.
- Change position frequently. Take a break, get up and stretch your legs.
- Adjust the chair to a comfortable position for typing. Keep your arms almost horizontal and adjust the screen so that your eyes are approximately at the same height as the top of the computer screen.
- When using the keyboard don't overstretch to use it. Move the keyboard into a comfortable position and make sure there is sufficient space in front of it. Try to learn how to type correctly. This is more efficient and you will distribute the stress across your fingers rather than concentrating it on one or two fingers. Be gentle with the keys! Avoid hitting the keys too hard, as this will only cause additional stress and injury.
- Use a document holder to reduce the stress on your neck when you look down.

Equipment and environment

The following guide to the working conditions can help to avoid many of the problems of health and safety which can occur in the workplace.

- **Monitor**   A poorly adjusted monitor causes not only visual fatigue but can lead to physical injury as the user strains to look up or down at the screen. The monitor should be adjusted to suit the height of each user.

- **Chair** To maintain a correct posture and avoid the problems of backache the chairs should have the following characteristics:
  - They should provide sufficient support for the back of the individual user and be adjustable in both height and seat backrest.
  - They should not be fixed and should be have castors to allow easy movement.
- **Keyboard** A poorly adjusted keyboard risks straining a user's wrists and fingers, which could lead to injury. Keyboards should be placed at the correct height and should be separate from the computer screen. Underneath the keyboard there are feet which can be adjusted to set the keyboard at an angle or to keep it flat to meet the preferences of the user. There must be sufficient room for the keyboard, and in front of it to support the wrists when not typing.
- **Incorrect desk height** The desk should be large enough to accommodate the computer and peripherals, such as scanner and printer, and leave sufficient working space. It should be adjustable for the height of the user and allow sufficient space for the chair.
- **Poor ventilation and heating** Physical discomfort can be caused if the office is too hot or too cold. Do not place a computer in a room too close to a radiator that is too hot. Do not place the computer near an outside door as it may make you uncomfortably cold. It is uncomfortable for the user, and the computer equipment itself can be damaged if there are too many variations in room temperature.

  There should be sufficient air circulation in the room – it is unpleasant and unproductive to work in stuffy, airless surroundings.
- **Avoid excessive noise** Excessive noise can lead to headaches and user stress; keep the noise down. Computer equipment manufactured in the last few years meets tougher noise regulations; in the past older dot matrix printers were very noisy and their sound had to be reduced by using acoustic hoods.

Information: A good working environment

A good working environment is one which has been ergonomically planned taking account of the different needs of each individual. It should be designed to achieve the following.

- It must be clean and safe from hazards and meet current health and safety standards.
- Equipment should be regularly checked and maintained.
- Procedures must be reviewed and updated where required.
- Users should receive sufficient training to ensure that current practices are met.
- Individuals should take personal responsibility to ensure they adhere to all health and safety regulations and take personal care to avoid visual and physical injury.

→ Check your knowledge

1 Describe what makes a good working environment.

2 What is ergonomics?

3 Describe the Workplace (Health, Safety and Welfare) Regulations, 1992.

4 State four ways you can reduce physical fatigue.

Multiple-choice test and practice assignments

To achieve this unit you need to pass one set assignment and a multiple-choice paper which covers the underpinning knowledge. The multiple choice is pass or fail grade and for the set assignment you can attain a pass, credit or distinction grade.

Multiple-choice test

1 A kilobyte is equal to
   a 1024 bytes
   b 100 bytes
   c 1000 bits
   d 1002 bytes

2 A CPU is a
   a client program unit
   b complex process unit
   c central processing unit
   d computer processing unit

3 Which of the following describes RAM?
   a permanent memory
   b a temporary storage
   c non-volatile
   d you cannot write to it

4 Which of the following is **not** an advantage of a network?
   a file sharing
   b sending electronic mail
   c sharing hardware
   d complex to maintain

5 What is GUI?
   a guaranteed user interface
   b graphical user interchange
   c graphical uniform interface
   d graphical user interface

6 Which is not a data format in a database?
   a date
   b text
   c memo
   d align

7 The software used to display web pages is called
   a modem
   b internet
   c browser
   d e-commerce

8 What is a search engine?

    a software that finds viruses

    b a network operating system

    c a program used to search for web pages

    d windows file management software

9 Which statement is **not** one of the eight principles of the Data Protection Act? Data should be:

    a fairly and lawfully processed

    b processed for unlimited purposes

    c not kept for longer than necessary

    d processed in line with your rights

10 Which of the following statements is correct?

    a You do have to pay a fee if you want to use shareware after a trial period

    b You don't have to pay a fee if you want to use shareware after a trial period

    c Freeware can be distributed at a profit

    d Freeware allows you to change the code

11 Which file is not a graphics format?

    a jpeg

    b tiff

    c matt

    d bmp

12 Which of the following does not prevent loss or corruption of data?

    a backing up your files

    b copyrighting your files

    c using a virus protection software

    d protecting files from environmental damage

13 A screensaver can

    a reduce the monitor purchase price

    b be different on each computer

    c permanently place an image onto the screen

    d turn the computer power off

14 A disadvantage of a network is

    a cost of initial equipment

    b e-mail

    c sharing of hardware

    d team working

15 To maintain privacy on the network you should

    a not change your password frequently

    b change your password frequently

    c write your password down

    d use your name as the password

16 To set the file attributes to write protection

    a hides the file from view

    b sets a password on the file

    c allows a user to look at the file and change it

    d does not allow changes to the data

17 Hazards should be reported to the

    a anointed person

    b appointed person

    c associate person

    d allotted person

18 Which of the following is a safe practice in a computer room?

    a trailing cables across the floor

    b blocked fire exits

    c use of electrical adapters

    d adjustable computer chairs

19 Which of the following describes a good practice in the workplace?

    a continue working at a computer until the job is finished

    b have frequent breaks away from the computer

    c you can use any type of chair to work at a computer

    d position your computer screen facing the window

20 RSI is a type of

    a storage device

    b network protocol

    c physical injury

    d application program

Practice assignment 1

Before you start your assignment make sure you have carefully read all the instructions. If you are unsure as to what is required, check with your tutor before you start the assignment.

Time allowed: 4 hours

Introduction

A brief scenario of the task is given and the assignment is broken down into six parts. You must observe health and safety at all times.

1 Task A requires you to work with hardware.

2 Task B requires you to use file management.

3 Task C requires you to use the word processing application using mail merge.

4 Task D requires you to use a spreadsheet application.

5 Task E requires you to use a spreadsheet application.

6 Task F requires you to identify health and safety precautions when using a computer and identify correct cleaning techniques for computer equipment.

> **Scenario**
> You are employed within the Marketing Department of Boris Badges, a company that produces badges and stationery. You assist in promoting the company's range of products. You also have responsibility to ensure that all staff working in the Marketing Department follow company guidelines in relation to safe working practices with IT equipment, and follow correct procedures for cleaning IT equipment.

Task A

The company has bought some additional computers to facilitate the introduction of the new range of badges.

1   Produce a checklist for new staff on how to assemble a computer. Include the keyboard, visual display unit, speakers and appropriate connections for each device.

2   Connect a printer to the computer and load the correct paper size.

3   Set the printer as the default printer and produce a screenshot labelled **Screenshot 1**, showing the printer as the default printer.

4   Change the volume settings for the audio (sound playback) to the maximum setting. Produce a screenshot to display the new settings and label this **Screenshot 2**.

Task B

1   Create a new folder called Badges and create sub-folders within it called Kent, Sussex, Hants and Surrey. Produce a screenshot showing the sub-folders called **Screenshot 3**.

2   Move the letter to Mr Prior (as shown) to the Kent folder. Produce a screenshot that shows you have moved the file and label it **Screenshot 4**.

Boris Badges Limited
Dimension Street
This Town
AAA 123

Mr P Prior
Glebe House
Rectory Lane
Puddletown
BBB 345

18th September 2003

Dear Mr Prior

Many thanks for your letter dated 16th September 2003. The pin type for your Kent badge is no longer in production but there is an alternative fastening in our catalogue reference 298B, on page 13.

I trust this will meet your requirements and look forward to hearing from you.

Yours sincerely
BORIS BADGES LIMITED

3   Create a copy of this letter and move this to the Sussex folder.

4   Rename this file **Sussex Badge**. Produce a screenshot labelled **Screenshot 5** to show the letter inside the Sussex folder.

5 Copy the Sussex file letter to a floppy drive and rename this **Sussex copy**. Produce a screenshot of this and label it **Screenshot 6**.

6 Delete the Surrey folder as this is no longer required. Produce a screenshot labelled **Screenshot 7** to show the file has been deleted.

Task C

1 Create a letter outlining a delay in the distribution of the badges and use the database file **Customers in Hants** as the data source (Figure 9.1).

Figure 9.1 Customers in Hants database file

2 Create a new email addressed to the Marketing Manager and a copy to the General Office on the Sussex range of badges.

3 Attach one copy of the letter in the email.

Task D

Open the spreadsheet file Kent Badges (Figure 9.2).

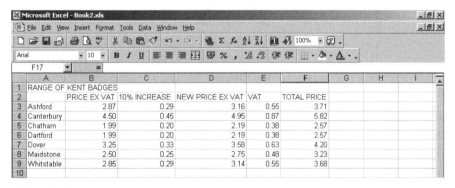

Figure 9.2 Kent Badges spreadsheet

1 Increase the total price by 2.5%.

2 Print a copy of the spreadsheet formulae to fit on one page.

3 Decrease the new price by 1% and print out the spreadsheet. Save the spreadsheet as **Kent New Prices**.

Task E

1 Produce a screenshot labelled **Screenshot 8** to display the attributes of the Kent New Prices file.

2 Make the Kent New Prices file read only. Produce a screenshot labelled **Screenshot 9** to show this.

3 Create a shortcut to the desktop. Create a screenshot to show this and label it **Screenshot 10**.

Task F

1 Produce three suggestions for reducing RSI when using a computer.

2 Outline the correct procedure on cleaning a keyboard and computer screen or mouse.

Practice assignment 2

In the following assignment you will practise some of the skills you have learned.

> **Scenario**
> Boris Badges produces a range of badges for various clubs and societies. You have been asked to assist in the administration.

Task A – Maintain a computer

1 A new computer has been acquired for the General Office. You have been asked to assemble it. Connect together the system unit, keyboard, mouse and printer.

2 Set the mouse to left hand use.

3 Verify that the keyboard language is set to English (United Kingdom). Produce a screenshot showing this.

4 Produce a memo which outlines *three* causes of RSI and how these can be prevented. Save this memo as **Health1**.

Task B – File management

1 Create new folders on the computer and name them Human Resources, Sales and Marketing, Production and General Office.

2 In each of these folders create separate sub-folders called Letters, Memos and Reports.

3 Produce a screenshot which displays the Reports sub-folder in the Production folder.

4 Copy the memo Health1 into the memo sub-folder of the Human Resources folder.

Task C – Spreadsheet

1 Open a spreadsheet application.

2 Enter the following data:

Salesperson	North	South	East	West	Total sales
Fred Bloggs	1111	5643	3244	7776	
John Smith	4321	9861	1572	2229	
Paula Jones	5412	9853	1119	9086	
Charlotte Black	9411	5421	8641	8907	

3 Create formulas to calculate the total sales, average, minimum and maximum sales for each salesperson.

4 Format the numbers to currency.

5 Create a formula to calculate a 2.5% commission on total sales.

6 View the formulae and print out a landscape copy.

7 Save the file as **January Sales** and save in the Sales and Marketing Reports sub-folder.

8 Close the spreadsheet application.

Task D – Electronic mail

1 Use an email application to create an email to the Sales Director and copy to the Sales Manager with the following text:

Please find attached January Sales Figures for the Sussex range of badges.

2 Attach the January Sales spreadsheet to the email.

3 Print a copy of the email.

Task E – Database and mail merge

1 Create a database with the following fields:

Customer ID

Title

Firstname

Surname

Street

Town

County

Postcode

Badge required

2 Enter the following records:

Mr	Fred Nicks	134a The Avenue	Bognor Regis	Sussex	PO86 4FR	Sussex
Mrs	Christine Tuck	65 The Street	Horsham	Sussex	HO76 9YY	Sussex
Mr	Paul Hammond	56 Oak Street	Canterbury	Kent	CT65 9HH	Kent
Mr	Juan Santos	88 Beech Avenue	Folkestone	Kent	FO86 1WW	Kent
Mr	David Chan	76 Harold Street	Folkestone	Kent	FO73 4RD	Kent
Miss	Julie Reed	12 Broad Avenue	Worthing	Sussex	BN99 1AA	Sussex
Ms	Heather Way	44 Apple Road	Worthing	Sussex	BN66 3SS	Sussex
Mrs	Mary Legge	1 The Walkway	Chichester	Sussex	CO11 4RR	Sussex
Mrs	Toni Smythe	1 Levett Road	Westbourne	Sussex	WO91 7GG	Sussex
Mrs	Heather Paterson	45 Twig Road	Ashford	Kent	RAS45 7YY	Kent

3 Save the file as **January Enquiries** in the Sales and Marketing Reports folder.

4 Produce a query to find all customers interested in the Sussex badges.

5 Save the query as **Sussex Customers**.

6 Close the database application.

7 Type in the following letter:

Dear

Thank you for your interest in the Sussex range of badges. Your order will be despatched to you within 14 days.

Yours sincerely

Valerie Johns

Boris Badges

8 Using the mail merge facility insert the data from the Sussex Customers file into the appropriate position in the letter.

9 Mail merge the document.

10 Print the mail-merged letters.

11 Save the file as **Mailmerge Sussex** in the Sales folder.

Solutions

Section 1

Check your knowledge 1

1 Input, Process, Output, Storage
2 False
3 False
4 True
5 False

Check your knowledge 2

1 See page 7.
2 See pages 9–11.
3 See pages 9–11.
4 See page 10.
5 See pages 10–11.
6 See page 11.

Section 2

Check your knowledge 1

1 A jagged underline indicates that there are grammatical errors in your text.
2 Access the **AutoCorrect** options and select the **Capitalize first letter of sentences** option.
3 A record is all the details and information about an item, person, etc. in the database. The fields are the individual parts which make up the details.
4 A cell is a box where you enter data.
5 See page 46.
6 The main document in standard letter format which will be merged with a data source of names and addresses of recipients.
7 See page 76.

Check your knowledge 2

1 See page 39.
2 See page 40.
3 Integrated software comprises separate application programs compatible with each other, allowing for data from one application program to be easily used by another. Microsoft Office with its individual word processing, spreadsheet, database and presentation graphics programs is an example of integrated software.
4 Projection devices magnify the display from the computer and project it on a large screen. They are used whenever a larger screen projection is required. Projection devices are used within the classroom for teaching purposes, for running PowerPoint presentations at conferences, presentations and exhibitions.
5 Bitmaps are graphical images made up from a series of dots (pixels). Microsoft Paint is an example of a program which uses bitmaps to create images.

   Vector graphics, unlike bitmaps, comprise solid lines based on xy coordinates. The advantage of using vector graphics is that they do not become distorted when enlarged.
6 Digital cameras have distinct advantages over film cameras in that you can take many pictures and reject those not required, saving the time and expense of developing the film.

Section 3

Check your knowledge

1 Details. The right windowpane displays all folders and displays additional files underneath the folders. In addition this view contains details of the file name, size, type, and modified date and time.
2 False
3 See Problem 3, page 108.
4 See Problem 1, page 107.
5 Provides a place to easily locate your programs.
6 Click on **Start**.

   Select Settings and click on **Taskbar and Start** menu.

   Select the **Advanced** tab.

   Click **Add**.

   Go to location.
7 The ability to have more than one program open at the same time and to be able to switch between them.
8 See Problem 5, page 108.
9 A small picture of the file.
10 Ctrl+P

Section 4

Check your knowledge

1 File attributes give information on how the file is to be used by the operating system.

2 An abbreviation used in searching for files.

3 False

4 Include all data. For example WP.* would include files called WP with any extension.

5 There are further sub-folders available.

Section 5

Check your knowledge

1 A local area network describes the connection of computers via cabling or wireless technology within a small geographical area, up to a distance of one kilometre. LANs are located in a small location, typically in a single building.

A wide area network describes the connection of computers through telecommunication links such as the public telephone system, over distances of more than one kilometre.

2 A computer, which is connected to a network, is called a workstation.

3 A client server is how programs and services are distributed from the server, which is a powerful computer, to the 'client', which is a workstation.

4 The most significant advantage is sharing.

Using a file server reduces the software cost, as programs held on the file server can be shared by all the workstations. In addition, it is easier to maintain integrity of data as all users can access the same data. This centralisation is also beneficial in that it is easier to control the security of programs and files.

Networks have some disadvantages, including the initial cost to install the network and the need for technical knowledge to maintain it.

If the main server develops a problem this can affect the whole network system.

5 Passwords and setting access rights.

6 To connect to the Internet you will need the following hardware and software:

computer, modem, telephone line connection, Internet Service Provider (ISP), web browser

7 URL (Uniform Address Locator), ISP is an Internet Service Provider, Intranet is an internal network, a set of rules for controlling the sending and receiving of data and error checking.

8 A web browser is a software program that allows users to read and browse for information on the World Wide Web.

9 Information on the World Wide Web is subject to copyright which must not be infringed. If you reproduce text or a photo on your website without obtaining the permission of the author, you will have broken copyright laws and may be prosecuted.

10 Carbon copy.

Section 6

Check your knowledge

1 Parallel port – also referred to as the LPT port (line terminal printing).

2 COM port (COMmunications port).

3 False

4 The printer which you will print from unless otherwise specified.

5 False. They are either 9 or 25 pin.

Section 7

Check your knowledge

1 See page 181.

2 By sliding across a small tab located at the corner of the disk.

3 See page 184.

4 See page 185.

5 See page 194.

6 See pages 193–198.

7 Tape backup unit, CD-R, CD-RW disk or zip disk.

Section 8

1 See page 205–207.

2 See page 205.

3 See page 208–209.

4 **a** Take regular breaks away from the computer.

b Maintain good posture.

c Ensure heating and lighting is suitable for the environment.

d Ensure noise is kept to a minimum.

Multiple-choice test

1 a	**6 d**	**11 c**	**16 d**
2 c	**7 c**	**12 b**	**17 b**
3 b	**8 c**	**13 b**	**18 d**
4 d	**9 b**	**14 a**	**19 b**
5 d	**10 a**	**15 b**	**20 c**